SUNDAY HOMILIES

YEAR C

George Ehusani

Foreword by John Cardinal Onaiyekan

Adonis & Abbey Publishers Ltd
24 Old Queen Street,
London SW1H 9HP
United Kingdom

Website: http://www.adonis-abbey.com
E-mail Address: editor@adonis-abbey.com

Nigeria:
No. 39 Jimmy Carter Street,
Suites C3 – C6 J-Plus Plaza
Asokoro, Abuja, Nigeria
Tel: +234 (0) 7058078841/08052035034

Copyright 2022 © George Ehusani

British Library Cataloguing-in-Publication Data
A catalogue record for this book is available from the British
Library
ISBN: 9781913976170
The moral right of the author has been asserted

All rights reserved. No part of this book may be reproduced, stored in a retrieval system or transmitted at any time or by any means without the prior permission of the publisher.

George Ehusani

SUNDAY HOMILIES

YEAR C

CONTENTS

FOREWORD VII
INTRODUCTION IX
1ST SUNDAY OF ADVENT 14
2ND SUNDAY OF ADVENT 19
3RD SUNDAY OF ADVENT 24
4TH SUNDAY OF ADVENT 29
THE SOLEMNITY OF CHRISTMAS 34
FEAST OF THE HOLY FAMILY 39
EPIPHANY OF THE LORD 44
FEAST OF THE BAPTISM OF THE LORD 48
1ST SUNDAY OF LENT 54
2ND SUNDAY OF LENT 58
3RD SUNDAY OF LENT 62
4TH SUNDAY OF LENT 68
5TH SUNDAY OF LENT 73
PASSION (PALM) SUNDAY 78
EASTER SUNDAY 85
2ND SUNDAY OF EASTER 90
3RD SUNDAY OF EASTER 95
4TH SUNDAY OF EASTER 99
5TH SUNDAY OF EASTER 104
6TH SUNDAY OF EASTER 110
7TH SUNDAY OF EASTER 115
PENTECOST SUNDAY 121

TRINITY SUNDAY	124
CORPUS CHRISTI	128
2ND SUNDAY OF THE YEAR	133
3RD SUNDAY OF THE YEAR	137
4TH SUNDAY OF THE YEAR	141
5 SUNDAY OF THE YEAR	146
6TH SUNDAY OF THE YEAR	151
7TH SUNDAY OF THE YEAR	157
8TH SUNDAY OF THE YEAR	162
9TH SUNDAY OF THE YEAR	166
10TH SUNDAY OF THE YEAR	171
11TH SUNDAY OF THE YEAR	175
12TH SUNDAY OF THE YEAR	180
13TH SUNDAY OF THE YEAR	184
14TH SUNDAY OF YTHE EAR	189
16TH SUNDAY OF THE YEAR	198
17TH SUNDAY OF THE YEAR	203
18TH SUNDAY OF THE YEAR	207
19TH SUNDAY OF THE YEAR	211
20TH SUNDAY OF THE YEAR	215
21ST SUNDAY OF THE YEAR	220
22ND SUNDAY OF THE YEAR	225
23RD SUNDAY OF THE YEAR	228
24TH SUNDAY OF THE YEAR	232
25TH SUNDAY OF THE YEAR	236
26TH SUNDAY OF THE YEAR	241
27TH SUNDAY OF THE YEAR	247

28TH SUNDAY OF THE YEAR 252

29TH SUNDAY OF THE YEAR 257

30TH SUNDAY OF THE YEAR 262

31ST SUNDAY OF THE YEAR 265

32ND SUNDAY OF THE YEAR 270

33RD SUNDAY OF THE YEAR 275

SOLEMNITY OF CHRIST THE KING... 280

SOLEMNITY OF MARY MOTHER OF GOD 284

SOLEMNITY OF THE BIRTH OF JOHN THE BAPTIST 288

SOLEMNITY OF SAINTS PETER AND PAUL 292

THE TRANSFIGURATION OF THE LORD 297

SOLEMNITY OF THE ASSUMPTION.. 302

SOLEMNITY OF ALL SAINTS.. 308

FEAST OF ALL SOULS 312

FOREWORD

Rev. Fr. George Ehusani has over the years become quite well known and respected as a powerful preacher and teacher of the faith. This has drawn a large crowd of eager spiritual fans into his Chapel at the Lux Terra Leadership Foundation, Abuja, Nigeria. His service of the Word of God has gone beyond his relatively small Lux Terra Chapel. His message is regularly transmitted on national TV stations, especially the Africa Independent Television (AIT), Lumen Christi Television, and the Catholic Television Abuja (CTV).

He has also effectively launched himself into the social media where large numbers, especially of the younger generation access his postings regularly with "like" and "subscribe." His message has gone far and wide, all-over Nigeria and beyond to the ends of the earth! Through him, the mandate of Christ to preach the good news to all nations is being fulfilled in our day.

Effective though the electronic media has become, it has not yet spelt the end of the print media, which the Lord himself has used in the Scriptures he has left for us as record of his words and deeds for our salvation. It is therefore a great joy that Fr. George has prepared for us a "hard copy" of the precious message that God has inspired him to deliver to our world. Yes, "to our world" not only to the congregation of worshippers who attend his services. Fr. George has a great gift of applying the Scripture and Liturgical messages to the concrete situations of the men and women of today. He resolutely and pungently delivers the truth of the Gospel, both bitter and sweet, in clear terms and skillful words, to all and sundry. Let those who have ears to hear listen to the Word of God – and be saved!

This publication is a precious collection of homilies covering the three years cycle of our Catholic Liturgical Calendar. It is a fountain of sound doctrine and good teaching, not only for Catholics but also for all men and women of goodwill, who fear the Lord and seek his face. Such people are badly needed today in our nation and in our world. May their tribe increase, and may the Lord give success to the further work of the hands and mind of our dear Fr. George. Amen.

+ John Cardinal Onaiyekan
Archbishop Emeritus of Abuja

INTRODUCTION

The Sunday homilies contained in these three volumes (Liturgical Year A, B & C), are a transcribed and edited form of actual homilies I delivered at the Chapel of Lux Terra Leadership Foundation, Abuja, Nigeria, during a period of three Liturgical years. I am grateful to God in Christ, whose living Word I have come to experience as Good News that I cannot keep to myself, but which I must share with others, using the opportunity and privilege I have as a priest who has the responsibility of preaching the Word at every Sunday Liturgy in the course of the year. Through my Christian journey and my life as a priest of over forty years, I have constantly benefited from the wisdom of innumerable Christian thinkers through the ages, and especially priests whose homilies, meditations, and exhortations I have benefited from immensely in my own desire for a deeper knowledge of and relationship with Jesus Christ the Son of God and Saviour of the world.

In the actual preparation of each one of the homilies however, I had cause to refer regularly to some of the following publications among others: *His Word Lives* by Vima Dasan, S.J., (St. Pauls, UK, 1998); *Sharing the Word Through the Liturgical Year* by Gustavo Gutierrez, (Orbis Books, New York, 1997); *Pray with the Bible*, Volume I-VIII by Noel Quesson, (Theological Publications in India, Bangalore, 1994); *Praying and Preaching the Sunday Gospel* by Joseph G. Donders, (Orbis Books, New York, 1988); *Seasons of the Word* by Denis McBride, C.SS.R., (Redemptorist Publications, UK, 1991); *Preaching the Lectionary* by Reginald H. Fuller, (The Liturgical Press, Collegeville, Minnesota, 1984); *This is the Gospel of the Lord* by Francis J. Moloney, (St. Paul Publications, Australia, 1993); *New Sunday and Holy Day Liturgies* Year A, B and C, by Flor McCarthy, OSB, (Dominican Publications, Dublin, 1999 & 2000). I am grateful to these and other writers whose insights into various aspects of the liturgical readings have helped to shape my Christian spirituality and in turn have influenced my homilies and writings.

I am also grateful to the regular members of the Chaplaincy of Lux Terra Leadership Foundation in Abuja, who constituted the direct audience when the homilies contained in these volumes were first delivered. Their active participation during the homily time, and the questions raised as well as the critical feedback they often offered during the discussions that ensued after mass each Sunday, very often helped to sharpen my thoughts and enrich those same homilies when next they were delivered. Also, at this point I must not forget to thank my "virtual parishioners" – those across the world who watch my homilies on television and on various social media platforms, and sometimes give some feedbacks. The awareness that my homilies are being watched or listened to by many more people than those sitting before me at the Lux Terra Chaplaincy, constantly influenced the scope of the issues touched upon or the commentaries made on the readings from one Sunday to the other.

I must express my profound gratitude to the many friends and parishioners who encouraged me many years ago to start recording my homilies. I am grateful to Chief Raymond Dokpesi and the management team of Africa Independent Television who for many years now have generously accommodated my Sunday Homilies on their station. I cannot but mention here Uju Obuekwe and Mike Egbe, who played critical roles in helping to bring about what later became a weekly preaching engagement on television. Perhaps this homily books would not have come about if I did not start keeping a record of each Sunday homily in accordance with their advice, encouragement, and support. I am grateful to all those who have assisted Mike Egbe in the Media Department of Lux Terra, including Jacob Aje, Robinson Okeke, Anthony Oni, Charles Ode and Francis Tokede and other staff and volunteers at Lux Terra Leadership Foundation.

The painstaking process of transcribing and editing the homilies in these volumes turned out to be the most difficult and time consuming of all. At the centre of this assignment is Mr. Omagbitse Barrow, a parishioner who sat through and listened to each one of the homilies, and thereafter worked over a two-year period on their transcription and initial editing, as well as on the structure in which the homilies should each appear. I am highly indebted to him. I am grateful to Father Anthony Azuwike of Veritas University, Abuja, who assisted Mr. Barrow with some part of the initial editing work. I am also grateful to Mr. Gregory Aiyemo and my brother Father Richard Ehusani, who did the enormous task of proof-reading the entire material before going to press. This publication would never have seen the light of day without their invaluable contribution.

I must express my sincere appreciation to the Archbishop Emeritus of Abuja, John Cardinal Onaiyekan, who graciously accepted to glance through the entire manuscript and write a forward to the homily series. I am most grateful.

I see the publication of these three volumes as my own little gesture of appreciation for what I have received from God and from others. They are part of my modest contribution to the great task of passing on Christ's message of truth and life. May the mustard seed that is being sowed through these publications bear abundant fruits in the hearts and lives of all the clergy and lay faithful who read them. Amen.

Father George Ehusani

Season of Advent

1st Sunday of Advent

Stay Awake

Readings: Jeremiah 33:14-16 | Psalm 25 | 1 Thessalonians 3:12-4:2 | Luke 21:25-28, 34-36

Summary:

Advent is the period of joyful expectation of the fulfilment of the promises of old. It is a season pregnant with possibilities. Just as the sight of a pregnant woman evokes joyful expectation, new possibilities, excitement, and longing for something refreshingly new, Advent is a time to look forward to something different.

Advent: A Season of Joyful Expectation

The season of Advent is a time to anticipate a new world order in our families, in our country, and in the world. It is a time to dream dreams of the new heavens and the new earth. It reminds us of springtime and the budding of flowers, even when everything is dried up; it reminds us of the sunshine even when it is all dark.

At Advent, we engage in prophetic imagination, the expectation of light despite our present darkness, of a joy that would dislodge our present sorrows. In the hearts of all who engage in this imagination, God shall reign, righteousness and integrity shall be at home, and justice and peace shall flow like water.

At Advent we celebrate the generations of faithful people, the heroes and heroines of our faith, who waited with profound longing for the coming of the Saviour and waited on God through the most trying times of conquest, enslavement, deportation to Babylon, and the desecration of their cherished temple.

At advent we celebrate our own deepest longings for a time when Christ's work on earth will be complete and God will be all in all. We celebrate our dreams and aspirations for the reign of integrity, justice, and peace in our country and in the world. We celebrate our dreams for a just society, a society where there is adequate welfare for all citizens, especially the lowly poor and the sick. Until these dreams are realized, we will keep on dreaming like Isaiah, Jeremiah, Baruch, Zephaniah, Zachariah, John the Baptist, and such modern-day prophets as Martin Luther King Jr.

Advent: A Time for Sober Reflection

Advent is also a time for sober reflection. It is characterised by wakefulness, watchfulness, vigilance, prayer, fasting, and penance. At Advent, we reflect on the meaning of the Incarnation, on the goal and mission of the Christian Church in the period "in-between" the first coming of Christ and his second coming. We reflect on the meaning and purpose of our individual (Christian) lives so we may fix our yes firmly on the prize, which is eternal life in Christ, instead of being weighed down by superficial concerns.

The End Time

At the beginning of Advent, we read of the terrible signs and images of human suffering and cosmic disorder that will precede the end-time (Luke 21:25-28). Christians are however supposed to understand the end-time events positively and not negatively, because Jesus does not want such gloomy pictures of the future to paralyse us with fear, but to influence our lives in the present and refocus our attention on what is important.

The frightening events Jesus spoke about in the Gospel are meant to inspire us into doing something positive in the present. Whereas the end-time events spell doom and gloom for the unfaithful and for those whose hearts are hardened, the same events herald the liberation and salvation of the faithful, who should await the end-time with confidence, vigilance, and prayer.

The Period In-Between

At Advent, we prepare for the celebration of the First Coming of Jesus Christ (in humility and weakness), and we anticipate his Second Coming (in majesty and power). We celebrate the prophecies of Isaiah, Jeremiah, Baruch, Zephaniah, Zachariah, and John the Baptist about the Messianic times. We reflect on the words of Jesus Christ and of St. Paul about the required conduct for the subjects of the kingdom in the period in-between. The time in-between the two comings of Christ is the time of the Christian community and Christian activity. This is when Christians are to act because when the Lord comes back all Christian activities will cease. So, it is not surprising that during this period in-between there is a lot of debauchery, infidelity, promiscuity, corruption, falsehood, and violence.

Right now is the time when Christian action is most needed and useful, the period of Christian activity. Evil still pervades the land; darkness still holds many people captive in the form of hatred and un-forgiveness, ethnic prejudice and social injustice, corruption, sexual immorality, greed and avarice, wickedness and hatred, idolatry and occultism, and violence and crime.

In this time in-between there will be widespread iniquity and corruption, but the Christian is called to be a sign of contradiction. This is our calling, but we find this life of contradiction very hard because we remain in the world and in the flesh, even though we are not of the world. Unfortunately, we compromise so easily and sell ourselves out so cheaply. But the good news is that we are not as weak as we think we are. We can do better. We as human beings are capable of, and indeed have often with the grace of God achieved heroic feats in various endeavours.

Advent is a time of commitment to the cultivation and promotion of such values of the kingdom as justice and integrity, holiness and righteousness, prayer and watchfulness, love and self-sacrifice, peace and solidarity, mercy, compassion and forgiveness.

To prepare for his second coming Jesus admonishes us to:

> Stay awake and not sleep-walk through life. To be awake spiritually is to be open, receptive, sensitive, active, and attentive to God and to others in love.
> Be watchful. This implies being wise and understanding, vigilant, alert, on guard, and responsible. It means to avoid

dissipation and drunkenness, getting our hearts coarsened by debauchery and the cares of this world.

The Lord will come back in glory. We do not know the day or the time, but in the meantime we must be ready. We should begin our faith journey with the end in view. If we are faithful to Christ and the values of his kingdom, when the end-time events begin to happen we would be able to stand erect, hold our heads high, and remain firm and confident amid the chaos.

Advent points our attention to the future coming of Christ and teaches us to live each day with our gaze firmly fixed on the goal which is the Kingdom of God. It teaches us to begin each day and each year with our everlasting union with God in view, because when we get too engrossed in simply satisfying our earthly cravings, *the day* will come upon us unprepared, and we will be shut out of His kingdom of love, peace and eternal glory.

The only way to be prepared for an unpredictable future is to be faithful in the present. It is to make ourselves ready by being active agents of love, justice, peace, and reconciliation. It is to be daily conscious that this world is not our home, that this world is passing away, and that we have an eternal home with Christ in heaven.

Conclusion

There is truly only one gift at Christmas, and it is Jesus Christ. He is the sole reason for Christmas, and Advent prepares us to receive this Gift. For true Christians, the end time is not the end; it is the beginning of genuine freedom for true disciples of Jesus. The end is not a moment of terror and judgement, it is the moment of salvation, and we ought to embrace it with gratitude.

Questions to Ponder

1. What is the theme of the Advent Season in general?
2. In what way is the prophesy of Jeremiah in today's 1st Reading (Jeremiah 33:14-16) a source of encouragement to all Christians in difficult situations?
3. Jesus says: "Take care, lest your hearts be weighed down with dissipation, drunkenness, and the cares of this life…"

(a). By what kind of life can this happen?
(b). What must we do about it today?
4. What is the one word or phrase that adequately captures all the readings of this Sunday?

Additional Reading
Isaiah 9:1; Matthew 24:37-44; Romans 13:11-14; 2 Peter 3:4-14

2nd Sunday of Advent

Jesus is Coming. Repent!

Readings: Baruch 5:1-9 | Psalm 126 | Philippians 1:4-6, 8-11 | Luke 3:1-6

Summary:

The Holy One of God, the Anointed One, the King of kings, the Prince of peace, the Messiah and the Saviour is coming, and He will right all wrongs. He will bring back the exiles to their own land and destroy their enemies. He will heal the sick, bandage the wounded, protect the orphan, and defend the widow. He will rebuild the Temple of Jerusalem. He will save men and women from the destruction which their sins have brought upon them.

Has God Forgotten his People?

The thought of being forgotten is an extremely painful one. No human being ever likes to be forgotten. In times of failure and distress, such as the onset of some terminal illness, personal tragedy or major disappointment, we often think that God has forgotten us, or that he does not love and care about us any longer. That is how many of the Jews felt in the 2nd Century before Christ, when Prophet Baruch was writing.

The kingdom of Israel had repeatedly fallen to foreign powers. The holy city, Jerusalem, had been destroyed with the Temple reduced to rubble, and their sons and daughters deported. In their despondency, they wondered where God was and what had become of his promises to their ancestors. Then many of them conclude that God has forgotten his people!

It was at this point that Prophet Baruch arose to assure the people that God had not forgotten them. He affirmed the presence of God in their midst and encouraged them not to lose heart. He further promised them that God will bring their sons and daughters back from exile. It took two centuries before these prophecies were fulfilled in Jesus. Though the people to whom he prophesied had died, God nevertheless remembered his promises, since with him a thousand years is like one day.

Israel and the Great Expectation

Christianity is built upon the great expectation of the fulfilment of the promises made to the chosen people of God and renewed from generation to generation through the prophets. So, what the prophets did was to keep hope alive. This is what we all must constantly do as Christians in moments of tribulations. God does not forget his promises. He did not forget the promises made to Abraham, Isaac, and Jacob. Nor did He forget the promises made to David, particularly in 2 Samuel 7. As the people experienced the humiliation of poverty, illness, conquest, enslavement, exile, deportation, and destruction of their temple, they were sustained by the great expectation of the coming of the Messiah promised to David.

The virtue of hope is a key Christian virtue. Every Christian must be full of hope because that is the only thing that will see them through the dark. When hope is gone, life is ended. When we hear about someone committing suicide, it often means that long before the action, hope has been lost. Christians must therefore be champions of hope, helping suffering people around them to persevere in hope.

The great expectation sustained the "remnant few" in Jerusalem who remained faithful to the covenant when the leaders of Israel forgot the ways of God, becoming corrupt, oppressive, idolatrous and the majority of the people submitting themselves to sin, immorality and injustice.

The history of our religion from the Judeo-Christian times shows that many leaders can often miss the way and it is generally some simple devotees that sustain the faith through challenging times. God does not respect the hierarchy of human beings. That is why Jesus Christ came, not from the house of the Chief Priest, but from the house of lowly Mary and Joseph.

Each of us should see ourselves as among the remnant few that are called upon to sustain the Christian faith during the period of trouble and distress. We should all aim to be like the prophets who spoke of the coming of the Messiah when most of the people were at the point of discouragement and disillusionment. The prophets were not the official religious leaders in Israel, but often lay members. Prophet Amos, for instance, was a farmer. While the official priests and leaders told the people what they wanted to hear, prophets like Amos, Baruch, and Isaiah told the truth. They often looked the people in the eye and told them that if they did not change their destructive ways, they would die. This is what it means to prophesy or to speak for God.

Our Own Expectations
Like the Jews of old, we too experience failure, disappointment, and one deprivation or the other. The reality of life often falls short of our dreams and expectations. We experience the sudden death of a loved one; we experience poverty and unemployment, failure in business or career, failure in marriage and family life, loneliness and abandonment, persecution or discrimination, and all kinds of social injustices.

No human being has it all. Something is often missing in the life of every one of us, even the wealthiest and the most successful, the most powerful and the most influential. We all sometimes cry, mourn, lament, and regret. Many people experience life as a burden: full of pain and anguish. The beautiful world which God created (see Genesis 1 and 2) is often experienced by many as a jungle, a wasteland, and a battlefield. It is full of oppression, corruption, immorality, injustice, violence, and war. Men and women are constantly longing for something more, looking forward to a better life, and expecting greater fulfilment. Many come to recognise with the prophets that we cannot help ourselves, that we need divine intervention, that we need a saviour.

The prophets insist that the coming of the Messiah will fulfil the hopes of all mankind, bring about deep inner peace, establish the conditions for lasting happiness, and be the source of eternal salvation. We join the prophets at Advent in dreaming, imagining and celebrating the messianic times when humanity will once again be reconciled to its God, and love, mercy, and compassion will reign in the hearts of people.

Prepare the Way of the Lord
Advent challenges us to bear witness to the Christian life of faith even as we live in an environment of doubt and fear; and to bear witness to Christian hope even as we live in an age of discouragement and despair. To facilitate the realisation of God's promise, we have a role to play ourselves. John the Baptist says that we must prepare the way of the Lord. We must pull down the mountains, fill up the valleys, and straighten all crooked roads. What these mean in concrete terms is that we must experience conversion in our beliefs and values, our attitudes and habits, our passions and preoccupations, as well as our daily engagements and relationships. We must live blameless lives, aim ourselves in the right direction, and commit ourselves to the right path.

To pave the way for the divine visitation, we must love tenderly. This means that we must pull down the mountains of selfishness and greed, flatten the hills of ethnic prejudice and discrimination, fill up the valleys of hatred, envy, and jealousy, and straighten all twisted and tangled relationships. We must endeavor to weed out the thorn bushes of adultery and fornication, and light up the way with sacrificial love, mercy, and compassion. To pave the way for the divine visitation, we must do justice. This means that we must pull down the mountains of falsehood and fraud, flatten the hills of political manipulation and economic exploitation, fill up the massive gaps between the rich and the poor, straighten all the crooked roads of corruption, and light up the landscape with commitment to the cause of the common good.

To pave the way for the divine visitation, we must walk humbly with our God. This means that we must pull down the mountains of pride and arrogance, flatten the hills of extravagance and ostentation, fill up the valleys of distinction between people, straighten the crooked roads with obedience to God's commandments, the practice of the sacraments of Reconciliation and the Eucharist, devotion to prayer and bible study, as well as periodic fasting and works of penance.

Conclusion

Advent challenges us to bear witness to the love of God even as we are surrounded by hate and enmity; to bear witness to the truth of God even as our society survives on lies and falsehood; to bear witness to the peace of Christ even as the sound of war and violent conflict continues to rage; and to bear witness to the light of Christ even as darkness surrounds us like a rampart.

Questions to Ponder

1. Mention one key word or phrase from any of the readings that adequately captures the theme of this Sunday.
2. What is St. Paul's message in the second reading (Philippians 1:4-6, 8-11)?
3. The good news of Advent is that God is about to visit his people, and their profound desires for happiness will be met. (a) What is God promising to do to bring this about? (b) What are the people expected to do?
4. John the Baptist called for repentance in readiness for the Lord's coming. He spoke of pulling down mountains and filling up valleys; what does this prophetic message mean for us in our concrete circumstances in Nigeria today?

Additional Reading

Isaiah 40:1-5; Isaiah 52:7; Micah 6:8; Romans 13:11-14

3rd Sunday of Advent

Rejoice, The Lord is Near

Readings: Zephaniah 3:14-18 | Isaiah 12 (Psalm) | Philippians 4:4-7 | Luke 3:10-18

Summary:
In the first reading from the Prophet Zephaniah, the people of Israel are encouraged to rejoice because God is with them and will he take care of them. In the letter to the Philippians, St Paul encourages Christians to rejoice and not to worry, but put to their trust in God. The Gospel is about John the Baptist challenging the people to change their ways as he prepared for the coming of Christ.

Rejoicing in Hope
Modern discoveries in neuroscience reveal that people who are not agitated and anxious for anything often live healthier, longer lives. Believers who rejoice in hope even while confronted with challenges in life are in this category. The joy of these people is based on their faith, trust and confidence that the God who has promised to deliver his people, is faithful to his promises. St. Paul knew how to cope with little or nothing, and how to enjoy abundance. If we have his attitude of detachment (knowing how to cope with hunger and with being well fed, as he describes in Romans 14:8 and Philippians 4:12), then our life will be less burdensome. We will often be overwhelmed by God's mysterious love, a love which makes God rejoice over us with gladness, and dance for joy as on a day of festival! (Zephaniah 3:17).

When in the 2nd Reading, St. Paul calls on believers to rejoice, he says it is because the Lord is near, and that it shall all be well. Believers must be wary of an all too narrow materialistic concept of success and well-being. Instead, we must remain open to the mysterious ways of our faithful God. In all circumstances, we are expected to simply do what we can, and leave the rest to God who has the whole world in his hands. St. Paul therefore insists that for believers, there is no need to worry. All we need do when we have put in our best, is pray with thanksgiving in our hearts.

For John the Baptist, the way to true happiness is the way of repentance from sin and conversion to selfless love, generosity, kindness, truth, honesty, justice, mercy, humility, and compassion. And it is by such disposition that we can fittingly prepare for the coming of the Messiah.

Christ, Agent of Total Transformation
God has made provision for his creatures in accordance with their unique circumstances. That is why Jesus enjoins us in Matthew 6:25-34 not to worry. Worry is the greatest obstacle to living a happy life. Those who want to be part of the happy dispensation which Jesus has come to inaugurate, must change and take on a new way of life in which they trust God more and worry less.

In Luke 3:10-14, when the people asked John what they must do to be saved, he mapped out for them a totally new way of living and relating with other people. Believing in Jesus Christ calls for a total transformation. Unfortunately, many Christians today think that they can simply add Christ to their lives without subtracting sin or undergoing a major turnaround. In the words of St. Paul, we are to take on the person of Christ, having now been grafted into him at conversion.

It means that Christianity is about changing from who we used to be to the new person that Christ desires us to be. This change ought not to be superficial but holistic. But because many often experience this change only at the superficial level, they feel agitated, anxious, and in distress over every little inconvenience or provocation, in such a way that there is often hardly any difference in the moral behaviour of many Christians when compared to the non-Christians in their societies. Yet, the religion of Jesus Christ is evidenced in the change that it brings about in one's life. Where this change is lacking what it means is that we are giving a counter witness to Christ and scandalizing both young Christians and non-Christians alike.

The Desire for Happiness

Happiness is a universal desire. All human beings desire it, but many today believe that religion is an oppressive force, and that the true practice of the Christian religion hinders their freedom. People think that true fidelity to Christ will end up depriving them of joy and happiness. Such impression is often because people so easily confuse pleasure with happiness. In today's second reading, St. Paul tells us where true happiness resides. He encourages believers who find themselves in any kind of need and or difficult situation to rejoice despite their circumstances. It is only with strong faith in God and faithful practice of authentic religion that such can be realized.

Jesus says that he has come that we may have life and have it more abundantly (John 10:10). In Luke 4:18-19, he says that he has come to set captives free, to open the eyes of the blind, to heal the lame, to preach good news to the poor, and He says also that, "If the Son sets you free, you are free indeed" (John 8:36). A firm belief in these promises often result in inner joy and happiness, even when believers are going through major trials.

God is literally begging his children to come into his embrace, for that is where we would find happiness. We can find true happiness only in God because He is the one that designed us, and it is in Him alone that we can find fulfilment. We often behave however like our first parents (Adam and Eve), who thought that they could find happiness and fulfilment outside the parameters set by their Creator.

Jesus' Own Happiness

Successful people through history do appreciate the notion of deferred gratification, accepting to suffer today, for the joy that awaits them in the future. St Paul and many other saints of our faith teach us that happiness can only be found in the Lord and nowhere else, and that it is only by living a life consistent with the values and ethos of the kingdom, such as sacrificial love, service, humility, purity, compassion, forgiveness, and non-violence, etc., that we can find true happiness, and not in the blind pursuit of wealth, pleasure, and power. Happiness comes from sharing not hoarding; from giving, not receiving; from serving others, not being served by others; and from promoting the welfare of others, not seeking our own welfare.

Happiness comes from bearing the pains of others, denying ourselves some pleasure and comfort for the sake of others; and not from making others suffer for our own selfish gains. What God wants is that we be happy, but such happiness does not necessarily come through material wealth or physical well-being. It turns out that the more detached one is from material possessions or the more content one is with little, the easier it is for one to be happy.

Authentic happiness results from godly living. Truly religious people should be among the happiest people in the world, because properly understood, faith in God is a liberating force. What makes people unhappy often include their bad habits and inordinate inclinations, as well as their inability to maintain healthy detachment from the things of the world. Once one is not entangled with too many things, one can more easily find happiness. True religion liberates us from these entanglements, helping us to live one day at a time with Jesus. True faith liberates us from all the forces that enslave and cause us much distress. True faith helps us to find our joy in the Lord.

The Pathway to Happiness

All the prophets of old, as well as John the Baptist, the Lord Jesus and his Apostles, have taught us that authentic happiness lies in living a life consistent with God's purpose and our beliefs. Psalm 1 is a guide for anyone who wants to tread this path. It spells out the source of happiness. Psalm 119 further says that they are happy who follow God's law. So, anyone who really wants to know what happiness is should look at the Scriptures.

Happiness is not some shallow self-indulgence. There can be no happiness if the things we do are different from the things we believe. Once such internal conflicts exist within us, it will not be easy for us to find true happiness. This is because a certain measure of sadness does descend upon us when we refuse to love even though we believe that love is our vocation, and yes, a dose of sadness descends upon us when we refuse to share, though we know that we are called to be generous and charitable.

For the Christian, God's presence is the source of the most profound happiness. When Prophet Isaiah says Jerusalem should shout for joy, he explains that it is because the Holy One is in their midst. And when St Paul tells the Philippians to rejoice in the Lord, he explains that this is because the Lord is nearby.

The joy that every human heart longs for, the joy that this world cannot give, is the joy that comes from a sense of God and His love for us. So, when Christ has taken up residence in our hearts, the external expression is joy. Where God is present, there is joy: the joy of love, the joy of a clean conscience, the joy of a grateful heart, the joy of a trustful soul.

Conclusion

Where God is present, sorrow and mourning disappear, because God heals our broken hearts and repairs our broken bodies with the touch of love. Where God is present, greed and avarice are replaced by selflessness and sacrificial love. Where God is present, oppression and intimidation are replaced by mercy and compassion, which bring joy to many. Where God is present, social injustice and economic exploitation are replaced by justice and equity, which enable many to live their lives to the full.

Questions to Ponder

1. It's the Rejoice Sunday. We believers are to rejoice even though our social circumstances remain the same.
   a. What is the basis of this rejoicing?
   b. How are we to find joy?
2. What, according to the readings of today, does it mean to be happy in the Lord?
3. Think of a single word or phrase that adequately captures the entire message of John the Baptist.
4. What (if anything) is going to change in the conduct of your life after hearing this message?

Additional Reading

Matthew 5:1-12; Mark 1:14-15; Isaiah 25:6-9; Luke 7:24-28.

4th Sunday of Advent

I am the Handmaid of the Lord

Readings: Micah 5:2-5 | Psalm 80 | Hebrews 10: 5-10 | Luke 1: 39-45

Summary:

Elizabeth and Mary trusted that God was at work in their lives. They knew that God was up to something, that he was advancing his purpose in the world, and that they had a role to play in the realization of this divine purpose. They offered their bodies for God's purpose, seeing themselves as only instruments in God's hands. As Christmas approaches, we ask ourselves: To what extent am I surrendered to God?

Elizabeth and Mary: Two Personalities, One Purpose

Mary received the message of the Angel Gabriel and set out quickly to Judea to visit her cousin Elizabeth who had also conceived by the power of the Holy Spirit. She went to share her joy with Elizabeth and to also share in Elizabeth's joy. Her visit brings such profound joy that even the child in Elizabeth's womb leapt for joy. Mary brought joy to Elizabeth, to John the Baptist, and to the world. With Mary's visitation they were bursting with excitement.

Mary's visit caused Elizabeth to be filled with the Holy Spirit. She sacrificed her comfort to ease Elizabeth's burdens and bring her joy. She inconvenienced herself to make another person comfortable, such that even the child in the womb leapt for joy. Thus, joy is the first response to the coming of the Messiah – the realisation of God's promised visitation.

One of the earliest Encyclicals of Pope Francis is known as *Evangelii Gaudium,* meaning "The Joy of the Gospel." In it he notes that wherever the gospel is preached, or received, it brings real joy irrespective of the circumstances of the society at that time. Preparing for Christmas should mean that we experience the joy of knowing that God so loved the world that he sent his only Son (John 3:16);

and that the people who walked in darkness have seen a great light (Isaiah 9:2).

We are not told that Mary brought any material gifts. But she brought just one thing to Elizabeth: the gift of herself. She gave Elizabeth her very presence, her love, her time, and her attention. Her presence gave Elizabeth strength, encouragement, and inspiration. Mary's response to God's giving of his son is to give what she had to her neighbour, Elizabeth. What is our own response to the gift of God's son which we celebrate at Christmas? Will our life remain the same? Will our relationships remain the same? What can we do with the gift of God's son? These are pertinent questions begging for answers as we look forward to celebrating Christmas.

Mary's Religious Disposition
The Angel Gabriel called Mary "highly favoured one," and three times in today's gospel, Mary is called blessed. This is the reason for her widespread veneration and exaltation. Mary is blessed because she was the vessel that bore the Saviour; she had faith enough to accept God's strange will (see Luke 1:45; Hebrews 10:5-10); she is the mother of Christ, and therefore the mother of God; and the fruit of her womb is blessed.

Mary emptied herself completely to be full of grace. This is an indicator that the best way to receive the blessings of God is to open oneself up (to be completely receptive), and to believe God simply because he is God. Mary saw herself as a lowly handmaid and trusted that God knows best. She placed herself at God's disposal and made a free choice to obey God's will.

Mary's response to God's invitation was: 'Yes, here I am. I am available. I will do as you say.' This is what her "I am the handmaid of the Lord, let it be done to me according to your word" implies. Her obedience brought upon her immense beauty and glory but also a dose of pain and hardship. Most mothers would not want the kind of pain and hardship she went through. Yet she accepted God's strange and unpredictable ways.

When Mary first said yes to the Lord, she had no idea what the implications would be. She had to renew her "Yes" at every point as the full implications were gradually revealed. Mary's yes was the beginning of everything that would happen to her for the rest of her life. Her yes would transform every moment of her life thereafter in a way that she could never have imagined. Mary's obedience was loving, trusting, persevering and long-suffering.

Our Own Yes to the Lord
Every time we participate at the sacrament of baptism or renew our baptismal vows, are we really committed to living up to the implications of the "Yes" we confess as the implications gradually unfold? As the events of life unfurl with trials and temptations, are we ready to continue to say yes? The need to continually pray for the virtues of fortitude and long-suffering, so we may remain faithful to God in the face hardship, cannot be overemphasized.

Like Mary, we too have said "Yes" to the Lord, and we continue to do so, at our conversion, baptism, matrimony, ordination, and at the sacrament of reconciliation. We say yes to the Lord each day and each Sunday at Mass. We say yes to the Lord at our private prayers and devotions. Our original "Yes" is like a leap in the dark. As the full implications of what we profess begin to unfold, our reaction must be that of constantly renewing our commitment to fidelity, in season and out of season, come what may. Our *yes* must somehow align with the *yes* of Mary, who even at the point of her son's death, stood firmly with him (at the foot of the cross) with unwavering faith and trust in God's mysterious plans and purposes.

To share in the joy and grace of Mary, we must choose to obey God at every turn in our lives, with all the attendant challenges. Obedience to God is risk-taking, because you never know all the implications, just like Mary never knew all the implications of her original "Yes." But those who take risks in doing God's will are never disappointed. Like Mary, they always win favour with God!

Conclusion
True happiness is to be found in the loving acceptance of duty, and in fidelity to one's commitment. Happiness is not found in evading duty or running away from responsibility. The more difficult the task to which we devote ourselves, the more joy and happiness will result. Christian values are often hard. Absolute fidelity to one's

commitment is hard. But we shall eventually overcome when we are persistent and focused on God. With God all things are possible. May the word take flesh in each one of us!

Questions to Ponder
1. Identify one single phrase from any of the readings that adequately captures the theme of all of today's readings?
2. Distinguish between the sacrifices of the O.T. and the sacrifice of Jesus. What does the sacrifice of Jesus consist in?
3. What are the similarities in the religious disposition of Mary and Elizabeth? What does the choice of the two women teach us about the ways of our God?
4. As we prepare to celebrate Christmas – the feast of the word made flesh – in what ways can the Word take flesh today in your life as a Christian and in the life of our society?

Additional Reading
Isaiah 7:14; 9:5-6; 11:1-9; Hebrews 10:7

Season of Christmas

The Solemnity of Christmas

The Word Became Flesh

Readings for Vigil Mass: Isaiah 62:1-5 | Psalm 89 | Acts 13:16-17, 22-25 | Matthew 1:1-25
Readings for Mass in the Midnight: Isaiah 9:1-6 | Psalm 96 | Titus 2:11-14 | Luke 2:1-14
Readings for Mass During the Day: Isaiah 52:7-10 | Psalm 98 | Hebrews 1:1-6 | John 1:1-18

Summary:

The first readings at the Vigil, Midnight and Day Masses celebrating the momentous event of Christmas are from Isaiah, the quintessential Messianic Prophet. The child to be born of a virgin is the promised Messiah, the Prince of peace and the Everlasting King from the house of David. He is to be called Immanuel (God is with us).

The second readings for the Vigil and Midnight Masses are from Acts and St. Paul's letter to Titus where he discusses the gratuitous nature of our salvation in Christ, and the transformation expected of us who enjoy this salvation in Christ. The second reading for the Mass during the day is from the Letter to the Hebrews, where the author begins his epistle by making a firm declaration that the God who through history had revealed himself in many and various ways through the prophets, has now spoken to us by his Son!

The Gospel readings for the Vigil and Midnight Masses are from Matthew and Luke respectively, where the birth of the child Jesus is announced, and where we are introduced to the Shepherds who were the first beneficiaries of the Good News as announced by the angels. In the Mass during the day, we read from the prologue of John's Gospel, "In the beginning was the Word, the Word was with God, and the Word was God... And the Word became flesh and lived among us..."

The Word Became Flesh and Dwelt Among Us

*"Go tell it on the mountain / Over the hills and everywhere
God tell it on the mountain / That Jesus Christ is born."*

We celebrate with songs of praise, thanksgiving, and adoration the portentous event of the Incarnation – the coming as man of the Son of God, to save the world, as the prophets had foretold. The event of Christmas is so great, so phenomenal, so gracious, so awe-inspiring, that we cannot but open our lips and raise our voices in union with the angels, to praise the Lord by whose tremendous love *"the Word became Flesh and dwelt among us"* (John 1:14). This is the day we celebrate the birth as man of the One upon whom all dominion is laid - the Wonderful Counsellor, the Mighty God, the Eternal Father, and the Prince of peace (Isaiah 9:6).

On Christmas day we read the passage of Hebrews 1:1-2 which says, "At various times in the past and in various different ways, God spoke to our ancestors through the prophets; but in our own time, the last days, he has spoken to us through his Son, the Son that he has appointed to inherit everything, and through whom he made everything there is." As the saying goes: In Christ, God became man "so that the children of men may become children of God." With the birth of Jesus Christ - the Way the Truth and the Life, and with his saving ministry and his eventual death and resurrection, God has revealed himself definitively to his people.

The central message of the Gospel of St. John, and indeed of the entire Christian Scriptures is that "the people that walked in darkness have seen a great light, and upon those who dwelt in the land of deep shadows, a great light has shone" (Isaiah 9:2). A great light has dawned upon the earth and all humanity, because "the Word became flesh and dwelt among us!" (John 1:1-18). This is not to be taken simply as a metaphor. No. At Christmas we Christians are celebrating a real historical fact that the only begotten Son of the Almighty God took flesh, was born in human form, and dwelt in our midst for 33 years!

Jesus was born as a helpless child at a lowly manger in Bethlehem, to poor and humble Mary and Joseph. He was born like all children, weak and vulnerable, and so he required parental care and protection. He grew up in a particular place called Nazareth, eating their food and taking their wine. He even learnt to do some Carpentry, the trade of his foster father Joseph. Yes, the incarnation implies that our eternal God broke into time and related with a particular people, taking into consideration their cultural, economic, and socio-political context. Thus, ours is a God who loves his people, and who meets them where they are.

Since the mystery of God itself remains impenetrable and inexpressible, the expression of our relationship with the unseen God must have to do in large measure with people, those whom we believe are created along with us in the image and likeness of God. If God created all human beings in his own image and likeness; if he has lavished his divine love on all human beings without exception; and if he has sent his Son into the world to die on the Cross, to save all human beings without exception, then it means that all human beings are lovable by virtue of simply being human. We can therefore not claim to belong to the God who sent his Son into the world to save all human beings and yet refuse to love any human being. This is one of the social implications of believing in the incarnation. This is perhaps why the celebration of Christmas has always been characterised by the exchange of gifts, alms giving and works of charity, mercy, and compassion in general.

Belonging to God means having a heightened awareness of the intricate bond that unites all the children of God without exception, and having preferential affinity with the poor, the weak, the sick, the distressed, the handicapped, and the marginalised. This is the logic of St. James when he writes that the practice of religion that is not accompanied by a commitment towards a more wholesome humanity is "worthless." He says that "pure, unspoiled religion in the eyes of God our Father is this: coming to the help of the orphans and widows in their hardships" (James 1:27). The incarnation therefore challenges us to take another look at the various cultural, social, and even religious practices and structures that alienate some people and deny others of their equal dignity as children of our one God and Father. For believers in the incarnation, there should be no room for ethnic, religious or class divisions. Ethnic prejudices and biases should be considered a scandal among Christians. None of us who professes faith in the one Lord and

God, who shares in the one Baptism and in the one Eucharistic Body of Christ, should be guilty of such prejudices and biases.

The circumstances of the contemporary Church and Society challenge those of us celebrating Christmas to allow our faith *take flesh* in us. We Christians must constantly reflect on the dynamics of "incarnational discipleship," a discipleship whose passion for justice, equity, well-being, and salvation of everyone one of God's children, should provoke concrete prophetic action towards realizing the liberation of the oppressed, the conversion of the oppressor, the empowerment of the poor, and the practice of authentic religion. We have often paid only lip service to the social imperative of the incarnation and the Gospel of Jesus Christ. We have often lived like hypocrites, preferring to have our little pleasures and comforts, rather than rocking the boat and getting hurt. Though we live in a world of sin or in an evil empire which is made up of unjust and evil structures, we have often preferred to avoid any confrontation with the status quo, and rather to flow with the tide. To that extent we have often conducted our affairs as if the incarnation did not take place.

Now is the time to take the event of the incarnation seriously. Jesus Christ came into the world to liberate the whole person - mind and spirit, body and soul. He came to liberate the whole person with his or her daily concerns and aspirations and his or her dreams of ultimate fulfilment. We must do something today to promote that total liberation in our environment. We must do something to defend the defenceless in our society, including unborn children, orphans, widows, the aged, the handicapped, the sick, prisoners, strangers, and refugees. We must do something about our economic structures which often leave most people permanently on the margins of society. As we celebrate Christmas, we must each strive to contribute our quota towards the emergence of a more just, more equitable and more humane society. The God who became man and dwelt among us, is still with us. We must therefore endeavour to light a candle today to make our world a better place.

Conclusion

On this day the whole world shines with joy, meaning, hope, and love. And all this because of the 'great joy' that was announced to the shepherds, and that is now announced to us. We rejoice because Jesus Christ came into the world to liberate the whole person - mind and spirit, body and soul. He came to liberate the whole person with his or her daily concerns and aspirations and his or her dreams of ultimate fulfilment. As liberated people, we must use our freedom to do God's will.

Questions to Ponder
1. What one word or phrase summarises the Christmas season for you?
2. In Titus 2:11-14, St Paul reminds us of what is expected of us if we are to enjoy the salvation won for us by Christ. What is this expectation, and how are you living up to it?
3. The birth of Christ in a manger demonstrates his identification with the poor and lowly of the earth. Discuss.

Additional Reading
Isaiah 9:1-6, 52:7-10, 62:1-5 | Psalm 89 | Matthew 1:1-25 | Luke 2:1-14 | John 1:1-18 | Acts 13:16-17, 22-25 | Titus 2:11-14 | Hebrews 1:1-6

Feast of the Holy Family

The Example of the Holy Family

Readings: 1 Samuel 1:20-22, 24-28 | Psalm 84 |
1 John 3:1-2, 21-24 | Luke 2:41-52

Summary:

The first reading (from the first book of Samuel) is about the birth of the child Samuel, and how after weaning the child, the mother Hannah had him consecration to God in accordance with her promise when she asked the Lord for him. In the second reading John the evangelist insists that we are God's children, and that we should always live with the dignity befitting our status as children of God. The Gospel narrates the story of the twelve-year-old Jesus getting lost in Jerusalem at the end of a pilgrimage to the city, causing Mary and Joseph great anxiety and distress. The story shows that challenges in family life, including misunderstandings, can occur even in the best of families. The loss, and the eventual discovery of Jesus in the Temple, was an occasion for the family to know something more about the real identity of Jesus.

Holy Family: A Paradigm for Christian Families

As we celebrate the feast of the Holy Family, we reflect on the exemplary life of Jesus, Mary, and Joseph, as the first Christian family, the ideal family, the prototype family, the paradigm that all human families must emulate, if our world is ever going to know true peace and lasting joy. As we recall the family life of Jesus, Mary and Joseph, we celebrate the preponderance of faith, hope, love, mutual respect and fear of the Lord in this first Christian family, which challenges all men and women to build their marriage and family life on the pattern laid down by Jesus, Mary and Joseph.

This celebration is important for all of us, as we live in a world that is becoming increasingly selfish, increasingly self-seeking, and self-centred. The ideals and values of Christian marriage and family life are becoming more and more difficult for the men and women of our age. Our secular society often considers the pains and sacrifices that go with marriage and family life an unnecessary burden that must be rejected. The men and women of our generation often want to have their pleasures, and they are often not ready to make any serious sacrifices for the sake of the spouse or the child. They are often not ready to forgive the spouse for hurts done them. They often expect too much from their spouse, while they themselves are not ready to give much. That is why traditional family life, which is the lasting union of man, woman and children, is becoming an endangered species. That is why there is so much crisis in many families and among many couples. That is why the rate of failure in marriage and divorce is so high in our society. Indeed, there is a general crisis of commitment among the men and women of our generation, and this is reflected in a most pathetic way in marriage and family life.

It is within the context of a generation that is weighed down by a crisis of commitment, a generation where trial marriages and divorce have become an everyday occurrence, a generation where the unfortunate phenomenon of single parenthood is becoming prevalent; it is within the context of an exaggerated secularism, where traditional family values are discountenanced along with their spiritual and moral counterparts, that we celebrate the feast of the Holy Family. Jesus, Mary and Joseph challenge the men and women of our generation with the words of Proverbs 1:7 that, "The fear of the Lord is the beginning of wisdom."

The totality of Christian living is indeed a sign of contradiction for the world. For whereas the world runs away from suffering and pain, the Christian has the cross as the means of his or her salvation, for we know that nothing good comes easy. Christian marriage is a task, an enormous task. It may be a bed of roses, but it must be recognised that roses have thorns. The attempt by many people to enjoy the rose and yet reject the thorns is the root of the crisis in marriage and the family life in our age. Christian marriage is a life of love. Christian love takes time to grow and mature. Christian love involves sacrifice, including the sacrifice involved in raising children, and the sacrifice involved in forgiving an offending spouse. To forgive an unfaithful spouse is not easy by any stretch of the imagination. To forgive an abusive spouse will take the grace of God and the maturity of Christian love. Yet it is the life of sacrifice, of mutual forgiveness, of patience, and of the fear of the Lord, that is presented to us today as the model for all believers.

Reflecting on the difficulties that go with marriage in Christ, especially its permanence and indissolubility, the disciples said to Jesus: "If that is how things are between husband and wife, it is advisable not to marry." The reply that Jesus gave them was that "It is not everyone who can accept what I have said, but only those to whom it is granted" (Matthew 19:10-11). Christian marriage is therefore a vocation for Christians. Those who do not have the life of Christ in them cannot possibly understand or appreciate the dynamics of Christian marriage. Christian marriage is a grace, a gift of God to those he has chosen. Success in Christian marriage is not something we can achieve by mere willpower. Success in Christian marriage and family is to be guaranteed by God who himself is love, and who alone can teach us how to love, and how to raise a family in love. The success of every Christian family shall be the work of God who makes all things happen.

The Psalmist says that "Unless the Lord builds a house, the labourers labour in vain" (Psalm 127:1-2). Many of us can and indeed do build houses, but none of us can on our own build a home. We need the divine input to build a home. We need the love of God, we need the fear of the Lord, we need the grace of God, we need commitment to the way of Jesus the Son of God, to build a home. In John 15:1-12 Jesus emphasises the fact that we are only branches. He is the vine. If we are united with him like a branch to the vine, we shall bear fruits in plenty. But cut off from him we can do nothing. God is love, and he is the source, the fountain, and the summit of love. Only those who seek God, and who abide in God and his ways shall succeed in living a life of love.

Human relations will be better ordered where there is wholesome respect for God and his will. The love for and fear of the Lord inspire mutual respect and mutual forgiveness which are necessary conditions for a peaceful home. Those who fear the Lord will not be tempted to put themselves in his place. Those who fear the Lord are more easily disposed to love their neighbour. Those who fear the Lord shall be endowed with the same grace that sustained Jesus, Mary and Joseph in Nazareth. Indeed, piety is the true foundation of both family life and social life. Piety is the sure way to political stability and economic prosperity. Piety is the foundation of individual and communal peace.

Christian families must be always united with God in prayer. They must learn to pray together, for the family that prays together, stays together. The communion of life which the Christian family is, makes it a school of love. In Christian marriage and family life, the members gradually learn the meaning of the words of St. Paul in I Corinthians 13:4-7 that "Love is always patient and kind; love is never jealous; love is not boastful or conceited, love is never rude and never seeks its own advantage, love does not take offence or store up grievances. Love does not rejoice at wrongdoing but finds its joy in truth. Love is always ready to make allowances, to trust, to hope and to endure whatever comes. Love never comes to an end..."

The Christian family is the proper place to conquer selfishness and greed since the husband, wife and children are compelled by their faith in God and their marital/family commitment to share their lives together. The Christian family is the proper place to overcome inordinate anger and the spirit of vengeance since the divine commitment compels them to forgive one another after every hurt. The Christian family is the proper place to learn to rejoice with those who rejoice, and to mourn with those who mourn. The husband, wife or child in the Christian family is not only a neighbour, but also a friend, for whom one should be ready to lay down his or her life. The Christian family is therefore a place to grow in holiness of life. That is why Christian marriage is seen by the Church as a vocation. Fidelity in Christian marriage and family should bring fulfilment, and peace, and should ultimately lead the couple and their children to God. The Christian family is therefore the divinely provided context in which the Christian child may grow to physical, mental and spiritual maturity. Proverbs 22:6 says that if you train a child in the ways of God when he is young, he will not depart from it when he grows old.

Conclusion

The Holy Family shows us what a Christian family should be. As the wife is the support of her husband, the husband is to practice the virtues of those who share Christ's life: heartfelt compassion, kindness, humility, gentleness, patience, and forgiveness — all of them essential for family life. Over and above all these, the Christian family should put on the most important garment of all, love. The same reciprocity applies to children. Children are to obey their parents and obey the Lord. In the Christian family, Jesus is always an unseen presence. May God teach us the sanctity of human love, show us the value of family life, and help us to live in peace with everyone in the human family. Amen.

Questions to Ponder
1. List the ingredients of a good Christian family as shown in today's readings.
2. Jesus wants to occupy the central place in our marriages and in our family relationships.
   a) What obstacles do we sometimes put on his way; and
   b) How are we to overcome those obstacles?
3. What role must I play as a committed Christian towards restoring traditional Christian family values to our society in this age of widespread marital crises, infidelity, easy divorce, and the normalization of multiple sexual perversions?
4. The text of Ephesians 5:22 that says, "Wives be subject to your husbands…" is one of the most misunderstood passages in the scriptures. Discuss.

Additional Reading
Proverbs 22:16; Psalm 127:1-2; John 15:1-8; Ephesians 5:21-6:4

Epiphany of the Lord

The Revelation of Jesus

Readings: Isaiah 60:1-6 | Psalm 72 | Ephesians 3:2-3, 5-6 | Matthew 2:1-12

Summary:

Epiphany is the manifestation of Jesus Christ in the darkness of the world. It is an open invitation to men and women to come and bathe in the light of Christ. Jesus himself said that we are the light of the world. We are to abandon our works of darkness, come and bathe in the light of Christ, and go around shining in that light.

The Great Manifestation

The Church is missionary in nature; we exist to evangelise (Matthew 28:19). A Church that is not actively engaged in evangelisation is dead. Part of this missionary mandate is to proclaim that Christ is revealed to all peoples, not only to the Jews as some of them believed, but to the Samaritans and Gentiles as well. The Incarnation is God's great act of salvation. At some point in history, God intervened in a phenomenal manner to right the wrongs done in the Garden of Eden by our first parents. His Son took flesh and dwelt amongst us as John the Evangelist tells us in John 1:1-18. This momentous event is what we celebrate at Christmas.

With the incarnation, the light has shone in darkness and darkness cannot overpower it. The glory of the Lord has risen upon the world and, as Isaiah prophesied, the people that walked in darkness have seen a great light. This great act of God, this revelation of God in Christ, is the real meaning of Christmas. We celebrate at the incarnation the revelation in our time of the mystery that was hidden for ages. The mystery according to St. Paul is that Jews and Gentiles are now to share the salvation of Christ on an equal footing (Ephesians 3:1-6). God desires to save everyone equally. Everyone is called and baptized on an equal footing, because salvation in Christ is a hope for all, and not a privilege for some. It is available for anyone who, like the Magi, has faith and responds fittingly to Christ's invitation.

Radiating Christ's Light

The light of Christ is present in every community of faith that welcomes all people, all races and ethnic groups, and all classes of people with their unique cultures and perceptions. We are to be very careful to provide equally for all in the church. We must have a place especially for the least of Christ's brethren. A Christian community that has no programmes with and for the poor and the needy is failing to witness to Christ. Churches must not gauge how well they are doing by how much wealth they have, but by how much they have reached out to the poor with the little they have.

The Wise Men

The Wise Men (the Magi) from the east neither had the Hebrew Scriptures nor did they read what the prophets had said about Christ. Instead, they had the newborn king revealed to them through nature – the star – and they recognised him as Saviour of the world. At this recognition, they paid him homage and offered him gifts. These non-Jews are models of faith. They represent all nations and peoples. The Wise Men stand for the introduction of Gentiles to Christ and his salvation. They are a confirmation of Jesus' declaration that "many will come from east and west and take their places at the feast with Abraham, Isaac, and Jacob" (Matthew 8:11). Indeed, in the Magi, "all nations have seen the salvation of our God, and all nations shall fall prostrate before God."

The Wise Men's Generosity

When they saw the child Jesus, the Magi opened their treasures and offered him gifts. This happens when people truly discover Christ. They burst into life, and the treasures of goodness which were hitherto buried inside them are suddenly opened. When people truly discover Christ, they joyfully offer gifts to the Lord and to their brothers and sisters, especially those who are poor, sick, lonely, or lowly. Jesus who was born in a manger, challenges us to share our gifts and talents with one another. It is in giving that we are enriched, and we discover our own gifts. Christian charity is not an investment with the hope of getting something back. It is giving without expecting anything in return. Many people of diverse religious traditions strongly believe that those who are stingy are robbing themselves, because when we give without expecting a reward, something returns. When people do not know how to give, they miss one significant channel of joy in life – the joy of giving.

The Transformation
After meeting the child Jesus, the Magi traveled back home by another way! They cut off all contact with the evil king. They acquired a new world view. They were transformed by their encounter with the Lord. Jesus says, "I am the light of the world, no one who follows me will ever walk in darkness" (John 8:12). All the things we hold in high esteem will diminish considerably when we meet Jesus. When we follow the path of the Magi to see God, it changes everything; what gives our neighbours joy may no longer be what gives us joy. Rather, our joy would come on account of a new mentality, a new set of values, a new set of goals, a new roadmap. It is impossible to encounter Christ truly without it affecting the way we live.

Conclusion
The world still gropes in darkness, with many engaged in the blind pursuit of power, pleasure, and wealth. Those of us however, who have seen the light of Christ, cannot keep this light to ourselves. We have work to do. We must show the world the light, spreading Christ's message of salvation and giving credible witness to his Gospel of life.

Questions to Ponder
1. What is the key message of the 2nd Reading of today from Ephesians 3:2-6? What is the mystery made known to St. Paul?

2. How do all the readings of today demonstrate that Christ is the King and Saviour of all the peoples of the world?
3. Jesus Christ says that no one who follows him will ever walk in darkness. In what ways are some people walking in darkness and still claiming to be followers of Christ?
4. In the difficult economic, political, and security circumstances of our world today, how (as a committed Christian) would you shine your light before men and women?

Additional Reading
Psalm 72:17 | Isaiah 2:1-4 | Matthew 8:11-12 | Mark 7:24-30 | John 8:12

Feast of the Baptism of the Lord

The Meaning of Jesus' Baptism

Readings: Isaiah 40:1-5, 9-11 | Psalm 104 | Titus 2:11-14, 3:4-7 | Luke 3:15-16, 21-22

Summary:

The feast of Jesus' baptism should remind us of our own baptism and its meaning. As Jesus' knowledge and beliefs regarding who he is helped him to live out his mission, so must our own knowledge of who we are truly influence our life and conduct. We must endeavour to be recognised as baptised people from the conduct of our lives.

John's Baptism: A Baptism of Repentance

John came to prepare the way for the Messiah whose coming was imminent. He preached conversion from sin, and at the River Jordan, administered the baptism of repentance. Many people came to him, confessed their sins, and received baptism (Matthew 3:5-6). Jesus joined the queue and submitted himself for baptism. John protested, but Jesus insisted that it should be so to fulfil all righteousness (Matthew 3:15).

Meaning of Jesus' Baptism

Jesus was sinless and needed no cleansing (Hebrews 4:15). So, what was the significance of his baptism?

- Jesus' baptism marked the end of the Old Testament and the beginning of the New Testament. The old covenant ended with the activities of John the Baptist.
- It was the inauguration of Jesus' ministry. He was shown to John and to Israel, and was affirmed as the beloved Son of

God. Jesus thus began his ministry with the Father's authority and love.
- It is to fulfil God's saving plan, and an act of obedience and humility (see Psalm 40:7-8; 42:1-4; John 4:34; 8:29).
- It is a symbolic act of solidarity with sinners.
- It is to show his followers how important baptism is.

The Significance of the Baptism of Jesus

As Jesus came out of the water, three significant things happened: the heavens were opened; the Spirit of God descended upon him; and the voice of the Father was heard saying: "This is my son, the beloved, in whom I am well pleased. My favour rests on him." The suffering children of Israel had always looked forward to the messianic time when God will bring them through the waters (like the waters of Egypt, the River Nile, the Red Sea crossing from slavery to freedom), when God's spirit will rest upon them, and when God will tear the heavens open and come down. They looked forward to when God will intervene in their circumstances and not keep quiet any longer.

It is against the background of this and similar Old Testament prophesies that we can understand Jesus' baptism. At the baptism, Christ's full identity was revealed, God's love and favour upon him was affirmed, and his saving mission was confirmed. God expressed his delight in Jesus even before he began his life-giving ministry that will entail rejection, suffering and death. These are all important for understanding what will happen at the crucifixion on Calvary. It assures Christians that God's favour was upon Jesus even as he went through rejection, persecution, and execution at Calvary.

Being Assured of God's Love

It is important to be convinced of God's tender love. If we are sufficiently convinced of the tender love of our God, then it is easier to pass through tribulations triumphantly. But we may not be able to endure trials, tribulations, and persecution as Christians, if we are not deeply convinced of God's love.

What happened at the Baptism of Jesus, and at his Transfiguration, where Moses and Elijah appeared, and a voice came from the cloud saying, "This is my beloved son...," were all meant to strengthen Jesus in his mission and assure him of God's loving presence.

At his Presentation, when Simeon said to Mary, the mother of Jesus, "...a sword shall pierce through your heart," Mary pondered these words in her heart. She did not understand them, but she knew the love of God. Empowered by this knowledge of God's love, she was able to say, "I am the handmaid of the Lord. Be it done to me according to your word."

In the same way, we do not have to understand everything that will happen to us. When things begin to happen in our lives that we do not understand, it is easier to remain faithful when we stand solidly on the foundation of the love of God. It is a terrible thing when people think that they are not loved. The consequences are devastating. All Jesus did throughout his ministry flowed from a clear understanding of who he is and how much the Father loved him.

Similarly, it is to the extent that we know who we are that we do what we do. Understanding who we are in the presence of God dictates the rest of our life. It determines our reaction when we do not get what we feel we deserve. Jesus knew that he is Son of God, called, not to prestige, power, and privilege, but to service and self-giving. In the Garden of Gethsemane, he knelt and cried out, "Let this cup pass me by. However, not my will, but yours be done." He knew that God's will has to take precedence over his own will, and knowing God's love for him, he freely obeyed.

Jesus' Identity and Mission

Jesus fulfils in his person the mission of the Servant of Yahweh seen in Isaiah 42. His mission was to change the world, to transform it, to bring justice to all nations, and to bring out of the dungeon those who live in darkness.

Every human being has a purpose in life even though some do not have an inkling as to what theirs is. We are called to commit ourselves to goals that are bigger than ourselves, because when we only commit ourselves to cheap goals like money making and social popularity, sooner than later, we run into some crisis of meaning.

The Meaning of our Own Baptism

Christians are not baptised for the same reason that Jesus and the Jews who came to John were baptised. Our baptism is in obedience to Christ's command in Matthew 28:19 and John 3:5. Our baptism brings about the remission of sins (Acts 2:38; 22:16). When in the name of Jesus Christ and in the Holy Spirit we are baptised, all our sins are wiped away. Baptism wipes away the original sin inherited from our first parents, as well as all the actual sins we ourselves have committed. That is how important baptism is. When we are baptized, we are united with Christ in his death and in his resurrection. We become adopted children of God and heirs of the kingdom with Christ.

Through baptism, we come into union with the community of faith and become part of the new universal family (Acts 2: 42-45), where God has no favourites and there is no segregation. Thus, baptism is the joyous beginning of a lifetime of love, service, and sacrifice. At baptism, we share in God's life and we are pointed in a particular direction – the direction of full, abundant, and eternal life meant for all God's children.

At baptism, we become disciples of Jesus called to love God and one another. We are called to fight against all evils, including the evil of corruption and immorality. In a world as ours that is so well endowed by God, the economic deprivation and impoverishment of a large proportion of people remains a major scandal. Our baptism challenges us to fight against this evil. Every Christian is commissioned by virtue of his or her baptism to be a social justice advocate, fighting for the rights of the lowly poor in society, including, the strangers and refugees, the widows and orphans, the aged, and the destitute. We should make choices daily that will not increase the problems of these categories of people, but rather choices that will help alleviate their problems.

Baptism is God's authoritative declaration in material form of a spiritual reality (an outward sign of an inward grace). At baptism sins are forgiven, and the baptised person is given a pledge of eternal life (this is the inner reality). The pouring of water and pronunciation of the Trinitarian Formula (in the name of the Father, and of the Son, and of the Holy Spirit), is the outer form of this inner reality that takes place.

Our Baptism, Our Identity and Mission

By virtue of our baptism, we have been purified by water, and enlightened by the Holy Spirit. We are now empowered even as ordinary men and women to do extraordinary things, and to transform the world for God. We are now like Christ, and everything we do, henceforth, must flow from who we have become. We are no longer ordinary or secular, and nothing about us is profane anymore, because, when we were baptised, we took upon ourselves not only the name of Christ, but also his character.

Conclusion

We are reminded today that we are God's beloved children, called to reject evil in all its manifestations, including hatred and vengeance, greed and avarice, lust and sensuality, etc. We are called to follow Jesus Christ, working closely with him, to bring about the kingdom of God: a kingdom of love, justice, solidarity, reconciliation, and peace.

Questions to Ponder

1. Our 1st Reading (Isaiah 40:1-11) graphically portrays the tender heart of our loving God. Discuss briefly.
2. What does your baptism mean to you? Are there any privileges and obligations attached to your Christian baptism? List some of them.
3. John the Baptist says regarding Jesus: "He will baptise you with the Holy Spirit and with fire" (Luke 3:16). What does this mean?
4. Peter says, "The truth I have come to realise is that God has no favorites..." (Acts 10:1). What are the implications of this truth for our daily lives as Christians?

Additional Reading

Matthew 17:1-8; 28:18-20; Romans 6:3-4

Season of Lent

1st Sunday of Lent

A Time to Conquer Sin

Readings: Deuteronomy 26:4-10 | Psalm 91 | Romans 10: 8-13 | Luke 4:1-13

Summary:

Our primitive instincts seek to rivet us to earth but the spirit of God makes us soar beyond the earth and look towards heaven. God created us and put us on earth to serve Him and so inherit our eternal destiny with him in heaven.

Overcoming Temptation

Jesus Christ was led to the desert by the Spirit, and he fasted for forty days and forty nights in preparation for his ministry. His sojourn in the desert exposed him to the desert experiences of hunger and frugality. The desert in its characteristic way always brings one back to the basics of life. It saw John the Baptist eating locusts and wild honey. There Jesus had a critical encounter with the forces of evil. He had a fierce battle with Satan over the human instinct for sensual pleasure, wealth, and power. But because Jesus was prepared through prayer and fasting, self-abnegation, self-mastery, and mastery over the primitive instincts, which the forty days and forty nights were meant to achieve, he overcame the tempter on each count with the following words:

"Man does not live on bread alone…"
"You shall not put the Lord your God to the test"
"You must worship the Lord your God and him alone must you serve"
(Luke 4: 1-13).

Lent – Time for Self-Mastery
Lent is a time to celebrate Jesus' conquest of evil. It is typically a time set aside for a communal struggle against sin. It is a time of withdrawal, a time to be with God our source of strength and power, a time to grow in discipline and to conquer our *concupiscence*.

Concupiscence refers to the primitive instincts that often lead us to seek inordinate power to control, dominate, manipulate, oppress, and destroy others. It refers to the unruly passions that nurture and sustain greed, avarice, consumerism, materialism, anger, and hate. It refers to the carnal desires that propel adultery, fornication, pornography and other perverse forms of sexual gratification, drunkenness, addiction to drugs, alcohol, and various forms of unrestrained, senseless, and inordinate entertainment.

Concupiscence sums up what the Scriptures identify as *the lust of the flesh*, *the lust of the eyes*, and *the pride of life* (1 John 2:16). These are the roots of the seven deadly (or cardinal) sins which are pride, covetousness, lust, anger, gluttony, envy, and slot.

Sin is often an addiction. It easily becomes obsessive, and it is the reason why people commit the same sins repeatedly. Every sinner is a slave in need of freedom. The good news however is that Jesus has died for us and has set us free from sin. He assures us of this when he says: "If the Son sets you free, you shall be free indeed" (John 8:36). Jesus also declares that he came that we may have life and have it to the full (John 10:10). It is in this same vein that St. Paul says: "It is for freedom that Christ has set us free. Do not fasten yourselves back to the yoke of slavery" (Galatians 5:1).

Jesus Conquered Satan
Following his desert experience, Christ defeated Satan and demonstrated to us how to conquer our lusts, overcome our obsessions, triumph over all compulsions, and obtain (inner) freedom. He shows us how to overcome all inordinate passions for pleasure, all evil inclinations for power and control, and all destructive instincts for wealth accumulation. Christ taught us that we cannot fight the devil with the instruments or tactics of the devil. He fought back the devil's temptations by practicing the opposite virtues. Against inordinate sensual pleasure, Christ demonstrated the virtues

of chastity, purity, and modesty; against inordinate power and ambition, Christ demonstrated the virtues of humility, obedience, and service; and against inordinate wealth accumulation, Christ demonstrated the virtues of willful poverty, frugality, and detachment.

Conquering the Forces that Enslave Us

Lent is the most auspicious time to reflect on, and strive to live by the example of Jesus' desert experience, to celebrate the vicarious suffering and death of Jesus in a special way, to reflect on the destructiveness of sin, preach more passionately repentance from sin and conversion to Christ, to make reparation for our individual and social sins, and to conquer selfishness, pride, greed for money, and lust for pleasure.

Lent provides an opportunity for us to take a trip into the wilderness of our lives, to leave our past behind and start anew, to sow seeds of God's words and reap abundant fruits at Easter. It also provides an opportunity for us to train in discipline and the practice of other virtues, to grow into spiritual maturity, and to emerge stronger at Easter.

Lent is the time to confront the reality of human depravity with the truth of Christ's holiness, to confront the world of wealth, power, and inordinate ambition with Christ's message of poverty, service, and humility. It is the time to confront a world degraded by promiscuity and rampant immorality with Christ's message of chastity, purity, modesty, and abstinence.

Lent is an appropriate time to confront the contradiction of rampant religiosity side by side with widespread corruption and immorality. It is the time to confront the evil of male chauvinism, and the oppression and subjugation of women in some of our societies. It is the time to confront racial and ethnic bigotry and long-standing group antipathies, and work for healing, reconciliation, and peace. Lent is the time to confront social indiscipline and the predilection in many to lie, cheat, and pursue instant gratification.

Conclusion

Lent is a most opportune time to confront the corporate abuse of the poor and neglect of the common good, and remind all believers that by dying on the cross, Christ has set us free, and so we have no business remaining slaves of sin. Lent is therefore the time to make considerable progress in living out Jesus' civilisation of love.

Questions to Ponder

1. In one sentence, summarise the message of the 2nd Reading (Romans 10:8-13).
2. "Don't fight the devil with the devil if you want to defeat the devil." Explain this admonition, using today's Gospel.
3. Jesus was tempted with the three-fold lusts that plague humanity: the lust of the flesh, the lust of the eyes, and the pride of life.
   (a). What do they mean?
   (b). How can we, like Jesus, overcome them?
4. "Lent is the period when we celebrate the Heart of the Christian struggle." Explain.

Additional Reading
Romans 12:21, 13:12-13; 1 Corinthians 9:27; 2 Peter 1:5-6

2nd Sunday of Lent

The Glory of Christ is Revealed

Readings: Genesis 15:5-12, 17-18 | Psalm 27 | Philippians 3:17–4:1 | Luke 9:28-36

Summary:

In the first reading, God makes a covenant with Abram, promising him a multitude of descendants that will outnumber the stars in the skies. In the second reading, St. Paul encourages us to focus on heavenly things and the things of God, promising us that Jesus will transform our lowly human bodies to be like His. The Gospel reading is about the Transfiguration, where Moses and Elijah appeared with Jesus on the mountain.

Bridging the Old and the New

The event of the Transfiguration is set on Jesus' Road to Jerusalem. Jesus had done a lot of work in Judea, and he was heading for Jerusalem where he was bound to face a violent death like all other prophets before him. He had been in Galilee, teaching and performing miracles. He had gained quite some popularity, but also, he had made a lot of enemies among the religious authorities. Jesus had many enemies, but he didn't focus on the enemies. He focused on God, whom he knew was going to take care of the enemies.

He was committed to his Father's will, and he was determined to carry it out. On his way to Jerusalem, Jesus went up to the mountain to reflect and to pray over the adversity that was soon to follow. He went up there to seek the face of the loving Father, to find encouragement and support. And as he prayed, he was transfigured.

Jesus' face shone like the light and his clothes became dazzlingly white. There appeared with him Moses and Elijah, and then the voice of the Father was heard from heaven which said, "This is my son the chosen one, listen to him" (Mark 9:7). It was a glorious moment for the disciples. They were confounded, mesmerized, and overwhelmed with joy. The event was beyond description.

Moses and Elijah represent the Law and the Prophets. The first five books of the Bible – Genesis, Exodus, Leviticus, Numbers, and Deuteronomy are the Law, and all the other parts of the Old Testament are known as the Prophets. So, the appearance of Moses and Elijah was to confirm that indeed Jesus was the expected One. Moses and Elijah are the two most respected Old Testament personalities. Their presence links the Old Covenant to the New Covenant. Their presence confirms the authority of Jesus, and proves that, in Jesus, the Law and the Prophets have found their fulfilment.

The hour of light on Mount Tabor was meant to help Jesus face the coming hour of darkness. Memories of this event of the Transfiguration were to sustain Jesus through the harsh and cruel moments of betrayal, rejection, condemnation, abandonment, crucifixion, and death at Calvary.

Prayer is always the source of strength for the believer against the enemy, and everyone who really spends time in prayer is transfigured in some way. Believers are transformed as they spend time waiting on the Lord in prayer. The classic definition of prayer is that it is the lifting of the heart and mind to God. Everyone who lifts his or her heart and mind to God and spends some time in God's graceful presence is transfigured and transformed. Every one of us needs an encounter with the Lord, an encounter as profound as Jesus' encounter at the Transfiguration, an encounter as profound as St. Paul's encounter on the road to Damascus, or that of Peter, Andrew, James, and John at the Sea of Galilee.

Meaning of the Transfiguration

We all deserve occasionally to have such rich experiences of encounter with God, so that at moments of difficulty, we can refer to and be strengthened by what we had seen and heard. The Transfiguration was meant to confirm that the cause Jesus undertook was right, and to strengthen his disciples for the scandal of the cross. After receiving the Holy Spirit at Pentecost, the disciples of Jesus tried to do everything well – they lived lives of humility and frugality, and they travelled far and wide to preach the good news. Many of them were brutally tortured and/or killed in the most savage manner. Looking at the experiences they had with Jesus, and the lives of holiness they led, it may be difficult to understand or explain their immense suffering. Yet, their Transfiguration experience on Mount Tabor, appear to have strengthened them for the crosses they were to bear. It is such an experience that will help us and strengthen us too as we go through in our own time the sufferings that come on account of our faith commitment to Christ.

With the Transfiguration, the disciples got a glimpse of the glory of the risen Lord. They saw themselves reflected in the image of Jesus' transformed self. They felt that if their Lord and Master is transformed this way, and if they follow him faithfully, then a similar transformation is awaiting them. From their experience, the disciples knew that they had a potential. They knew they could become much more than they were, and that they could do much more than anyone in the world expected of them.

Finding Strength for Our Crosses

Life for many of us could sometimes be very hard. Many people face poverty and unemployment, failure in career or business, loneliness and rejection, persecution and unfair judgment, humiliation and condemnation, problem marriage and challenging children, as well as sickness and pain. When we find ourselves in such difficulties, we are challenged to go up to the "mountain" metaphorically, to reflect and to pray. From the mountaintop as it were, we can often see far beyond the immediate horizon. We can often see the larger picture. We can often seek the face of God and receive some needed assurance. At difficult times in our lives, we are challenged to "go up the mountain," to receive the light of hope, to listen, and to hear those consoling words of the Father, *"You are my beloved son/daughter. My favour rests on you."*

The Lenten season is our own time of ascent to the mountaintop; it is the communal time for all Christians to ascend to the mountaintop. Lent reminds us that we are citizens of heaven. It is a time to engage in prayer, works of penance, and alms giving. Lent is the time to conquer our concupiscence with the grace of God. It is the time to practice the virtues and the ethos of our heavenly homeland. It is the time to practice the kind of life we shall be living in heaven. Lent is the time to practice the fear of the Lord, true piety, and true worship. It is the time to practice love and compassion, service and sacrifice, obedience and humility, kindness and generosity.

Conclusion
The Transfiguration was a bridge between the Old and the New Testament. The events of the transfiguration gave Jesus the hope and energy that he needed to go through the passion. We too need a transfiguration event in our lives by being in God's presence and seeking an encounter with him. This experience will help us remain firmly rooted in our love for God and help us through the various challenges we must face. To achieve this, we must constantly lift our hearts and minds to God in prayer and to savour God's beautiful presence, surrendering to him as Jesus did.

Questions To Ponder
1. What relationship is there between the first reading and the Gospel reading today?
2. From our readings today, what does a real encounter with God consist of?
3. What is the key point raised by St Paul in today's second reading?
4. What message will you send to your family, friends, and colleagues during this season of lent based on today's readings?

Additional Reading
Exodus 34:29-35; 2 Kings 2; Mark 9:2-10; Acts 15:14-18; 1 Corinthians 15:20-28

3rd Sunday of Lent

Repent or Perish

Readings: Exodus 3:1-8, 13-15 | Psalm 103 | 1 Corinthians 10:1–6,10-12 | Luke 13:1-9

Summary:

The Lenten period is a privileged opportunity for new growth in Christian discipline, patience, courage, charity, purity, prayer life, and holiness. Lent calls us to conversion from being self-centred to being God-centred, from slavery to sin and selfishness to a life of freedom and grace, from a life of barrenness to a life of fruitfulness, and from an all-too-earthly preoccupation to a life oriented towards the Kingdom of God.

The Immense Goodness and Compassion of Our God

The goodness of God is expressed in the concern shown for his people. He revealed himself to Moses in Exodus Chapter 3, as a God whose fire of love is never diminished. He says he is the "I Am Who Am," meaning the God whose love is constant and ever-present, a God who was, who is, who is to come. The Lord says: "I have indeed seen the misery of my people in Egypt. I have heard them crying for help on account of their taskmasters. Yes, I am aware of their sufferings. And I have come down to rescue them from the clutches of the Egyptians… and bring them to a country flowing with milk and honey…" (Exodus 3:7-9).

God then sends Moses to champion this cause of liberation. He delivered them from Pharaoh with a mighty hand, led them through the Red Sea dry-shod, guided them with a pillar of cloud by day and a pillar of fire by night, provided manna for them, gave them water from the rocks, led them out of slavery into the Promised Land flowing with milk and honey, and conquered the inhabitants of the various territories along the way (the Philistines, Jebusites, Ammonites, and Perizzites).

The children of Israel were expected to respond to God's love and compassion with goodness, fidelity, and obedience, the normal expectation of anyone who has received so much beneficence from their Lord. But they did not. Instead, they responded to God's immense goodness and compassion with infidelity, wickedness, idolatry, and rebellion.

God's Patience and Forbearance
Again, and again the people sinned: they violated the commandments, complained loudly against God, worshipped other gods, and committed all manner of abominations. Many times, God threatened them with destruction but at the intercession of Moses his servant, he often relented. Yet the people sinned again and again until there was no more remedy possible. Our God is indeed all tenderness, patient, long-suffering, slow to anger, and abundant in mercy. It however gets to a point when nothing can be done again, as the people seem determined to self-destruct.

The Wages of Sin is Death
The consequence of their sin was that the generation of Israelites who left Egypt did not reach the Promised Land. They did not live to see the inheritance. The Lord handed them over to the powers of their enemies. They all perished in the desert (Joshua 5:6). St. Paul's teaching in Romans 6:23 affirms that "the wages of sin is death, but that the gift of God is eternal life." As God delivered the people of old through Moses, he saves us in Jesus Christ. We have been saved from slavery to sin, and we are now en-route to the promised land of heaven. Just as the Israelites passed through the Red Sea, and were *baptised* in Moses, we too have passed through the waters of baptism and are baptised in Christ. As they were fed with manna from heaven, we are being fed with the body of Christ. As they were guided with a pillar of cloud in the day and a pillar of fire at night, we are being guided by the Word of God which is a lamp for our feet and a light for our path (Psalm 119:105).

Our Faith Must Bear Fruit

Our salvation in Christ cannot be taken for granted. Our religious activism makes little sense if we are not bearing the appropriate fruits. We are not saved simply because we are the new people of God. Our faith must bear fruit (Matthew 21:18-46) and our lives must radiate the glory of God (Matthew 5:14-16) because we are the light of the world. As we serve a God of love, Jesus commands us to love one another as he has loved us. He went on to say that all men will know that we are his disciples if we love one another in the same way as he has loved us (John 13:34-35).

Unless You Repent You Will Perish Likewise

Reacting to the tragic events reported in today's Gospel, Jesus denounces the popular belief that tragedies and misfortunes are inflicted by God as punishment for individual sins. In response to the story of the Galileans whose blood Pilate had mingled with their sacrifices, Jesus told them not to be deceived into thinking that the victims were worse sinners than other Galileans at that time. For Jesus, everyone's sin is grave enough and deserves death but for God's mercy. He then warned his audience at the time, and ourselves today, that, "Unless you repent, you will perish likewise" (Luke 13:3, 5).

God's mercy and compassion may allow us a second chance; it may allow us a third, fourth, sixth, and even perhaps a tenth chance, but sooner or later, there will be the last chance. God is prepared to allow a little delay here and a little indecision there, a little procrastination here and a little failure there, as well as a little backsliding here and there. But one day shall be the last day.

The frightening thing is that we do not know when that day will come. What we know is that God is patient with those of us alive today: there is still time to repent, and that time is now. But time is getting shorter with each passing day for each one of us. There is a cut-off point, just as with the fig tree in today's gospel, a point at which God's patience will run out and the tree which does not produce fruits will be cut down.

While We Were Yet Sinners…
God is good, loving, and compassionate. He has shown his goodness in countless ways, and above all by sending his only Son to die for us, "while we were yet sinners." And John says that God sent his only Son that those who believe in him may not perish but may have everlasting life (Romans 5:8 and John 3:16).

Christians are called to respond to God's goodness with similar goodness in our hearts. With our baptism we are expected to put on the mind and heart of Christ and act as Christ would. Therefore St. Paul in Philippians 2:21 says that life for him now is Christ, and in Galatians 2:19 he says that he has been crucified in Christ and that the life he lives now is no longer his own but a life that is buried and risen in Christ. To be worthy of his kingdom, therefore, Christ urges us to love our neighbour as he loves us and to pay attention to our needy brothers and sisters. He warns us against hatred, selfishness, and unforgiveness.

Taming the Flesh to Grow the Spirit
It is natural that the more the body or the material aspect of one's existence is given free rein, the less one's spirit grows. It has been demonstrated by wise men and women all through the ages that when human beings overindulge their bodies or engage in the pleasures of the flesh without sufficient restraint, their spirits hardly grow. That is why sages, spiritualists, and mystics through the ages often recognised the critical place of fasting and other acts of penance in fostering spiritual growth. For Christians, fasting is not limited to skipping food and drink, but also restraining one's appetite for wealth accumulation and excessive entertainment, and even restraining oneself from talking too much! It is believed that such mortification of the body facilitates spiritual growth and maturity.

Carrying the Cross of Jesus Daily
Christ teaches that our bodies are to be kept holy and that only the pure shall see God. But many Christians are hooked to a life of

fornication, masturbation, adultery, pornography, and ever newer expressions of sexual perversion. Jesus warns that no matter how ordinary or commonplace these perversions may be in our generation, they are still utterly evil. He asks us to seek first the kingdom and its righteousness, and all other things will follow. Still, many Christians today are caught up in the blind and unmitigated pursuit of material power and prestige. Many are ready to exchange their very souls for money and power, giving no heed to Jesus' admonitions.

Christ teaches us that unless we forgive those who sin against us, our heavenly Father will not forgive us. Yet, many Christians have continued to store up offences and hurts of the neighbour, and others have continued to subject fellow sinners to the most ruthless treatments. Christ urges all who wish to follow him to carry their crosses every day, but many Christians abandon the Lord as soon as any hardship or difficulty arises.

Beware of False Security
The parable of the fig tree is a serious warning for those who take their salvation for granted, those who think that they are saved simply by saying that they believe and are born again (Matthew 7:21). We must however carry the cross of Jesus daily by standing for the truth; by keeping our bodies holy and pure; by denouncing all forms of sexual perversion as evil, even if one is a lone voice; by rejecting the primitive instinct to acquire wealth and material possessions for ourselves without consideration for those who lack basic needs in our societies; by refusing to succumb to inordinate desires for power and prestige; and by constantly forgiving those who hurt us as we have been forgiven.

There should be no false sense of security. Each Christian must make use of the opportunity that each day presents. None of us should fool ourselves into thinking that there is always a tomorrow. Time is limited, and no one has forever to accept God's offer. At the end of the day, it is by our fruits that we shall be known.

Conclusion

Committed Christians must learn to seize the opportunities that come their way and not foolishly keep thinking there will always be a tomorrow. It is certain that one day it will be our last chance. Refusing to repent or postponing repentance chance after chance, will have disastrous repercussions. When the day finally comes, we will either be glad for making the most of the opportunities that came our way, or regret shutting ourselves out!

Questions to Ponder

1. God told Moses that he was standing on holy ground. What is it that makes a place "holy ground?" Give examples.
2. Identify the two attributes of our God that feature prominently in today's readings.
3. What is repentance? What place does repentance have in Christian life? And how is this illustrated in today's readings?
4. What message will you share with your friends and neighbours today after reflecting on the readings of this 3rd Sunday of Lent?

Additional Reading

Mark 1:14-15, 8:36; John 15:1-8; 1 Corinthians 6:9-10; James 2:14-17

4th Sunday of Lent

Our God is Compassion and Love

Readings: Joshua 5:9a,10-12 | Psalm 34 | 2 Cor. 5:17-21 | Luke 15:1-3, 11-32

Summary:

Each year the Scripture readings during the season of Lent help us to reflect on where we are supposed to be and to ask such pertinent questions as: Who am I? Where have I come from? Where am I headed? Once we realise that mistakes have been made, that things are not the way they should be, or that we are not living the life we should, then there is need to change our course, no matter how painful the required change may be.

A Super Story of Love

The Parable of the Prodigal Son is a classic story that has been variously described as an illustration of the tender heart of God, the portrait of a tremendous lover, the story of the reckless lover, the story of the extravagant lover, the story of the kind father, the story of the merciful and forgiving father, and the story of the steadfast love of God.

Realisation, Repentance, and Reconciliation

Before anyone takes a step toward conversion there must first be an awakening, an awareness, or a realisation of where we are at that moment, and where we are supposed to be. This is the first stage in the journey of conversion and reconciliation. However, many people often lack this awareness. Many people are often not sufficiently aware of who they are, where they are, and where they are supposed to be headed. Many are simply sleep-walking through life. Some never really wake up all through their lives. Others only come to a measure of such awareness when they hit rock bottom as it were, on account of a major illness, accident, or misfortune.

From the time the young man in the Gospel story asked his father for a share of his property, to the point where he finished wasting the entire fortune, he was "asleep." He was not aware of himself or his purpose in life. He only woke up, after he hit rock bottom, and found himself in the company of the pigs.

As children of God, we were created for a specific purpose, which we must wake up to. Like the prodigal son who experienced ultimate degradation after giving free rein to his impulses and living foolishly and recklessly, when we commit sin we experience the loss of the state of grace, the loss of friendship with God, and the loss of our sense of purpose.

To live through life unaware is a terrible thing. It amounts to alienation from the source of ultimate meaning. The resultant effect is emptiness and futility. To redeem humanity from such fate is the reason for which Jesus Christ came to the world. The prodigal son recognised that a pig's pen is not where he belonged, as indeed should all of us who are presently in a state like his. At the point of realisation, one can decide to do nothing and watch the situation degenerate or summon the courage to move on to the next level, which is repentance. Repentance is a painful process that requires the grace of God to experience. To repent is to turn back, to make a U-turn and to move in the opposite direction.

Repentance demands a great deal of humility and courage. Many people in the same situation as the Prodigal son may still have some primitive pride and choose not to return to the father. Whereas the father is always waiting for the return of the lost son, some people on account of foolish pride and arrogance, would rather die in their terrible situation than return to God, even when they know that it is only in returning to the Father that they can truly find fulfilment.

Reconciliation is the logical consequence of genuine repentance. The Prodigal Son returned to his father and was received with great rejoicing. Following the realisation that he has sinned, and on account of the steps taken to turn around to righteousness and rectitude, reconciliation is achieved, the right order (broken by sin) is re-established, and peace is restored.

People often live in darkness and sin because of lack of realisation and awareness. For the period he was away from home, the Prodigal Son suffered a great deal. Perhaps he experienced some momentary, superficial pleasure, but his life was devoid of true joy. He soon lost his fair-weather friends, and he suffered hunger, loneliness, degradation, and the pain of guilt.

He returned to his father broken, empty-handed and in rags. He fell from grace to grass. All he had left was a humble, contrite heart. The Prodigal son had eaten the forbidden fruit, and rather than being satisfied, he was left with a bitter taste in his mouth, the taste of regret. His loving father, who all the while was waiting for him, recognised all these and that is why his heart collapsed as it were, at the sight of his returning son.

While the father knew that outside his house this young man will not be a happy person, his elder brother saw him as "enjoying" away from home. Whereas his father saw a suffering soul that was hungry for home, and he was so delighted to have the boy back, the elder brother seemed envious of the boy and angry at his return. But Christians ought to see sin differently. We should never use the word "enjoy" or "happy" for anyone who is living a life of sin.

The father who had been waiting for him all this while ran to the boy, embraced, and kissed him, and ordered that his dirty clothes be changed to a kingly apparel. This is very significant. It means that we can always approach our loving God, but once we come before him, we are obliged to live by his heavenly parameters.

The Tender Heart of God

The Parable of the Prodigal son is a graphic illustration of the tender heart of our God who is slow to anger, rich with mercy, forgiveness, and graciousness. He is a God who never stops loving us even in our sinfulness, because he recognises our weaknesses, and he suffers with us, even when our suffering is self-inflicted. The Prodigal son discovered that he was loved even in his sin.

The Free Gift of Love

An important lesson from the story of the Prodigal Son is that God's love is gratuitous, extravagant, bountiful, and generous. It is sheer grace. This explains how God could send his only son to die a shameful death for us sinners (John 3:16; Romans 5:8). It is one thing to be loved in one's goodness, but what an extraordinary experience to be loved in one's sinfulness!

Such love is like breeze to a dying fire or like rainfall on parched ground. Such is the love with which we have been loved in Christ Jesus. Like the Prodigal Son we have often done abominable things. We have often been unfaithful. We have often squandered God's grace and misused our gifts and talents. If the Lord were to mark our guilt, who among us would survive? Do we not all need more mercy than justice? Yet, God is generous in forgiving us, and it is through our sins that we most experience the immensity of God's goodness and compassion.

The elder son in the story represents the Pharisees and many of us who like to think that we are righteous and in good standing. The elder brother represents those of us who think that our good behaviour makes us worthy of God. He represents all who have no room in their hearts for forgiveness, all who show no mercy and compassion, all who give no second chance to offenders, all who think that sinners are damned and/or insist that offenders must always face the full wrath of the law.

Such persons find themselves inevitably sympathising with the elder son because of their arrogance and self-righteousness. Such persons do not understand the gratuitousness of God's love or the dynamics of God's compassion. Many persons like this claim to be religious. But how can anyone be religious and not be compassionate? How can anyone be religious and not have some of the tender heart of God? There are three major marks of a truly religious person, namely, tenderness of heart, mellowness of soul, and calmness of the spirit. These are the common denominators for anyone who claims to be religious.

The Mercy of God
Human beings need the mercy of God more than anything else. The way to demonstrate our appreciation for God's abundant mercy over us, is to show the same mercy to others. It is said that forgiveness is unlocking the door to set someone free, only to realise that you were

the prisoner all the while. As we are all beneficiaries of God's abundant mercy, it behoves on us to reciprocate in like manner, as we relate with our neighbours. The Church in its wisdom has given us a template to live Christ-like lives in the Corporal and Spiritual Works of Mercy. This Sunday presents us with an opportunity to reflect on our failings, to turn around like the prodigal son, and return to the loving embrace of our Heavenly Father.

Conclusion

The Parable of the Prodigal Son is one of the most moving parables of Jesus. It is a classic love story with a powerful lesson on God's infinite love and his willingness to forgive and forget. To live meaningful lives, we are called and charged to go forth and reciprocate the love and forgiveness of our Heavenly Father. May our own love affair be founded on God's love.

Questions to Ponder

1. What point does St. Paul make in the 2nd Reading (2 Corinthians 5:17-21)?
2. If you were to give your own title to the story of the Prodigal Son, what would it be?
3. The Elder son in the Gospel story symbolises the Justice of man but the Father represents the Justice of God. Explain.
4. What concrete steps can you take to make the merciful love of God your own lifestyle?

Additional Reading

Psalm 103:11; Matthew 5:7, 18:23-35; Luke 6:36-38, 15:4-10, 19:1-10

5th Sunday of Lent

Our God is Rich in Mercy

Readings: Isaiah 43:16-21 | Psalm 126 | Philippians 3:8-14 | John 8:1-11

Summary:

The encounter with Jesus is the beginning of new life for the woman caught in adultery. It signifies that every sinner has a future not just a past. In Christ we have endless possibilities: for goodness, for holiness, and for godliness. We must forget what lies behind and strain forward, like St. Paul, to what lies ahead.

Mercy – A Free Gift

The story is told of a young soldier who deserted Napoleon's army and was caught within a couple of hours. The punishment for desertion was death. The young soldier's mother pleaded with Napoleon to have mercy and to spare her son's life, but Napoleon told her that on account of the gravity of the offence, her son did not deserve mercy. She responded, "I know he does not deserve mercy; it would not be mercy if he deserved it."

What everyone deserves is justice. Mercy, on the other hand, is undeserved. It is a sheer gift. Mercy is the gracious disposition by which the wronged person unilaterally cancels out all the wrongs and transgressions of the offender. Mercy does not suggest that the guilty is not guilty; it recognises the guilt, but does not demand satisfaction for the wrong, the kind of satisfaction people demand when they insist that the offender should go to jail, or that he or she should be put to death in the case of a capital crime.

A Move to Trap Jesus

The Mosaic Law prescribes death by stoning for all who are guilty of adultery (see Deuteronomy 22:22-24 and Leviticus 20:10). The Pharisees and Scribes who brought the woman to Jesus knew the law, but they wanted to use the occasion to trap Jesus, because he had been talking about mercy and forgiveness. Since it is a clear instruction from Moses, they wanted to see if he was going to disobey the law of Moses. However, a lot of practices that have become acceptable and normative in many cultures could be inherently unjust or oppressive. John Paul II often spoke of such practices as "structures of sin," and Christians are supposed to be constantly challenging not only individual sin but also these structures of sin as well. We must take a critical look at some of the practices that are accepted in our societies, to see whether or not they can stand the test of Christ's civilisation of love.

Jesus had been preaching a lot about mercy, forgiveness, and compassion, and he had also been keeping the company of tax collectors, prostitutes, and others that were considered public sinners. The Pharisees and Scribes were curious to see how he was going to respond this time. They said to him: "Master, this woman was caught in the very act of committing adultery, and according to the law of Moses, such a woman is to be stoned to death. What do you say?"

Seeing how they had debased, humiliated, and dehumanised the woman, Jesus turns away in disgust. He neither looked at the woman nor at them. He simply wrote on the ground. But when they insisted, he raised his eyes and said to them: "If there is anyone who has not sinned, let him be the one to throw the first stone." He went back to writing on the ground. A lot has been written as to what Jesus was writing, and we may never know, but some say that he was listing the accusers' sins, and confronted with the truth of their own sinfulness, the accusers left one by one, disappearing as quickly as possible.

Neither Do I Condemn You
When Jesus raised his eyes again, he saw the woman standing there alone. He asked her: "Where are they? Has no one condemned you?" And she answered: "No one sir." Then he said: "Neither do I condemn you. Go and sin no more." Note that he pardoned her with a caveat: "…sin no more." In this way, Jesus forgives and rehabilitates her. He restores her God-given dignity and frees her from being an object of religious controversy. He relates with her as a person beloved by a God who hates sin but loves the sinner.

The Pharisees and Scribes wanted to apply the maximum possible sentence. They wanted to take her life, because for them she was a lost cause. They saw no other solution to her sinful life, but Jesus could see immense potential and endless possibilities in her, so he gives her another chance. He demonstrated the love of God, which is always available, and constantly calling the sinner to repentance.

Jesus' action does not in any way suggest that he condones the sin of adultery. Like the rabbis of old, he viewed adultery as a major contravention that contaminates, violates, and ruins the offender. In fact, he imposed higher standards of sexual morality on his followers than was found in the old law. For instance, his followers could be guilty of fornication or adultery if they do not sufficiently guard their thoughts with regards to the sexual appetite (Matthew 5:27-28; Luke 16:18).

Yet, Jesus rejects the wickedness of the Pharisees and Scribes and their cruelty towards the woman. He rejects the double standards and the selective justice by which they brought forward only the woman in a case that involved a man and a woman. He rejects their lack of compassion and kindness towards a woman that is already thoroughly humiliated. Jesus takes the controversy over the woman to a higher level by addressing their hypocrisy. He turns the table on her prosecutors, challenging them to look critically into themselves before taking such action against another. In this way he demonstrated to them that in the eyes of God, we are all sinners in need of forgiveness (Luke 6:36-38), "for all have sinned and fall short of the glory of God" (Romans 3:23).

We often stigmatise people who are guilty of certain categories of sin. We humiliate, torture, and execute, even sometimes by extra-judicial means, those guilty of certain sins. Many of those engaged in such callous and merciless acts see no contradiction between their actions and going to church to praise the God of Jesus Christ, reciting the Lord's Prayer, and asking for God's forgiveness.

A God of Mercy and Compassion

The greatest attributes of the God we serve are mercy and compassion (see 2 Chronicles 30:9; Psalm 100:5; 111:4). Our God is rich in mercy and compassion; his anger is for a while, but his mercy is everlasting. He is so merciful that he sent His only Son to die so that we may not have to bear the full consequence of our sins. He allowed His Son to be killed so that his kingdom of love and peace may be established (John 3:16).

Having sacrificed himself for us, the Son of God has made love, mercy, forgiveness, and compassion towards those who offend us a *conditio sine qua non* for admission into his kingdom. In Matthew 5:7 he says, "Blessed are the merciful for they shall obtain mercy," and in Luke 6:36,38 he says, "Be compassionate as your heavenly father is compassionate…, for the measure you give out is the measure you will receive." In the parable of the unforgiving debtor Jesus says, "that is how my heavenly father will deal with you unless you each forgive your brother or sister from your heart (Matthew 18:35). In what we have come to know as the Golden Rule, Jesus admonishes us to do unto others as we would like them to do unto us (Matthew 7:12).

A World in Need of Mercy and Compassion

In *Dives in Misericordia,* Pope John Paul II says that the greatest weakness of the world today is its lack of mercy. He observed that the pursuit of justice in the strict sense is not enough for a humane society. He calls on the world to go beyond strict distributive justice to embrace love which includes mercy, forgiveness, and compassion.

A world without forgiveness, says John Paul II, is a cold world of endless strife! We must ask God for mercy and change the situation. God's forgiveness is somewhat conditional on our own forgiveness (Matthew 6:12, Luke 11:4). If we refuse to forgive the sins of others, God can revoke the forgiveness he had given us. Dying of pain on the cross of Calvary, Jesus forgave his executioners, saying, "Forgive them, father, for they know not what they do" (Luke 23:34).

Conclusion

"God is so merciful toward us. We too should learn to be merciful, especially towards those who suffer," says Pope Francis. None of us deserves God's mercy, it is sheer grace. The works of mercy include giving and reaching out in love, even to those who hurt us.

Questions to Ponder
1. What is the relationship (if any) between last Sunday's Gospel – the Parable of the Prodigal Son – and today's Gospel – the woman caught in adultery?
2. What are the treasures that St. Paul now refers to as rubbish when compared to the glory of knowing Christ Jesus?
3. Identify the outstanding qualities that made St. Paul such a powerful witness of Christ?
4. What has changed so far and what more will change in your Christian life and practice as we progress in this Lenten season?

Additional Reading
Psalm 130:3; Matthew 6:9-13, 18:23-35; Luke 11:2-4, 23:34; Rom 3:23.

Passion (Palm) Sunday

The Passion of the Lord

Readings: Isaiah 50:4-7 | Psalm 22 | Philippians 2:6-11 | Luke 22:14–23:56

Summary:

In Christ the symbol of death, the cross, has become a symbol of life and love. The cross of horror has become the cross of hope, the tortured body has become the source of new life, and the gaping wounds of violence have become the fountain of forgiveness, healing, and reconciliation.

The Suffering Servant of Isaiah

The Suffering Servant is the one who is led through the path of pain and suffering like a lamb – dumb and docile to the slaughterhouse. He is one who endures insult and spitting, who offers his back to those who strike him, and his cheeks to those who pluck his beard. The Suffering Servant is, however, untouched by the insults because God is with him. He knows that he will be vindicated and will not be put to shame (see Isaiah 50:4-9).

Faith in the fact that there is a good, loving God who is the overarching controller of the universe, a God who will bring about justice in the end; and faith in the fact that good will ultimately triumph over evil, and that the triumph of evil is only a mirage, etc., are some of the reasons why some people survive devastating and traumatic events and are able to bounce back and move on, whereas others are crushed and completely destroyed by those same events.

The Suffering Servant knows that his "redeemer liveth," even though it has pleased him to crush this servant with suffering. Prosperity gospel advocates cannot understand what that clause, "it pleased the Lord to crush his servant with suffering" means. But this truth is part of what 1 Corinthians 1:18-25 refers to as the scandal of the cross: "...Christ crucified, a stumbling block to Jews and foolishness to Gentiles."

Yet the servant does not suffer in vain: he offers his life in loving service, taking the people's faults upon himself, and bearing their infirmities, he uses his suffering to justify many. At the end, the Suffering Servant shall have a long life; he shall see his heirs! (See Isaiah 53:10-11).But we know that Jesus died at age thirty-three. So, long life here must mean something else, and whatever it meant for Jesus, that is what it should mean to us his followers. If therefore I am a follower of Jesus, I have long life, even if I die at forty. What matters is living in Christ, for we know that when one is living in Christ one is alive, and that life is eternal. Eternal life for all of us Christians begins with the event of our baptism.

Humility: Jesus Emptied Himself

Jesus the King of kings comes to us as the Suffering Servant bearing the cross of human infirmity. He sacrificed himself out of love for us to gain us salvation. The Humility of Christ is celebrated in today's 2nd Reading. We are invited and challenged to have the same mind as Christ Jesus, to share in his suffering, and follow his example of obedience. Jesus did this to be in solidarity with, and to help, all those who suffer sickness and pain, those who live in poverty, those who are victims of social injustice and those who are neglected and discriminated against.

Lessons of the Passion Story

Palm Sunday launches us into the paschal mystery of the death that brought life and the humiliation that brought glorification. The story reminds us of the crowd of followers who shouted "Hosanna" for Jesus one day and "Crucify him" the next day, the cowardice of his followers who abandoned him, the wickedness of the religious leaders who plotted his death, and the cruelty of the soldiers who carried out the execution.

The focus of Palm Sunday is, however, on the person of Jesus, the central character of the story. We are reminded of his fidelity to his Father's will, his courage in the face of hardship, and his sheer goodness in the face of evil (as seen in his entreaty, "Father, forgive them for they know not what they do"). The goodness of Jesus' interior being expressed itself outside, even at the most difficult time of pain. Since Jesus was all good inside, nothing else could come out of his mouth, no matter the torture he experienced. It is impossible for Jesus to bear any grudge against his torturers, because of the transparent holiness, goodness and generosity of his entire being. We too need to pray for such internal goodness and holiness, so that goodness may proceed out of us, even at times of pain, tribulation and persecution.

Against the darkness of Calvary, the goodness of Jesus shines forth brightly. This is why the Friday of Jesus' crucifixion is called Good Friday. It is a Friday that shines brightly when everywhere is dark. It is love that transformed Jesus' violent death into a good thing. As he says, "There is no greater love than for a man to lay down his life for his friends."

From Palm Sunday to Easter Sunday, we celebrate the tremendous love of God that saved the world through the death of his Son. We celebrate in an ironical manner, the triumph of the cross, because the glory of Jesus cannot be separated from his passion. The glory of Jesus and his suffering are one, hence we cannot accept one and reject the other.

We cannot accept the Jesus of the resurrection and reject the Jesus of the cross; they go together. He says, "Anyone who wants to be a follower of mine must first deny himself, take up his cross daily, and follow me." We know that the death of Jesus was not a defeat but a victory: the victory of good over evil, of love over hate, of light over darkness, of life over death, and of mercy and forgiveness over the powers of destruction. So, the virtues that can transform the world are the opposite of the vices that have destroyed the world, namely, hatred, violence, and unforgiveness. We celebrate Jesus' response to hate and evil. He absorbed all the violence and transformed it with love. He had nothing but love to show because there was nothing but love in him. Even when they nailed him to the cross he kept on loving and forgiving.

The passion of Jesus gives courage, strength, and hope to all believers who suffer. It means that we are not alone. As a human being, Jesus suffered incredible pain: he was let down by his friends, betrayed by one of his followers, suffered incredible anguish in Gethsemane; he had no one to support him during his agony; he was subjected to a barrage of accusations; and he endured insults, blows, taunts, and spittle.

Love Gives Meaning to Suffering

Jesus suffered the shame of being condemned to death like a common criminal and was whipped severely and pierced with thorns and nails. He suffered incredibly. It is no mere drama. But his suffering would have had no meaning if he did not endure it with love. In the same vein, it is enduring our own sufferings with love that will give such suffering meaning. No one likes to suffer. Jesus prayed that the cup passes over him, but when the suffering became inevitable, he embraced it for the sake of those he loves.

Jesus is the good shepherd who out of love lays down his life for his sheep. This love inevitably brings pain, but it also brings joy. Christians must constantly submit their sufferings and pains in love to Jesus, knowing that the love of God transforms all suffering and pain into saving grace.

The Language of the Cross

> By his wounds we are healed, by his stripes we are made whole (Isaiah 53:5).
>
> While Jews demand miracles and Greeks demand wisdom, here we are preaching a crucified Christ (1 Corinthians 1:22-23).
>
> God's foolishness is wiser than human wisdom, and God's weakness is stronger than human strength (1 Corinthians 1:25).
>
> By virtue of the cross of Calvary, death is swallowed up in victory (1 Corinthians 15:54-56).
>
> God's power is at its best in weakness (2 Corinthians 12:9).

Conclusion

Perhaps the greatest Christian witness we are called upon to give before our power-hungry and hate-filled world is Jesus' life of love, humility and meekness. Many will continue to find this difficult to understand and accept. Yet it is part of the foolishness of God that is wiser than human wisdom which we celebrate on this Sunday and throughout the passion week. May our Palm Sunday celebration help us to appreciate ever more the ways of our God whose power is at its best in weakness. Amen!

Questions to Ponder
1. How does Jesus fit into the "Suffering Servant" image we see in today's passage from Isaiah?
2. What is the one thing that the 2nd Reading challenges us to have, to do, or to be?
3. Which of the last statements of Jesus on the Cross impresses you the most? And why?
4. In what ways can husbands lay heavy crosses on their wives or wives push husbands to Calvary? And how are today's readings a source of encouragement for all who suffer like this?

Additional Reading
Isaiah 42:1-4, 49:1-6, 50:4-9; Luke 9:23-26; John 3:16; Romans 5:8, 8:31-39.

Season of Easter

Easter Sunday

Christ is Risen, Alleluia

Readings: Acts 10:34a, 37-43 | Psalm 118 | Colossians 3:1-4 (or 1 Corinthians 5:6b-8) | John 20:1-9

Summary:

The first reading is part of the early post-Pentecost sermons of Peter. He summarised the spectacular life of Jesus, which ended in a brutal death at the hands of the Jews. But he said that the story of Jesus did not end with the inglorious death on the cross of Calvary. God raised him from the dead, allowing him to be seen by many witnesses, including Peter himself. Peter then declared that Jesus is the Messiah about whom all the prophets spoke. He then invited every one of his hearers to come and believe in him, so they may have their sins forgiven.

In the second reading, St. Paul tells us that by virtue of our Baptism, we Christians already share in the risen life of Christ. We are to abandon our old selves, with its worldly addictions and seek the things that are above, where Christ is now seated at the right hand of God.

The Gospel story is a record of the spectacular events of the morning of the resurrection, including the discovery first by Mary Magdalene, and subsequently Peter and John, that the tomb was empty. They saw the empty tomb, and they believed that he is alive! Until now they did not understand the Scriptures that Jesus must rise from the dead.

Christ is Risen, Alleluia!

Each year we celebrate the earth-shaking event of the rising from the dead of the Son of God, the Righteous One, who died a shameful death on the cross at the hands of cruel men. After spending himself preaching the love, the compassion and the forgiveness of God, healing the sick, feeding the hungry and affirming the weak and the poor, Christ the author of life was rejected by the Jews. He was betrayed by his own disciples, and handed over to Pilate, a pagan king, who got him tortured, humiliated, and crucified, along with two common criminals.

We celebrate on this Easter Sunday what happened three days after the terrible events in Jerusalem. While the disciples remained utterly shocked, frightened, and discouraged, and as they wondered among themselves what meaning there was in a life of holiness, humility and self-sacrifice, and what hope was in store for them, Jesus himself appeared to them individually and severally, and demonstrated that he had indeed risen from the dead as the Scriptures had foretold, and as he himself had said.

At some of the post-resurrection appearances, especially in the versions recorded in the Gospel of Luke 24, Jesus took time to explain to his disciples the meaning of his life, his death and his resurrection. He demonstrated to them how the Law of Moses, the Prophetic Writings, the Psalms and the Wisdom Literature, were all fulfilled in him. He sat his disciples down and explained that such passages as Deuteronomy 18:16-19, 21-23; Hosea 6:1; Isaiah 49-50; and 52:13; as well as Psalms 2-22, were all about himself. Most of these passages show that the suffering of the just man, far from being useless, is extraordinarily fruitful, as it often results in the salvation of many. He himself had taught them that "Unless a grain of wheat falls to the ground and dies, it remains only a single grain. But if it dies, it will yield fruit in plenty."

The message of the Resurrection is that through the cross, Jesus Christ the Son of God has taken away the sins of humanity. He has become our advocate with the Father by virtue of being the victim who takes away our sins (See John 1:29; John 11:51-52; Romans 3:25). He has taken upon himself the guilt of humanity, and by his precious blood, he has done the expiation for our sins. He has exchanged his own life for the life and freedom of each one of us. His death has reconciled humanity with God. By his suffering on the cross of Calvary, Jesus has removed the barrier that separated human beings from God. He has also broken down the evil wall that separated Jews from Gentiles, slaves from freeborn.

With the death and resurrection of Christ, a fundamental change has occurred in the scheme of things. A new relationship is now possible with God and with fellow men and women. Individual men and women, and indeed the whole human society may now enjoy a filial relationship with their God, and a relationship of brotherhood and sisterhood with one another. The only condition for our participation in this new dispensation is repentance and conversion from sin, and baptism in the name of Jesus.

Only Jesus could explain the events of the paschal mystery to his disciples. Only he could transform the profound mystery of his death and resurrection into a revelation of God's love. Only he could transform the fear and confusion of his disciples into understanding and confidence. And as soon as the disciples' eyes were opened to these truths, they became witnesses of the resurrection and of the message of repentance from sin. This is what we see in Peter's sermons as recorded in the Acts of the Apostles. Peter and his companions became witnesses to the meaning of all that had taken place in Galilee and in Jerusalem. They were not just eyewitnesses of the raw Paschal events. They were now equipped by Christ and the Spirit of God with the necessary wisdom, courage and confidence to interpret these events to their hearers. Rather than keep the good news to themselves, they preached it to all who had ears to hear.

We too are beneficiaries of the missionary assignment given to the disciples, which many of them discharged with great zeal and enthusiasm. Many disciples died in the process of proclaiming the good news, and as we say, the blood of the martyrs is the seed of the Church. Christians of all generations have the mission, the responsibility and the challenge to pass on the good news of the saving death and resurrection of Christ to others. This message has been kept alive by committed Christians in the course of the last 2000 years. We ourselves can keep the message alive by living it out and passing it on. This is how we keep the Gospel of Christ alive - by giving it away!

The earliest Church reached out from Jerusalem into the pagan world, which was enslaved to sin and blinded by corruption and superstition. They announced to them God's message of repentance and forgiveness. Many pagans got converted and they carried on the message. Like the early Church, modern Christianity is confronted with the challenge of preaching Christ amid a neo-pagan culture of widespread corruption, hedonism, occultism, materialism, consumerism, and violence. We are confronted today with a neo-pagan culture of inordinate lust for money, power, pleasure and security, with the attendant crimes of abortion, hired assassination, armed robbery, social manipulation and exploitation, widespread drug addiction, and a rising tide of suicide.

When Jesus sent his disciples out, he had in mind not only the Gentiles of the 1st Century, but also the millions of sinners in our own day who would need the washing of baptism for the forgiveness of sins. He had in mind the millions of sinners today who need to be plunged into the merciful love of God and into the Holy Spirit that gives life. In reflecting on the resurrection, we must ask ourselves today to what extent we are committed to living and spreading the good news of God's generosity in forgiveness and his call to repentance and conversion. For it is only by an ardent commitment to a life of repentance and conversion to Christ's civilisation of love that we shall truly show that we understand the meaning of the resurrection.

Finally, in a global environment gripped by widespread fear and anxiety over many uncertainties about the future of humanity, Christian believers in the Resurrection of Jesus are the harbingers of hope and confidence in God who is the Overarching Controller of the universe. We are the ones to announce to the world that because the Crucified One has risen from the dead, there is no need to panic. He has the whole world in his hands. He has conquered the principalities and powers, including the forces behind plagues and pestilences. He will see us through these perilous times. His voice echoes from the other side of Calvary, saying: Do not be afraid. Peace be with you. It shall all be well. May we soon experience in our very lives, in our homes, and in our country, many manifestations of Jesus' victory over the forces of darkness. Amen.

Conclusion

Christ is risen, Alleluia! The Cross of Calvary has become a symbol of glory, and this is the message the disciples have told through all generations. Many disciples died in the process of proclaiming this good news, and as we say, the blood of the martyrs is the seed of the Church. Christians of all generations have a lifetime mission, responsibility, and challenge, to pass on the good news of the saving death and resurrection of Christ to others. May we never fail to carry out this mission in word and in deed.

Questions to Ponder
1. The resurrection of Jesus is the centre of our faith. Discuss.
2. The Acts of the Apostles represents a second journey of Jesus through Apostles. How is Jesus' ministry to be carried on today?
3. After today's celebration of Easter, what message of comfort and encouragement would you send to a Christian friend or relation who is a victim of violence, or to someone suffering from an illness, poverty, unemployment, loneliness, childlessness, or persecution?

Additional Reading
Romans 6:3-11; 1 Corinthians 15:19-20; Galatians 5:1; Hebrews 13:8

2nd Sunday of Easter
(Divine Mercy Sunday)

My Lord and My God

Readings: Acts 5:12-16 | Psalm 118 | Revelation 1:9-11a, 12-13, 17-19 | John 20:19-31

Summary:

All our religious activities ought to bring us to the point where we have a physical encounter with the Lord. They are meant to bring us to the point where we exclaim in awe and worship with Thomas, "My Lord and my God." This is what the resurrection and appearances of Jesus was for the weak, frightened, and disillusioned disciples. It was for them a spectacular moment of divine encounter.

From Doubting to Believing Thomas

The doors were closed where the disciples were, for fear of the Jews and Jesus emerged in their midst for the first time after his resurrection. Thomas was not with them when they first saw him. He suffered an extra week of distress on account of the death of Jesus. His companions' efforts to get him out of his misery proved abortive when he insisted, "Unless I put my finger into his wound and put my hands on the side where the lance went, I will not believe." So, he was still mourning while others were already rejoicing.

Then Jesus appeared in their midst a second time with Thomas present, and after saying, "Peace be with you," he turned to Thomas and said, "Thomas, put your finger here. Look, here are my hands, doubt no longer but believe." It is striking to note that we are not told that Thomas eventually put his finger there. Perhaps once he saw Jesus, it was no longer necessary. All we are told is that Thomas immediately went on his knees and said, "My Lord and my God!" Jesus' response to the sudden devotion of Thomas was: "You believe because you have seen me. Happy are those who have not seen and yet believe" (John 20:29).

This is a very significant verse because all of us, including St. Paul (who never met Jesus physically), benefit from this declaration, and it authenticates the assertion that faith is believing things not seen (Hebrews 11:1). If you can see, touch, or feel a thing, then it is no more a matter of faith. So, when Thomas says unless I see… unless I touch… it sounds reasonable and logical as human beings are always curious and want material evidence. Unfortunately, many who claim to be believers are still at this point where they are constantly seeking for material evidence and proof in what is supposed to be a matter of faith.

My Lord and My God!
There are dimensions of reality which elude the physical senses, but which are nevertheless real. Reality is not limited to the material world. This is what Antoine de Saint-Exupery means when he writes in the *Little Prince* that, "It's only with the heart that one can see rightly, for what is essential is invisible to the eye."

Thomas soon discovered the stupidity of his ways. He soon discovered that he could not impose his limited human conditions on God. He had lost one week of joyful life in his doubt, grief, and isolation. On meeting with Jesus, however, he cried out in worship: "My Lord and my God!" Thomas' cry of faith became the most powerful proclamation of the identity of Christ. In the Catholic Church, when we raise the consecrated body of Jesus we echo the words of Thomas, "My Lord and my God!" This is how God turns things around. He has taken the words of a disbelieving man and etched them in gold.

Thomas moved in one instance from earthly "seeing" to spiritual "believing." He is one of the examples of the fact that when one encounters the risen Christ, one is not the same again. All Christians ought therefore to be constantly seeking an encounter with the Lord. Perhaps part of the reason many people are not able to give credible witness to Christ is that they have not had the privilege of such an encounter with the risen Lord as Thomas had.

Divine Encounter

When Thomas encountered Jesus, his fears vanished, his doubts disappeared, a new fire was lit in him, and he was instantly healed of his blindness. He suddenly recognised his need to be filled by God's surprising ways rather than insist that God meets his own conditions. But our God is so merciful that he waits for us to truly discover him and is ever ready to say to us, "Peace be with you." After the powerful encounter, Thomas was energised to go out and spread the good news. Legend has it that Thomas went as far as India with the Gospel of Christ, and that he was martyred there!

Like the doubting Thomas, many of us are often not there when Jesus comes by. It would be interesting to know where Thomas was for a whole week after the others had seen the risen Lord. The other ten disciples locked themselves up in the upper room, and at the appearance of Jesus they were consoled and overjoyed, while Thomas remained in mourning, and he refused to be consoled.

Thomas separated himself from the community and lost joy for one week. Like Thomas, many of us insist that God must behave only in ways that fit our expectations. Like Thomas, many of us refuse to go deeper to savour the mysterious ways of God. We remain on the superficial level of material proofs for God's presence. Sadly, if we remain on this level, we will never savour what St. Paul refers to as the mystery hidden from ages that has now been revealed.

The Dynamics of Christian Faith

Faith saw a virgin conceive the Son of God. Faith saw the crucified one back to life. Faith turned the early Christians from frightened disciples into bold and courageous martyrs of the faith. By faith, the mighty can be pulled down and the lowly raised up, water can be changed into wine, wine can be changed into the Blood of Christ, five loaves can be multiplied to feed five thousand, desperate situations can be overturned, and dead ends can become highways. By faith the early Christians went far beyond where their human abilities could carry them, and their activities changed the course of human history.

Christians hold that all appearances to the contrary notwithstanding, light will outshine darkness, truth will conquer falsehood, good will overcome evil, love will triumph over hate, the stone can be rolled away, and sinners can rise from the ashes of shame. By faith the mountains of selfishness and greed shall be removed, and the hills of corruption and indiscipline shall be leveled; hatred and vengeance shall be removed; and religious extremism and terrorism shall be destroyed. By faith, the multiple crises of leadership and politics and the many challenges with marriage and family in the modern world shall be resolved.

Faith takes us where our senses cannot go. Believing is much more than accepting something as real. It is developing the spiritual faculty to perceive the invisible reality at the heart of all things. Believing enables us to "see" beyond physical sight (John 6:40; 9:35-39).

Witnessing for Christ

The apostles had the privilege of "seeing" Jesus physically. But those who know Jesus through believing are equal to the apostles who knew him by sight. The world is full of *doubting Thomases*. Many people will not believe unless they can touch Christ' wounds and see the radiance of his face. But people can touch Christ's wounds and see the radiance of his face if Christ is alive and active in us. Pope Paul VI said, "The men and women of today are not looking for more teachers, but witnesses. And if they will listen to any teachers at all, it is because those teachers are also witnesses." There are too many teachers and churches all over the place, but what the world is looking for are those who give witness to Jesus.

Christ's Gift of Peace

Before leaving his disciples to face his suffering and death, Jesus spoke words of peace to his disciples:

> Peace I bequeath to you,
> My own peace I give you.
> The peace which the world
> cannot give, this is my gift to you.
> Do not let your hearts be troubled (John 14:27).

As Jesus appeared to his frightened and disillusioned disciples at various times and in various locations, his first words were, "Peace be with you;" "Do not be afraid, it is I." These are the same words he said to John in the Island of Patmos. As he appeared to Peter who denied him and as he met the other disciples who disserted him, he also uttered those consoling words: "Peace be with you!"

In John 20:19-29, he repeated those gracious words three times. Jesus' assurance of peace came at the disciples' greatest hour of need, when for them, all seemed to have ended in defeat and humiliation. These same words are a great source of hope for all believers who are suffering defeat and humiliation. He assures them of peace.

Jesus' words are a great source of hope for all of us at our greatest moments of need. Even today and always he is around to say to us, "Peace be with you!" Those who take the words of Jesus seriously can claim his peace amid tension and turmoil, as they are confronted by tragic circumstances, or as they experience failure and disappointment.

Conclusion

As he rose from the dead Jesus bore an olive branch announcing the defeat of Satan and the realisation in himself of God's promise of peace. The real peace which every human heart longs for, the true peace which families need, is now available in the risen Christ. Yes indeed, the lasting peace which has been the pre-occupation of genuine leaders in every age is now available in the risen Christ.

Questions to Ponder

1. What is the link between today's Gospel and the Church's Sacrament of Penance?
2. The world has a problem believing without seeing. How can my life contribute to making those around me believe in Christ without seeing him?
3. What is the message of Divine Mercy which we celebrate this Sunday?

Additional Reading

Mark 16:17-18; John 14:27; Romans 8:28-39; Hebrews 11:1-40

3rd Sunday of Easter

Do You Love Me More Than These Others?

Readings: Acts 5:27-32, 40-41 | Psalm 30 | Revelation 5:11-14 | John 21:1-19

Summary:

Peter is a great source of hope and consolation to all repentant sinners. In giving authority to the man who denied him publicly three times, Jesus wants to show that he was establishing his Church not on human strength but on his own love and faithfulness. He wants us to know that he is not placing a leader who is perfect over the Church, but one who must learn to rely on the strength that comes from God.

Love, Betrayal, and the Beauty of Reconciliation

Human love is fragile, but it can be a wonderful experience. It often starts with charm, passion, and romance, but can be rocked by failure, betrayal, and brokenness. It can also be rekindled with reconciliation, and possibly grow to an unusual level of heroism. As we journey through life, we sometimes experience hurt and betrayal, or we are let down by people we love and trust. When this happens, the reaction is usually shock and disappointment, anger and resentment, rejection and separation. Relationships can be permanently damaged after such an experience unless something decisive is done.

Reconciliation can restore broken relationships. Although it is difficult because it often demands the generosity and magnanimity to reach out to the other person, the willingness to forgive and forget the hurt, and the courage to risk trusting the person again, reconciliation is immeasurably rewarding. The fruits of reconciliation could be so enormous that, for some, it makes having a conflict a rewarding enterprise. It can bring the best out of people. Reconciliation brings about peace where there was war, love where there was hatred, good feeling where there was ill feeling, friendship where there was enmity, and understanding where there was misunderstanding.

The Call of Peter

The Gospels tell us that Peter was called twice: first, by the Sea of Galilee at the start of Jesus' ministry (Mark 1:16-18), and second, three years after (after Jesus' resurrection) by the Sea of Tiberias (John 21:15-19). Peter responded to the first call readily. He recognised and confessed Jesus as the Christ (Matthew 16:13-20) and declared his undying love for and loyalty to him.

However, because the cost of true love is enormous, when the painful demands of the call began to unfold, Peter fell. When the painful cost of Peter's love for Jesus dawned on him, he denied that he ever knew Jesus, and he denied him insistently three times (Matthew 26:73; John 18:15-17, 25-27). But when Jesus rose from the dead, he looked at Peter with love, and not with hate or resentment. Jesus did not condemn him or write him off; he did not even caution him against future betrayal. He simply asked Peter if he loves him and put him in charge of his Church.

It is our love for Jesus that provides the energy and passion to keep his commandments. It is their passion for and love of Jesus that made the disciples go through all their suffering with Christian fortitude. Loving the Lord is a fundamental precondition to living his life. It entails having a personal encounter with the Lord.

Such encounter transforms one and enables the person to see differently. At the second account of the calling of Peter he was wiser and humbler. His "Yes Lord," was more mature and more enlightened than the first time. Though he had displayed incredible weakness, cowardice, and unreliability, Jesus gave him a second chance because he knew that Peter was capable of something better and something greater.

The Lord knew that there was another side, a better side, to Peter. He knew that a brand-new Peter motivated by sacrificial love could emerge from the ashes of failure. So, with the three-fold "Do you love me?" Jesus erased Peter's three-fold denial.

The entire dialogue at the second calling of Peter places the responsibility of tending the sheep within the context of love. Loving the Lord is therefore the prerequisite for all missionary work and, indeed, all our Christian enterprise. All who truly love the Lord will also love and care for his "sheep."

That the Lord entrusted the love and care for his sheep to the man who denied him publicly three times is important for us who, when we witness some public scandal in the Church, or when some leaders misbehave seriously, we presumptuously declare that the end has come for Christianity or for the Church! We are often too quick to forget that Christianity was not built on any person's blood, but the blood of Jesus Christ.

Lessons from Peter's Reconciliation Experience

Peter's experience buttresses the fact that we are often not as brave and as strong as we presume ourselves to be. So, we need to be cautious and ever more humble as we live out our Christian commitments, recognising daily that our need for grace. We must also appreciate the fact that the Lord loves us even in our weaknesses and sinfulness (see 2 Tim 2:13), so we must learn to forgive ourselves and others of momentary weaknesses and failures.

It is very important to always bear it in mind that a person's fall is not the end of his or her life. But, like Jesus who fell three times on his way to Calvary, we must learn to pick ourselves up when we fall and forge ahead in life, knowing that the Lord is more interested in our future prospects than our past failures. The truth that love covers a multitude of sins and keeps the devil at bay (see 1 Peter 4:8), and that no one loves the Lord in a vacuum, is very instructive here.

Feed My Sheep

Loving the Lord always translates into the mission to reach out to his sheep, to witness to his name, and to make sacrifices for his sake. Thus, like Peter, we too can feed Jesus' sheep through acts of love as well as sharing our faith with our brothers and sisters. We can feed Jesus' sheep by training and mentoring the young people in our societies, using our own exemplary lives of virtue and devotion. We can feed Jesus' sheep by taking seriously Jesus' preferential option for the poor – caring for, and promoting the welfare of the poor, the sick, the aged, the handicapped, as well as the widows and orphans.

A critical dimension of the task of feeding Jesus' sheep could be demonstrated in the Christian's engagement with politics and governance, where the Christian citizen is called upon to shine the light of Christ by promoting kingdom values in public life. In the same way Christians are called upon to shine the light of Christ at work and in business, to rid society of corruption, greed, and avarice. We are called upon to shine the light of Christ in our family lives, giving witness to Christian sacrificial love, and displaying a high level of courage and fortitude when trials and tribulations come our way.

Conclusion

The question Jesus addressed to Peter is addressed to each of us too. We may be quick to say "Yes Lord, you know I love you," but do we know the implications of this love? We need to stop and reflect on how deep and how faithful our love for Christ is. The depth and profundity of our love only begin to show as we journey with Jesus through the challenging experiences of life.

Questions to Ponder

1. The disciples in the 1st Reading were glad to have had the honour of suffering in Jesus' name. How does this challenge our faith in Christ today?
2. Can we say that the question: "Simon…Do you love me more than these others do?" is addressed not only to Peter but to all Christians? If so, explain.
3. Why do you think Jesus went ahead to make Peter head of his Church – the man who denied him three times?
4. Give examples of circumstances in which Christians are called to obey God rather than man in our country today?

Additional Reading

John 15:12-13; Romans 8:31-39; 1 Peter 4:8; 1 John 4:10-16.

4th Sunday of Easter

The Good Shepherd

Readings: Acts 13:14, 43-52 | Psalm 100 | Revelation 7:9, 14-17 | John 10:27-30

Summary:

What distinguishes the good shepherd from a hireling is care. While the good shepherd cares, the hirelings do not. Hirelings are not motivated by love, and so when danger comes, they simply abandon the sheep and flee. But the care of the good shepherd is costly and risky. It often ends up consuming the life of the caregiver. This however does not stop the good shepherd because caring is what gives meaning and satisfaction to his life. He is motivated by the love that drives out all fear.

Distressed Sheep Without Shepherd

Fallen humanity is plagued by multiple crises, including natural and man-made disasters such as violent crimes and bloody conflicts, economic injustice and oppression, bad governance and youth restiveness, social insecurity and uncertainty, strange diseases and illnesses, as well as poverty and unemployment. We also experience marital crisis and family upheaval, loneliness and abandonment, demonic attack and occultic manipulation, and sinfulness and blindness, etc. These are among the many ills that distress humanity, often leaving men and women like sheep without a shepherd. Many are hungry for physical food, but many more are suffering the hunger of the heart for true love and affection.

Humanity is broken by sin and wrecked by wickedness. Many societies are poisoned by hatred and polluted by falsehood. Politics in many societies is afflicted by the lust for power and greed for money. The economy of many societies is devastated by corruption. So many people live sad, lonely, empty, and futile lives. Many have lost the sense of meaning and purpose in life. Many are therefore truly yearning for meaning, and in their desperation, they tend embrace whatever is the trending fad or fashion.

Thieves, Rogues, and Brigands

In their hunger for truth and in their thirst for meaning, many men and women have often fallen into the hands of fraudsters who pretend to have the answers to their problems and claim to be able to save humanity, but are only out to steal, kill, and destroy (John 10:10). Many men and women are in our being fed on poison. Others are wasting time and effort on what is not true and cannot bring satisfaction (Isaiah 55:1-3). There are now many quasi-religious groups, esoteric confraternities, magical cults, mystical forces, and pseudo-Christian movements all over the place, who are offering all kinds of prescriptions for freedom, peace and happiness, and claiming to be able to guide people unto green pasture and unto salvation.

People often flock to these "hirelings" out of desperation to solve the puzzles of life and ward off the threatening danger. But a Christian should not be desperate about anything, because it is such desperation that leads men and women to fall into the hands of the devil and his agents. The human being's restlessness and insecurity will persist, and his or her sense of futility will remain unabated, until he or she finally meets God. It is this realisation that prompted St. Augustine to say that "the Lord has created us for himself, and our hearts are restless until they rest in him." Such restlessness, when not properly channeled, leads many to those whom Jesus refers to as blind guides, thieves, rogues, brigands, and wolves in sheep's clothing.

Even within the Christian fold today, there are unfortunately many false prophets, fake preachers, mercenary priests, fraudulent evangelists, self-serving pastors, blind guides, quacks, and charlatans. We see them every day and everywhere, advertising themselves on regular and social media. They are recruiting millions of followers, from among people who are not standing on solid ground. These fake preachers and pastors are often stealing from the sheep, cheating them, leading them astray, destroying them, feeding fat on them, and allowing the Lord's sheep to die of hunger and starvation.

Jesus the Good Shepherd

It is within this context that Jesus introduces himself as the good shepherd who lays down his life for his sheep. The good shepherd loves and cares for his sheep by feeding the hungry, bandaging the wounded, making the weak strong, looking for the lost and leading them to green pasture. This is in contrast with the fraudulent shepherds, hirelings, thieves, rogues, and brigands who have no love, and do not care for the sheep, but who are only interested in what they stand to gain. We have often seen a lot of people who pretend to be leaders in Christian churches and all they care about is what they stand to gain.

The good shepherd on the other hand loves the sheep. His love for the sheep is so strong that the shepherd is prepared to die in defense of the sheep. Because of such extravagant love, the shepherd's own life matters less than that of his sheep. The good shepherd loves his work. To him shepherding is not a job, but a vocation which gives his life meaning. His work is difficult and risky (because he is exposed to wild animals whose target is to devour the sheep) but it brings satisfaction and meaning to the shepherd. Love is the source of the shepherd's strength. Love is the source of his courage. His love for his sheep conquers all difficulties, and with this love, no sacrifice is too great.

The work of shepherding is not always palatable or smooth sailing. In fact it promises to be very difficult, because nobody loves without experiencing pain. Yet the good shepherd is a combination of tenderness and toughness, care and self-sacrifice. Jesus is the true Shepherd who dies to save his sheep. He demonstrated through his suffering and death his exceptional love and care, his diligence and commitment, and his fearlessness and unusual courage as he defends the sheep against wild animals.

Brennan Manning, the American author who had a spectacular conversion experience, notes in his book titled, *The Relentless Tenderness of Christ,* that Christ is both tender and courageous. We therefore celebrate today the Good Shepherd as the answer to the profound longing of the human heart for true love and affection, for peace and security, for meaning and purpose, and for eternal salvation.

When in Matthew 9:36 Jesus saw the crowd, he felt compassion for them, because they were distressed and dejected like sheep without a shepherd. In several passages he says: "I am the way, and the truth, and the life" (John 14:6); "I am the bread of life. No one who comes to me will ever hunger" (John 6:35); "Let anyone who thirsts come to me" (John 7:37); "Come to me all who labour and are overburdened, and I will give you rest (Matthew 11:28).

Called to be Shepherds
Like Jesus the good shepherd, we are called to be caring shepherds to one another, especially the poor, the weak, the widow, the orphan, the sick, and the handicapped. We are called today to show true selfless love to all those around us and to serve them with all commitment, to care for them with all diligence - as parents, teachers, and elders; and as politicians and public office holders, corporate heads, doctors and nurses, Church leaders, and Church members.

For Christians, leadership (at all levels and in all spheres) is about shepherding. The leader is one who takes care of his sheep and leads them to green pasture. The distinguishing mark of a truly civilised society is the quality of care that is practiced in that society, and, as Jessy and Bryan Matteo *say*, "Even the smallest act of caring for another person is like a drop of water; it will make ripples through the entire pond." Those who occupy positions of leadership without this quality of care are thieves, rogues, and brigands.

Conclusion
Selfless service defines every Christian vocation. True leadership is about loving, caring, and sacrificing. It is about taking risks and, when necessary, dying for the sheep. If we run away from these, we run from things which give satisfaction and meaning to life. The true measure of societal advancement is how the society takes care of those whom Jesus Christ identifies as the least of his brethren - the poor, the widow, the orphan, the aged, the stranger and the handicapped. Those who work for the emergence of such caring societies are the true shepherds of our day, after the fashion of Jesus Christ the Good Shepherd.

Questions to Ponder
1. In today's 2nd Reading, (Revelation 7:14-17), John saw a multitude of people before the throne of God *"who have washed their robes and made them white in the blood of the Lamb."* What does this mean?
2. List three basic requirements of belonging to Jesus brought out in today's Gospel (John 10:27-30).
3. How does "the Good Shepherd" image of Jesus challenge the conduct of leadership at all levels and in all spheres of life today?
4. How are you striving to imitate Jesus the Good Shepherd before others at home, at work, in the Church and in the wider society?

Additional Reading
Psalm 23; Ezekiel 43:1-16; Luke 15:4-7, 19:10; John 8:12

5th Sunday of Easter

Love One Another

Readings: Acts 14:21-27 | Psalm 145 | Revelation 21:1-5 | John 13:31–35

Summary:

We are all capable of love to a heroic degree because God has planted love and goodness in each one of us. It is in our nature to love, but we often work against our very nature, refusing to be the best version of ourselves. Christianity calls us to a life of love and compassion, as well as mercy and forgiveness. This, in the language of modern psychology is our *true self*.

The Christian Community in Antioch

The early Christian community in Antioch has all the elements of an ideal Christian community. They had an ardent faith and hope in the risen Lord and love among themselves. There was mutual support as they shared their material resources and were sensitive to the needs of the poor, the orphan, and the widow among them. They had zeal for evangelization, which is why they commissioned Paul and Barnabas and sent them out on mission to the gentiles. Their zeal was such that every one of them was actively involved in the missionary project. Every one of them was a missionary. Thus, an ideal Christian community is one where everyone, every man, woman and child, is engaged as an agent of the gospel according to the gifts God has given them.

The Christian community in Antioch gave flesh to Jesus' statement that by the love we have for one another everyone will know that we are his disciples, and the result was that they were the first to be called Christians. They were called Christians because the non-Christians around them who had heard about Jesus and his deeds saw the same in these Antioch Christians. So, they described them as living like Christ. This is what the word *Christian* means.

Barnabas: Bearing Witness to Christ

One of the striking personalities who emerged from the Antioch community was Barnabas. He was described as "a good man, full of the Holy Spirit and of faith" (Acts 11:22-24). His generosity was remarkable. It is recorded that he sold his entire estate and laid the proceeds before the apostles (Acts 4:36-37). The number one mark of his Christian conversion is his generosity.

Generosity is one of the characteristic marks of a Christian. This is so because as soon as somebody meets Jesus Christ, material possessions begin to count for very little with such a person. That is why St. Paul could be content, whether well fed or hungry, whether in plenty or in need (Philippians 4:12). All that matters after an encounter with Christ is salvation and eternal life. These are the greatest treasures to be sought in Christ Jesus. It is impossible to be very spiritually conscious and still be very greedy, very materialistic, or very rapacious, because we often grow in spirit to the same proportion as we are able to moderate the flesh.

At his conversion, Barnabas trusted that God would take care of him. This belief was expressed practically in his selling his estates and bringing the proceeds to the apostles for the work of God. This concrete witnessing encouraged the apostles so much that they gave him the name, *Barnabas*, which means *son of encouragement*. He sure had an extraordinary gift of encouragement and used it for the work of God.

Encouragement Amid Challenges

While encouraging others he sure had his own unique challenges. That he was an encourager does not mean he was free from suffering. What it means is that, even in the face of his own challenges and suffering, he did not choose to focus on himself; rather he chose to reach out to people with the resources at his disposal.

Barnabas the encourager, along with Paul, went about putting fresh hearts into the early disciples, and his encouragement resulted in many people persevering in their faith. These were times of serious persecution for Christians, and it was Barnabas who helped Paul during the most critical moments of his ministry. Paul, initially an outlaw, was not easily welcomed by the early Christian community because of his antecedents. It was Barnabas that took him around and assured the people that the criminal they knew had become converted; that he was no longer a persecutor but a fervent disciple.

Barnabas invested time and energy in helping Paul to become the best he could be. He became a companion of Paul and was his source of strength and support. He was truly a son of encouragement and he helped Paul to live up to his new name and calling as an apostle of Christ.

Loving As Jesus Loves

The command to love God and one another is one the Israelites were familiar with. Leviticus 19:18 and Deuteronomy 6:5 are clear on the injunction to love one's neighbour and God. Yet Jesus called it a *new commandment*. What is new perhaps is that Jesus raised the standard with the clause, "as I have loved you."

The kind of love Jesus is demanding is new because it is a radical kind of love. It is love unto death. It is love that forgives the enemy, no matter the gravity of the offence, and frees people (the offender as well as the offended) from the prison of unforgiveness. It is the kind of love that is all merciful and compassionate.

Also, Jesus' charge is new because it calls for a daily response to God's invitation. It is an ongoing effort to get out of ourselves to make others the centre of our lives. By the dictates of this love, it is no longer enough that we share with the poor from the excess we have; we must also share with them from the little we have, because they have now become the centre of our lives.

The Perfect Model

Jesus came to make known the God who is love (1 John 4:8,16). He did this especially with the gift of himself unto death and taught that there is no greater love than for a man to lay down his life for his friends (John 15:13). St Paul explained the depth of this love when he wrote that what shows God's love for us is that while we were yet sinners Christ died for us (Romans 5:8).

Just like Jesus' example, how we love ought to become the channel by which others experience the love of God. We are the ones through whom the love of God is felt. It is our hearts and deeds that can reveal the love of God. The task of making God known did not end with the death of Jesus. Witnessing to Jesus' loving lifestyle must be the daily task of all who believe in him.

In fact, loving one another should be every Christian's very source of identity and power. Just as with Jesus, our love for one another reveals the face of the God who is love; it shows the greatness of God's love and confirms us to the world as the disciples of Jesus. Also, Jesus will be recognized and will continue to be present always among us his disciples if we love in the manner he did.

The Pain and Reward of Love
It is through sacrificial love, selfless service, and reaching out to others in spite of inconveniences to ourselves that Jesus will be recognized in our midst. Through such love we encourage one another during times of trial and tribulation and announce the coming of that beautiful day when the Lord will wipe away every tear (Isaiah 25:8). Reaching out to help others in loving service and generous understanding of others' pains, often lessens our own burdens. Every sincere gesture of affection or act of love for others, liberates us from the prison of selfishness, greed, and self-centeredness. And yet love is risky!

The first person to take the risk to love was God. God so loved human beings that he created us in his own image and decided to give us freedom. He did not stop there. He decided to take another risk and sent His Son to us His creatures. They treated him shabbily and eventually killed him. But God did not stop loving them. Such sacrificial love is what truly connects us to God and to one another.

The Sure Path to a Life of Bliss
The easiest way to find happiness is to reach out to help others, to love others, to do things selflessly for others. Nothing material, nothing tangible, brings us happiness; otherwise, many rich and famous celebrities would have no reason to be depressed or to be on drugs. Rather, what brings true happiness to us are often the things we do for others, especially when they are done selflessly.

The greatest gift anyone has or can receive is the gift of being loved. If receiving love from others can feel so great, then loving others will feel even greater, because we were made to love. We should be telling God daily in prayer: Lord, do not let me die until I have loved sufficiently. Please, do not let me die until I come out of myself and make the loving service of others the focus of my life.

Conclusion
Love elevates and brings out the best and brightest in us. Love is fire; it inflames our hearts and energizes our spirits. It warms our souls, generates passion in our lives, renders many tasks easy, and heals everyone (the giver as well as the receiver). Love is what gives meaning to all our life's preoccupations, and it is the secret of happiness. Jesus came into the world to reveal to us the face of the God who is love.

Questions to Ponder
1. Paul and Barnabas told the early Christians that it is through many tribulations that we must enter the Kingdom of God (Acts 14:22). What does this mean?
2. What vision was John describing in the 2nd Reading (Revelation 21:1-5)? And how is this vision Good News for us today?
3. What is it that makes Jesus' instruction: "Love one another as I have loved you" a new commandment?
4. With what spiritual resources (as seen in today's readings) can Christians go through this life bearing their sufferings and tribulations cheerfully?

Additional Reading
Deuteronomy 6:4-5; Micah 6:8; Matthew 5:44-45; John 13:12-15, 35; Acts 2:42-47, 4:32-35

6th Sunday of Easter

Promise of the Holy Spirit

Readings: Acts 15:1-2, 22-29 | Psalm 67 | Revelation 21:10-14, 22-23 | John 14:23-29

Summary:

Knowing that there will be many challenges ahead, including persecution, and conflicts within the Church, and that his disciples will have to struggle hard to keep faithful to him in the midst of the impending turmoil, Jesus assures his disciples that he will not abandon them, and that if they keep to his word they will be drawn into the love of his Father through the gift and the power of the Holy Spirit.

Jesus Promises the Holy Spirit

As the reality of Jesus' final departure dawned, the disciples became anxious and afraid, and this is understandable. They must have been afraid because they were not sure of what will become of them after his departure. On the other hand, Jesus knew that after his departure, everything will not be rosy, beautiful, and glorious for those he would leave behind. A case in point is the controversy in the 1st Reading that came up not long after Jesus left them. So, Jesus promised to send them help from above. This promised help is the third Person of the Trinity, the Holy Spirit.

It was through the inspiration of the Holy Spirit that the serious controversy in the 1st Reading was resolved. The Holy Spirit was at work, and it instructed the Church in Antioch to send Paul and Barnabas to the elders in Jerusalem for a decision. This is how the first council of the Church was convoked, the Council of Jerusalem. There were many other councils that came after this, including the councils of Nicaea and Ephesus that defined for us the Christian Creed.

Jesus promised his disciples that the Holy Spirit will be their advocate, defending them in times of trouble, so they did not need to be afraid of anything. From the time before he died to the time after he resurrected and appeared to his disciples, he kept telling them not to be afraid. Jesus promised them that the Holy Spirit will be their counselor, giving them wise counsel; it will be their guide, going before them and showing them the way; it will be their mentor, inspiring them to do right; it will be their teacher, reminding them of everything Jesus has taught them, as well as their advisor who will clarify issues for them.

Jesus promised to give them the peace the world cannot give, the peace that results from keeping his word and possessing his Spirit. These are powerful promises made not only to the early disciples, but to Christians of all ages.

The Holy Spirit's Abiding Presence

Jesus says that his physical presence would be replaced by the abiding presence of the Holy Spirit who will be sent by the Father in his name to be with us, so we may not be afraid. So, one evidence that we have the Holy Spirit is that even in critical situations, we will not be afraid or allow our hearts to be troubled. Another is that we will be able to remember all that Jesus taught and did. With the presence of the Holy Spirit, we are strengthened to keep the word and live in the love of Christ. The Holy Spirit renews the face of the earth and transforms the whole of humanity. The Holy Spirit is every believer's source of consolation when invoked.

The Holy Spirit is sent to build up the one, holy, Catholic, and apostolic church, as well as to sanctify believers in Christ, so that we may be purified and transformed into the likeness of God. In other words, the principal function of the Holy Spirit is to make Christians holy!

Authentic Religion

Religion is meant to promote godliness in believers. All religious activities, including fasting, private prayer and public worship, etc., are meant to lead people to God, and to help them achieve holiness of life. It turns out unfortunately that our show of piety is often not much more than a show! Many Christians find it difficult to live out the values and ideals of Christ. Mahatma Gandhi identified among his

Seven Deadly Social Sins, "Religion without Sacrifice," an anomaly that appears very rife in our own age. Sacrifice is at the core of all religious enterprise. Without sacrifice there is no religion. Our daily devotional activities are an expression of an inner desire to get closer to God, our desire to be godly, otherwise they do not qualify to be called religious activities.

The Holy Spirit has been sent to enable Christians live authentic Christian lives modelled after Jesus Christ who is the Way, the Truth, and the Life. The Holy Spirit is meant to sanctify us in Christ so that we may be purified and transformed into his likeness. Every outward expression of religiosity is supposed to spring forth from our transformed inner lives. The Psalmist prayed, "Let the words of my mouth and the meditation of my heart be acceptable in your sight, O Lord, my rock and my redeemer" (Psalm 19:14). It is part of the essence of religion that all the thoughts in our hearts, the words of our mouths, and indeed all our actions, should be so pure as to be acceptable to God.

Christian Unity Empowered by the Spirit

Jesus admonishes us to walk in the Spirit, that is, to do all things in the Holy Spirit. When we so walk in the Spirit, we live in union with Christ and with one another. Our disunity as Christians is therefore evidence that perhaps we are not walking in the Spirit. In unity, the disciples of Jesus and the early Church submitted to the authority of the elders under the guidance of the Holy Spirit. Guided by the Holy Spirit, they were able to resolve the controversy around the demand for the circumcision of gentile converts generated by the Judaizers. Unity in the Spirit produces harmony in the community, and from harmony comes the strength and the perseverance with which we can go through even the worst difficulties and come out victorious. The Holy Spirit is the Giver of Life. Without the Spirit we are spiritually dead. The Holy Spirit sanctifies us in Christ, and subjects us to him in humility and obedience.

The Shalom of Christ Jesus

On several occasions after the resurrection, Jesus greeted his disciples with the gracious word of peace, shalom! This word of peace turned their despair into hope, and their sadness into joy. Shalom refers to well-being, fullness of life, harmony, and peace. The peace Jesus Christ bequeathed to them is a state of universal completeness, a state of perfect well-being, a state in which nothing is lacking, a state of communion with God.

The peace of Christ is a comprehensive kind of peace that only God can give. This kind of peace cannot be attained by human effort. The peace of Christ does not consist in the absence of war. Rather it is possible even amid the drums of war. It does not consist in escape from reality. Rather it can be experienced amid the challenges of each day. The peace of Christ does not consist in material prosperity. It can even be experienced in the lowliest circumstances.

The peace of Jesus is described by St. Paul as the peace that surpasses all understanding (Philippians 4:7); and Jesus calls it the peace which the world cannot give (John 14:27). Since the world cannot give it, the world cannot take it away from any believer. The peace of Christ can exist even amid a troubled life and world, and the good news is that anyone, just anyone, who is living in Christ, whatever their circumstances may be, can claim this peace. As Christians, we do not need to have all our problems resolved before we can experience the peace of Christ. It is available to us in all circumstances.

Prerequisites for Peace
The peace of Christ is essentially internal. It is a state of inner equilibrium, resulting from a good, loving relationship with God and neighbour. Such peace cannot come from human beings or from any material entity. It is the gift of God. Christ's peace is essentially communion with God. Jesus had peace in himself, and he could offer us this peace, because he was in full communion with the Father.

Christians who strive to be in full communion with God will be full of peace and can promote peace among those in their environment. Christ was able to offer peace even as his enemies were closing in on him. He spoke words of peace to the women who were consoling him and offered words of peace even from the cross. True peace, the type that Jesus promises, therefore, results when one trusts in God and when the desire to please him is the most dominant desire in one's life.

A Gift and a Task
The peace of Christ is both a gift and a task, because once received we must also work with God's grace to dispense it in our various spheres of influence. As beneficiaries of Christ's peace, we have the vocation to be peacemakers who bring peace to the world around us, beginning from our homes, our offices, our societies, and our churches. We are called to be defenders and promoters of peace wherever we find ourselves.

Conclusion
If we do all things in the Spirit as the early disciples and Christian community did, we will enjoy the peace of Christ. If we do not, our hearts will be troubled, and we will live in fear. So, the peace of Christ comes when we submit ourselves to the will of God, and we are empowered by God and are in obedience to the Holy Spirit.

Questions to Ponder
1. What major differences can be seen in how the early Church resolved arguments and what is obtainable today?
2. In our world today, what is Jerusalem the holy city written in the book of Revelation in the 2nd Reading?
3. Who is the Holy Spirit to you?
4. Christians have been praying for peace in the world. What is your assessment of the success or not of these prayers?

Additional Reading
Deuteronomy 7:12-13; Sirach 4:10, 14; 2 Thessalonians 3:16, 14:1-3; Revelation 17:7, 13-15.

7th Sunday of Easter

That We May Dwell in Love and Unity

Readings: Acts 7:55-60 | Psalm 97 | Revelation 22:12-14, 16-17, 20-21 | John 17:20-26

Summary:

The priestly prayer of Jesus recorded in John chapter 17 indicates that it is the way we practice love, unity, care, concern, and compassion that will make the world to know that indeed Jesus is alive, and that we are his disciples. The early Christians in Antioch were first called Christians on account of how they were living the life of Christ. Christians of all generations are challenged to give loud witness to the love of Christ wherever they are, so they may be truly recognized as his followers.

The Spectacular Witness of Stephen

Stephen was a young, committed, courageous, and generous disciple of Christ. That is part of the reason he was chosen to be among the seven deacons. He bore witness to Christ in word and in action. He served Christ with his life, and he crowned this service with his death. He paid the ultimate price for his belief in Jesus Christ. In the face of a violent death, Stephen did not deny Christ. Perhaps he could have saved his life if he had kept quiet, just as many Christians keep quiet today to save their skin when they should rather speak up. But Stephen did not. He boldly held on to his conviction. He remembered Jesus' teaching that we should not be afraid of those who can kill the body but cannot kill the soul.

The manner of Stephen's death bears so much resemblance to the manner of Jesus' death. Like Jesus, Stephen was an innocent man accused of blasphemy and tried by the Sanhedrin. He died a violent death, outside the city. He prayed that God may forgive his killers and surrendered his soul into the hands of the Lord before he died.

Thus, the death of Stephen reflects the death of Jesus Christ, and to have died in almost exactly the same manner as Jesus did is real grace.

Stephen lived passionately for Christ and died gallantly with hope of ultimate victory in Christ. Every Christian that lives passionately for Christ, will expire gallantly, because one hardly becomes a hero in death if the person has not been a hero while alive.

The Beatific Vision

With his fearless preaching, Stephen proved his unwavering commitment to Christ. It was his fearless preaching that made the Jewish authorities decide to condemn him. Perhaps in reward for his exemplary discipleship, Stephen was granted a rare privilege, one that many saints long for, but did not receive: the privilege of beholding the glory of Christ while still in this world. He saw Jesus Christ standing at the right hand of God the Father!

This is a rare privilege, and no other thing must have mattered at that point, because the most profound desire of the human heart is to see the glorified Christ as Stephen did. This profound desire is linked to our purpose in the world, and until we discover that purpose, we shall keep desiring the profane.

Stephen died like a Christian by commending his spirit to God (Acts 7:59). He died bearing his pain with grace, forgiving his persecutors and murderers, and surrendering himself to God. He is a spectacular example of how every Christian should aspire to die. In other words, every believer in Christ should aspire to die focusing intently on the Lord, whatever the circumstance of their death may be; bearing their suffering with grace and submitting them to Jesus Christ who is available to help the believer carry them the cross. Christians should desire and pray to die while forgiving their enemies and committing their spirit into the hands of the loving and merciful God.

The Fruit of the Death of Stephen

Stephen was able to speak boldly even in the face of death because he believed that this world is not all there is, that in there is nothing in this world to compare to the new life that awaits him. Stephen knew that it was better to speak for the Lord in whose hands was his eternal destiny, than to bow to earthly powers who could not do more than they did to him. He knew as we all should know, that in Christ death is swallowed up in victory. St Paul says that death has lost its sting because of our faith in the resurrection.

The death of Stephen, which could be termed tragic, and which marked the beginning of an intense persecution of the early Christians, could also be understood as the beginning of the spread of the Church by which numerous Gentiles become Christians. God turned around what was a tragedy and brought out of it immense good. Paul teaches that God is able to turn all things unto good for those who love him (Romans 8:28). Thus, what every Christian should be desiring is to have their lives securely in the hands of God who is able to turn all their tribulations (as well as death, the worst of all machinations of the enemy) unto good. Christians should be able to declare with St. Paul that "if we live, we live to the Lord, and if we die, we die to the Lord" (Romans 14:8).

Today, many Christians live as though they no longer believe in the resurrection. They carry on their daily affairs with little or no consciousness of the afterlife. This is often reflected in the choices such Christians make when faced with challenging issues of life. The quality of our Christian life is to be measured not by what we profess with our lips, but by the fruits we bear (Matthew 7:15-18, 20). The reality of our world today is such that only a few Christians are called to physical martyrdom. But all of us are called to give courageous witness to the kingdom values taught by Jesus Christ, in an environment that is becoming increasingly averse to such spiritual values.

Jesus is Alive and He is Lord
The vision of St. Stephen in Acts 7 and the vision of John the Apostle in Revelation 22 highlight a central truth of our faith: The innocent Lord who was crucified, rose again from the dead and is exalted above all powers. He is seated at the right hand of God. He will come again in judgement. Jesus has already triumphed. He is king, but his kingship is still hidden from many. His kingship will be fully revealed when on the last day he comes in glory. The

world will only get to know of Jesus' glory and oneness with the Father as Christians practice the divine love that he taught and gave us as a commandment.

The wonderful spectacle of Christ in his glory that Stephen and John had a glimpse of in the 1st and 2nd readings of today, is part of the secret which no eye has seen, nor ear heard, nor the heart of man conceived; it is the pleasant surprise that God has prepared for those who love him (1 Corinthians 2:9). To see this glory should be the desire of our hearts. St. Augustine captured this ultimate desire when he said that God has created us for himself, and our hearts are restless until they rest in him.

Many human beings have continued to waste their lives on the pleasures of this world, which amount to vanity, while failing to recognise that the greatest treasure they ought to desire is the beatific vision, the vision of God in his glory. Many live blind, senseless and destructive lives, redoubling their efforts and forgetting their goal, thus ending up in futility.

Love and Unity Among Christians
Regarding the period between his first and second coming, Jesus prayed earnestly (in John 17) that his followers might live such lives of love, unity, and service as to convince the world that the Father sent him; that he is alive and present; that he is the resurrection and the life; that he loves the Father, that the Father loves him; and that he and the father are one. The world will not be convinced unless Christians begin to live lives of love, unity, and service. Jesus' prayer expresses his passionate concern for future generations of his followers, including ourselves. Thus, he prayed that we all may be one so that the Father's love for him may also be in us, and that the world may come to know this love through us (John 17:21, 26).

Besides, because Jesus knew that unity was vital to the success of the community he was leaving behind, he required that their unity had to be one based on love, so he gave them the commandment of love. Jesus wants our love and unity as Christians to make a major impact in the world. This is what it means to leave one's footprints in the sands of time. Jesus Christ wants us to make an impact here by our love.

Hindrances to the High Priestly Prayer

Jesus prayed for unity, not just for mutual tolerance. The unity the Lord prayed for involves solidarity, sharing, belonging, compassion, and shared joys and sorrows. But such unity is rendered impossible by selfishness, greed, pride, ethnic bigotry, and the lust for power. These are a major obstacle to true unity. The division among Christians is a major scandal and counter-witness. Christian unity is rendered more difficult today because of the proliferation of churches. It is bad enough that there are so many different churches, and we are not able to worship together. It is even worse that there is so much hatred, enmity, and acrimony among Christians. Thus, as we reflect on Jesus' prayer for Christian love and unity, we must each take this matter seriously and begin to take some initiatives within our various communities towards overcoming the division. Nothing is impossible with God. Unity can be achieved when different members of the Church begin to contribute their different gifts to attain a common goal and in mutual love and respect for one another.

The Communal Nature of Christianity

Everyone must contribute their talents, time, and resources towards the well-being, growth, and development of the Christian Church. There is therefore no room in the Church of Christ for backbenchers, passive onlookers, armchair critics or anonymous members. Our coming together, our fellowshipping is what makes us Church!

The men and women of our age often seek to divorce spirituality from community. People often want God, but they do not want the Christian community. But true believers in the God of Jesus Christ cannot want God while rejecting the community of God. Salvation in Christ is to be pursued in the context of a believing community. There is no such thing as a solitary Christian.

Christianity is a communitarian religion. It is about 'we and our God,' not about 'me' and 'my God.' We workshop our God within the context of the believing community. This is why the law to love one another is so central in our faith. It could even be argued that if the community is not important, then perhaps there would be no need to emphasise that we love one another. Christian spirituality is thus a communitarian enterprise, since the search for God is hardly a private search.

Conclusion
Jesus teaches that God saves us not just as individuals but as a community. How we relate with each other is part of how we relate with God. The conduct of our neighbours can be good, bad or ugly, but Jesus commands us to love them all the same. This is not easy. But that is why it is a commandment. Real Christian sacrificial love is hard work!

Questions to Ponder
1. What role did Stephen play in the life of Saul of Tarsus? Is anyone watching your way of life?
2. What are the causes of disunity in our faith/Christianity and what are the remedies?
3. How do you deal with constant provocation in order to achieve unity?

Additional Reading
Exodus 24:16ff; Daniel 12:10; Isaiah 40:10, 41:4, 44:6; Galatians 1:13ff; Hebrews 13:12ff

Pentecost Sunday

Filled with the Holy Spirit

Readings: Acts 2:1-11 | Psalm 104 | Romans 8:8-17 | John 20:19-23

Summary:

Jesus gave a clear distinction between life in the flesh and life in the spirit, and St. Paul elaborates on this point in the first part of today's 2nd Reading. For him, anyone who lives in the flesh is in enmity with God. To live in friendship with God one must live in the spirit, because what is born of the flesh is flesh and what is born of the spirit is spirit.

Who the Holy Spirit Is?

The Holy Spirit is the paraclete. He is our advocate, the one who pleads our cause. He is our defender in times of trial. He is our comforter. He is our vindicator, the one who bears witness in us to Christ's message of salvation. The Holy Spirit is the spirit of truth.

Jesus says that all those who are on the side of the truth will believe in him and will come to him. It is the spirit that will lead us to that truth and will remind us of all that Jesus taught us. He will show that everything Jesus said is right and will show the world how wrong it has been. For example the institution of marriage and family life are threatened by various perversions that are widespread in our day, but the Holy Spirit will show the world how wrong it is, and how right Jesus is. It is He who will lead the disciples to the fullness of truth.

The Holy Spirit will confirm all that Jesus taught and bring about for every age a renewed and deeper understanding of the revelation of God in Christ. The disciples had only a superficial understanding of who Jesus was, until the outpouring of the Spirit on Pentecost day, in fulfilment of the promise Jesus made to them before he ascended to the Father. He said to them, "Not many days from now you will receive power when the Holy Spirit comes upon you, then you shall be my witnesses" (Acts 1:8). With the outpouring of the Holy Spirit, they were emboldened: they preached the gospel boldly and fearlessly, and they received thousands of new converts to Christianity.

Pentecost – The Outpouring of New Life

In John 3:5 Jesus says to Nicodemus, "In all truth I tell you, no one can enter the kingdom of God without being born of water and the Spirit; what is born of human nature is human; what is born of the spirit is spirit." The Holy Spirit was given to believers as the first fruits of Christ's redemptive work. He whets the appetite of Christians for the kingdom. He is the pledge of the rich blessings that await the faithful in the kingdom and the first taste of the Beatific Vision.

The Breath and Fire of God

The Holy Spirit is the breath of God blowing through the world, re-creating, renewing and sustaining it. He is the fire of God's love that enlightens humanity, conquering the darkness of hate, and overcoming sin and corruption. He is the water from the fountain of God, purifying, energising, and inspiring new godly conduct in believers.

Pentecost Marks a New Beginning

Pentecost celebrates a new beginning. It is the beginning of the Church. It is a new creation, and the overturning of the divisions amongst people of old, symbolised by the collapse of the Tower of Babel (Genesis 11:1-9). With the event of Pentecost, God has intervened powerfully in the world, re-moulding humanity, re-designing the world, and renewing believers. The Holy Spirit is our source of strength, enabling Christians to become signs of contradiction to the negative currents of their age.

A World in Need

The world needs spirit-filled Christians to infuse Christ's spirit of life into dying persons (`who are going around with no sense of purpose or meaning), dying families (where there is no love), and dying societies (plagued by multiple evil). The world needs spirit-filled Christians to witness powerfully to a life of discipline, holiness, and wholeness in a world of rampant sin, corruption, violence, racial/ethnic and religious bigotry. Our societies are grappling with too many issues, which are only symptoms of the real problem, the widespread abandonment of the way of God, which Moses told the Jews is the way of life!

Many people are stuck with the fruits of self-indulgence listed in Galatians 5:16-17. These are: sexual vice, impurity, sensuality, worship of false gods, antagonism, rivalry, jealousy, bad temper, quarrels, disagreements, factions, malice, drunkenness, and orgies. On the other hand, the fruits of the Spirit are love, joy, peace, patience, goodness, faithfulness, gentleness and self-control (Galatians 5:22-23). In addition to the fruits are the gifts of the Spirit which are wisdom, understanding, knowledge, fortitude, good counsel, piety, and the fear of God. A society that demonstrates these fruits and gifts in plenty, is usually a society at peace.

Conclusion

The world needs spirit-filled Christians to witness powerfully to a life of discipline, holiness, and wholeness in a world of rampant sin, corruption, and violence. It is the task of every baptised Christian, relying on the Holy Spirit, to champion this cause while looking forward in hope to the eternal glory of the beatific vision.

Questions to Ponder

1. Why is fire a fitting symbol of the Holy Spirit and what do we mean when we speak of the fire of the Holy Spirit?
2. How as a Christian can I be sure that I am under the influence of the Holy Spirit in the conduct of my life?
3. List the functions of the Holy Spirit in the Christian church and in the life of Christians.
4. Identify and distinguish between the fruits of the Holy Spirit and the gifts of the Holy Spirit.

Additional Reading Joel 2:28-29; John 14:15-26, 16:12-13; Acts 1:5-8; Romans 8:5-22; Galatians 5:19-23

Sundays in Ordinary Time

Trinity Sunday

The Revelation of the Holy Trinity

Readings: Proverbs 8:22-31 | Psalm 8 | Romans 5:1-5 | John 16:12-15

Summary:

Our first reading for this day is in praise of Lady Wisdom which played a critical role at creation. It is this Old Testament reflection on wisdom personified that constitutes the window to what will eventually become the revelation of the mystery of the Trinity. In the second reading St. Paul discusses the relationship of love (with God) which the death of Christ has made possible, and the hope of victory which this gives us in our time of suffering and tribulation. And in the Gospel, Jesus tells his disciples that the Holy Spirit will help Christian believers come to a full understanding of everything that he has revealed to us about the Father. The second and third readings are selected for today most likely because in them the three persons of the Blessed Trinity are mentioned.

The Revelation of The Trinity

We read at the beginning of the Letter to the Hebrews: "Long ago God spoke to our ancestors in many and various ways by the prophets, but in these last days he has spoken to us by a Son, whom he appointed heir of all things, through whom he has created the world" (Hebrews 1:1-2). This means that God's mysterious personality which has been a matter of utmost secrecy through all the ages has now been revealed with the coming of Jesus Christ. By virtue of our faith in Jesus therefore, we now share the privilege of knowing God, not only in his works, but also in his person, in his inner being, as a *community of persons.*

We have the privilege of sharing in the love which binds together the Father, Son and Spirit. Jesus drew the attention of his disciples to this unique privilege when in Luke 10:23-24 he said to them: "Happy the eyes that see what you see, for I tell you that many prophets and kings wanted to see what you see, and never saw it, to hear what you hear, and never heard it." The good news proclaimed by the Christian doctrine of the Trinity is that the God who was inaccessible to previous generations of humanity, the God whose name was "Unapproachable Light," has now revealed himself in his personality and relatedness and has now invited us to share in the Love that is the secret of this personality and relatedness.

The Trinity is not a mathematical super-equation for the elite among us or for those schooled in theology. It is not even a speculation into the mystery of God's nature, but a practical statement of how Christians have experienced the reality of God. It is about a truth, hidden from the learned and clever, but revealed to simple people by the power of faith. The revelation of the Trinity is an invitation for believers to share in the love life that is characteristic of Trinitarian relationship. The revelation of the Trinity is a declaration that God loves us so much that he shares with us what he cherishes the most - that is Jesus Christ his Son. Jesus, in turn, gives us the Spirit through whom we learn to pattern ourselves on God's likeness and begin to partake in eternal life.

The revelation of the Trinity is an invitation for us to climb higher into the realm of the divine, where only unselfish love reigns. God intends to be present among us, so that we may reach beyond ourselves. Our human words are incapable of expressing the ineffable quality of the love which binds together Father, Son and Spirit, and makes them one. But by virtue of our baptism, we are now able to enter such an intimate relationship with the Triune God, as children of the Father, brothers and sisters of Jesus Christ the Son, and temples of the Holy Spirit. Therefore, far from being a teaching on the abstract nature of God, the doctrine of the Trinity is about God's life with us and our life with God and with each other. The doctrine of the Trinity is thus a call to live according to love. Loving is the highest form of understanding. Our love for God should prompt us to deepen our knowledge of him.

What are the implications of knowing the Triune God who is infinite in glory, eternal in majesty, and boundless in mercy? What are the implications of knowing God whose other name is Love, and whose life is one of perpetual life-giving love? If the Godhead is a community of persons, loving one another in the unity of the Holy Spirit, what practical challenges does this revelation of the nature of God pose for the Christian family and Christian community living? If indeed we Christians have been baptised (plunged) into this Trinity of Love, in what practical ways do we bear witness to God's tremendous love?

Much more than any other doctrine, belief in the Trinity unites all Christians, as it expresses our common understanding of God, and distinguishes us from adherents of other religions, including Muslims, Jews and Jehovah's Witnesses, who struggle to worship the God of Abraham, Isaac, Jacob and Ishmael. By the doctrine of the Trinity, we Christians believe that besides God the Father, we also have Jesus Christ who is more than just a prophet or a holy man. He is as we read in the Nicene Creed: *"the only Son of God, eternally begotten of the Father, God from God, Light from Light, true God from true God. Begotten, not made, of one being with the Father. Through him all things were made…"* We believe also in the Holy Spirit, *"the Lord, the giver of life, who proceeds from the Father and the Son. With the Father and the Son he is worshipped and glorified. He it was who spoke through the prophets…"* We know all these to be true by virtue of our faith in the ultimate revelation brought to us through Jesus Christ.

Conclusion

From contemplating the Trinity as revealed, the unity in the Blessed Trinity stands out. Therefore, as people called to a relationship with the Trinity, we are to witness to this unity by modeling the life of the three divine Persons in God who, though separate, are one in essence and intensely active in love. God calls us to be united in a community of active love, even as the three Persons in God. As believers in the Trinity, we are challenged today to make our faith in God real by our love for and our openness to others.

Questions to Ponder

1. How would you explain the revelation of the Blessed Trinity to a non-believer?

2. What shared qualities of the three persons in one God challenge Christians the most today?
3. "Belief in the Trinity is a fundamental element of our Christian identity and worship." Discuss.

Additional Reading
Matthew 28:19; John 14:26; Acts 2:33-36; 2 Corinthians 13:13

Corpus Christi

The Body and Blood of Christ
Readings: Genesis 14:18-20 | Psalm 110 |
1 Corinthians 11:23-26 | Luke 9:11-17

Summary:

Eucharistia in Greek means thanksgiving. Our Eucharistic celebrations are a celebration of the passion, death, and resurrection of Jesus Christ. They are occasions when we make communal thanksgiving to God for the gift of his Son Jesus Christ, who offered his body and blood on the cross of Calvary to save us from damnation and make us God's adopted children. Properly understood therefore, our gathering each day and each Sunday for mass is a thanksgiving enterprise. And the person who leads us in this thanksgiving (eucharistic) sacrifice, is Jesus himself, the new High Priest, who is both the priest that is offering the sacrifice, and the victim that is sacrificed.

A Priest like Melchizedek of Old

Our first reading from the book of Genesis introduces us to an ancient priest-king, Melchizedek, the King of Salem, as he presents gifts of bread and wine to Abraham, after which he pronounced a blessing over him. Salem means peace and it is the ancient name for Jerusalem. In Christian tradition, Melchizedek represents Christ the eternal king and the bread and wine he offered represent the Eucharist.

The priesthood and the offering of sacrifice go together. There is no priesthood without sacrifice. The reason why any religion has priests is so they may offer sacrifices. Sacrifice is at the root of all religion. It is a core element of all religious practice. If there is no offering of sacrifice, there is truly no religion. Religion without sacrifice is an anomaly.

In the old order, the traditional priests offered sacrifices, often of animals' blood or whole burnt offerings. However, with the coming of Jesus, the sacrifices of old have been abolished. The sacrifice we now offer is the one sacrifice that Jesus offered, which is his own body and blood. So, the priest in the New Testament tradition takes his priesthood from Jesus Christ, the High Priest who offered his body and blood for the salvation of the world. The New Testament era priest does not offer something new. He is only commemorating or "memorialising" the one sacrifice that Jesus offered on the cross of Calvary, in accordance to his direct instruction that we do this "in memory of me."

A Miracle of Mercy

The people were drawn to Jesus by the power of his words and the warmth of his person. When they found out that he and his disciples were in Bethsaida they followed him there. The heart of Jesus collapsed at the sight of their suffering. He was moved with mercy and compassion, because the people were harassed and dejected like sheep without a shepherd.

So, he gathered them around himself (over five thousand of them), taught them about the kingdom, and healed their sick. By the time he was done, it was too late, and they were hungry. He knew that some of them may collapse on the way if he accepted his disciples' suggestion to send them away, and so in his mercy and compassion, he worked a miracle. He multiplied a little boy's offering and fed the multitude.

Our world today has continued to harbour a multitude of people who are harassed and dejected. It is our duty to be compassionate toward them and to be willing to offer the little we have like the boy who offered his five loaves and two fish, and trust God to work a miracle. Allowing our hearts to collapse at the sight of another's suffering and doing something about it (however little), is what it means to be compassionate.

Do This in Memory of Me

The elements of the miracle of the loaves prefigure the institution of the Holy Eucharist. In the second reading as well as in all three accounts of the Last Supper in the synoptic gospels – Matthew 26:26-28, Mark 14:22-24, and Luke 22:19-20 – Jesus gives himself away as food and drink to his followers. In effect, Jesus charges his followers to keep his memory alive by gathering regularly to break bread and eat it in his name. This gathering was a very significant dimension of the early Church's life (see Acts 2:42-45 and 1 Corinthians 11:17-33). Jesus' charge is to the effect that "whatever else you do, you must keep my memory alive by eating this bread and drinking this cup."

This is how the Catholic Church understands "Do this in memory of me," and therefore we celebrate the Eucharist daily. The disciples continued to gather in communities (every day and especially on Sundays) to keep the memory of the passion and death of Jesus Christ alive in the breaking of bread. Our gathering is a powerful declaration that we are privileged beneficiaries of the saving mission of Jesus Christ. We are overwhelmed by the tremendous love or God which made him send his Son to die for us while we were yet sinners (Romans 5:8). We are keeping this memory alive, holding it sacred, celebrating it anew, and in this way receiving new life from it.

As we celebrate this great event in the history of humankind, and as we memorialise the sacrificial death of Jesus that won new life for humanity, we ourselves are gaining new life. We dare not forget to keep this memory alive, for as often as we do it, we do it in memory of Jesus' suffering, death, and resurrection. We believe that Jesus becomes really and truly present (in his body, blood, soul and divinity) every time we break bread in his name and in his memory. It is the core belief of the Church that when we pronounce those sacred words, *transubstantiation* takes place, that is, the bread and wine become the body and blood of Christ.

We recognise that the Eucharist is a dangerous memory. It is dangerous in the sense that Jesus has charged us to remember what he has done for us through his passion, death, and resurrection, and to go and do the same. The charge is that we go and do the same for others. Jesus has shown us that there is no greater love than for one to lay down his life for his friends. As the body of Jesus becomes bread broken for our salvation and for the salvation of the world, we too are to accept to become bread broken for our brothers and sisters.

Different Levels of Meaning of "Body of Christ"
The Body of Christ (Corpus Christi) at one and the same time refers to:

> The Human Body of Jesus Christ who walked this earth – the one that Joseph of Arimathea buried, and the women went to anoint.
>
> The Resurrected and changed Body of Jesus Christ – the one that passed through closed doors and was lifted to heaven at Ascension.
>
> The Mystical Body of Christ – the Church or the body of believers.
>
> The Blessed Sacrament – the Body of Christ which we celebrate today.

The Eucharist is a communion. As we eat the Body of Christ, an intimate bond is established with God in Christ. We become one with him. All of us who share the one Body of Christ invariably become one body with one another, because we all share in this intimate bond of unity in Christ.

Conclusion
The Eucharist is called *communion* because as we eat the Body of Christ, we become one with him: an intimate bond is established with God in Christ. All of us who share in the Body of Christ therefore invariably become one body with one another. The same intimate bond is established between us. This has serious implications for our love and unity, for our sense of family and community, and for our readiness to care for one another.

Questions to Ponder
1. What is the difference between the Manna given in the desert and the Body of Christ we receive today?
2. Identify at least three levels of meaning for the Body of Christ.
3. What are the implications of sharing in the Body and Blood of Christ for:
   (a) our relationship with God.

(b) our relationship with fellow Christians.
4. It is commonly believed today that "we are what we eat." How does this apply with regard to the Eucharist?

Additional Reading
Exodus 16:1-30; Matthew 5:3-13, 26:26-29; Mark 14:22-25; Luke 22:14-20; Acts 2:42-45, 4:32-35; 1 Corinthians 11:23-33.

2nd Sunday of the Year

Changing Water into Wine

Readings: Isaiah 62:1-5 | Psalm 96 | 1 Corinthians 12:4-11 | John 2:1-11

Summary:

What Jesus did at Cana in Galilee is called a "sign." He gave this first sign to show that the time has come, the long-awaited Bridegroom is here to claim his bride, Israel. He will bring the people to himself in a new way. It signifies that the wedding feast is on; the period of fasting is over. It is now the time of generosity and abundance (see Luke 5:34; John 1:16; 6:1-13; 10:10).

The Prophecy of Isaiah

Isaiah prophesied at a time of great distress when the people of Israel were experiencing their lowest moment in history. Jerusalem had been destroyed and the people were humiliated in Babylon where they were sent on exile. Many people reasoned that Israel, once recognised as God's beloved bride, has been forgotten. She is now like a widow bereft of children.

But Isaiah declared that God has not forgotten them, and that when the time comes God will take Israel to himself as a bridegroom takes a new bride, amid great rejoicing. He reassured them that God will change their circumstances and gladden their hearts with new wine as on a wedding feast.

The image of rich wine supplied in abundance is a familiar one depicting the messianic times. The abundant supply of rich wine symbolises the joyous arrival of God, and the display of God's favour and abundant generosity. Earlier references include Isaiah 25:6-8 where we read: "On this mountain the Lord of hosts will provide for all peoples a feast of rich food and choice wine, juicy rich food and pure choice wine." And also Isaiah 55:1-3, where the prophet says:

> Oh, come to the water all you who are thirsty;
> though you have no money, come!
> Buy and eat; come, buy wine and milk
> without money, free!
> Why spend money on what cannot nourish
> and your wages on what fails to satisfy?
> Listen carefully to me, and you will have
> good things to eat and rich food to enjoy…

Again, in Amos 9:14 we read: "I will restore my people Israel, they shall rebuild and inhabit their ruined cities, plant vineyards and drink the wine." And the Prophet Joel says, "I am sending you grain, new wine, and oil, and you will be satisfied by them. Never again will I make you a disgrace among the nations" (Joel 2:19).

Thus, amid widespread hopelessness and distress, these prophesies offer hope that with the new marriage of God and his people which the Messiah will bring about, there will be a change of fortune, there will be a cleansing of the land, and God will become one with his people. Israel looked forward to the realisation of this prophesy with great hope. It is this prophecy that is fulfilled in Christ Jesus at the very beginning of his public ministry as he attended a wedding feast at Cana in Galilee.

Compassion: Key to Jesus' Miracles
With his presence at Cana, Jesus demonstrates that the prophecies of Isaiah are being fulfilled. Prompted by compassion, Mary goes to Jesus and says: "They have no wine." Jesus replied: "Woman, why turn to me? My hour has not yet come!" But he goes ahead to perform the miracle.

With compassion, all things are possible. The miracles of Jesus were always prompted by compassion. He did not perform any miracle to show off his power. In John 6:1-13 Jesus was moved with compassion when he saw the crowd that had been with him and were now very hungry, and there was nowhere nearby to find food for all of them to eat. So, he multiplied the five loaves and two fish that were available there, and successfully fed the multitude of people that made up the crowd.

At the wedding in Cana, something awkward and terribly embarrassing happened: the hosts ran out of wine! The compassionate Mother of Jesus noticed that something was wrong. She felt the embarrassment of the hosts and did something about it. She had empathy and was sensitive to their needs.

It would have been the shame of a lifetime for the young couple. They were about to be thoroughly humiliated and would have been the subject of public ridicule. But just then, at the instance of his mother, Jesus intervened and saved the situation. He intervened to bring joy and gladness to a couple who would otherwise have been highly embarrassed, and they would have had their wedding day ruined. He transformed their fortunes unto good and the guests were filled with gladness. Jesus can also intervene in our own circumstances.

The miracle of Cana demonstrates that in Jesus, there is a new epiphany: a great light has dawned on the people; God has appeared among them, and great things happen when God mixes with humanity. At the event in Cana, the God revealed to us is not a frightful, vengeful, punitive God that needs to be appeased so that we may have peace, but a God of compassion that comes to save his people from humiliating and embarrassing situations.

Do Whatever He Tells You
Obedience is a critical virtue for those who would receive God's miracles. Mary the mother of Jesus knows this very well, and she tells the servants, "Do whatever he tells you." When they obeyed Jesus' command to fill six empty jars with water, a miracle happened. These servants were therefore part of the miracle because they obeyed.

Conclusion
Many Christians today have run out of wine on account of poverty and unemployment, loneliness and rejection, failure and disappointment, and widespread anxiety and fear. But the good news is that God can transform their circumstances and bring them joy and gladness. He can turn their water into choice wine, if they go to him and do whatever he tells them.

Questions to Ponder
1. What does "Wedding Feast" represent in the prophecies of Isaiah, and in the life and mission of Christ?
2. Identify the Christian virtues demonstrated in the story of Jesus' 1st miracle at Cana.
3. Jesus came to change our water into wine. In what ways can we Christians today help change other people's water into wine?
4. What spiritual gift do you have? And how are you using such gifts to glorify God and build up the Church and humanity in general?

Additional Reading
Psalm 23; Matthew 11:28-30; John 6:1-13, 10:10, 15:1-7

3rd Sunday of the Year

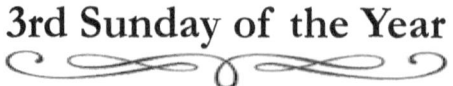

Bringing the Good News to the Poor

Readings: Nehemiah 8:2-4a, 5-6, 8-10 | Psalm 19 |
1 Cor. 12:12-30 | Luke 1:1-4; 4:14-21

Summary:

When the people of Israel had the opportunity after a very long time to hear the word of God read to them, many of the people were moved to tears, but Nehemiah, Ezra the priest, and the Levites admonish the people not to weep, because the joy of the Lord must be their strength, and the day (of the presentation of the Law), is holy to the Lord their God. St. Paul on his part reminds the people of Corinth, as he reminds us, that as Christians we make up the body of Christ. In the Gospel story, Jesus outlines his mission statement, adopting as it were the Messiah's programme of action as prophesied in Isaiah 61:1-2, and declaring that in Him prophesy has become reality.

The Anointed One of Isaiah

Jesus was a faithful Jew who went to the synagogue every Sabbath. Although the Gospel of Mark (1:14-15) presents Jesus as emerging from the desert and declaring that, "The kingdom of God is at hand, repent and believe the good news," on this particular occasion, Luke (4:18) says that he went to the Synagogue where he stood up to read from the scroll of the Prophet Isaiah. Unrolling the scroll, he read from the place where it is written that the Anointed One of God, *the Christ* will be endowed with the Spirit of God, and he will be the personification of God's mercy and compassion.

Jesus came as the perfect image of God who is the "Father of orphans, Defender of the widow, and Friend of the poor." He brings God's love and affection, as well as God's tenderness and compassion to the people, and he announces the good news to the poor. The immediate challenge is that we can hardly claim to be Christians if we are not united with God the Father in his role as

Father of the orphans, Defender of the widow, and Friend of the poor. Such is the identity of the God we serve, and it should also be the identity as well as the mission of all of us who are united with him in Christ.

Jesus read to his listeners in Nazareth: "The Spirit of the Lord is upon me, because he has anointed me to bring good news to the poor, to proclaim liberty to captives, to open the eyes of the blind, to let the oppressed go free and, to proclaim a year of favour for the Lord." When he finished reading, he handed the scroll over to the attendants and sat down. By now all eyes were on him. Then he made a most spectacular claim: "This scripture is being fulfilled today even as you listen!" The congregation was left in shock, for Jesus was announcing to them that in him, the prophesy has become reality, and that word and deed have become one. He was declaring that in him the promise is fulfilled!

Jesus' declaration after reading the Isaiah text meant that the time has come, the day of the Lord is here; this is the year of God's favour for everyone, especially the lowly poor and the weak. Jesus meant to say that with his coming, captives shall be liberated, the blind shall have new sight, the oppressed and downtrodden shall all be freed, and the poor shall hear the Good News preached to them. These are exactly the things that Isaiah said the Anointed One would do, and Jesus proclaims that He, the Anointed One is here.

So, Jesus adopted the prophecy of Isaiah (61:1-7) as his mission statement, his missionary agenda or his programme of action. He will deliver his people from oppressive situations, bring hope where there is hopelessness and despair, restore dignity to the poor and marginalised and thus inaugurate God's kingdom of righteousness, justice, love and peace. In John 10:10 he declares that whereas the thief comes to steal, to kill, and to destroy, he has come that we may have life and have it more abundantly. In John 8: 36, he says that if the son sets us free, we shall be free indeed!

Jesus' Preferential Option for the Poor
Armed with the Spirit, Jesus' principal mission is to bring the Good News to the poor. We celebrate this mission of Jesus prominently in today's liturgy. In Luke 4:18-19, he proclaims that he was sent, not to

the powerful, but to the poor, the lowly, the oppressed and the afflicted. In Matthew 9:12, he declares that he came not for the healthy, but the sick. He will confront squarely situations of sin and iniquity, poverty and disease, ignorance and blindness, injustice and oppression. Jesus identifies himself closely with those who suffer these deprivations and transforms their circumstances.

When John's disciples came to ask: "Are you the Messiah or are we to wait for another?" he answered them: "Go and tell John what you hear and see: the blind receive their sight, the lame walk, lepers are cleansed, the deaf hear, the dead are raised to life, the poor have the good news proclaimed to them" (Matthew 11:4-5).

In both his teaching and healing ministries Jesus constantly identified with the poor and lowly. He was indeed the visible image of the invisible God who, according to Mary in the Magnificat, pulls down the mighty from their thrones and raises up the lowly (Luke 1:46-55). In a world of aggressive competition for wealth, power and prestige, we need followers of Jesus who would inspire the men and women of the world to moderate those primitive passions and inordinate inclinations that are destroying the human society.

Jesus links blessedness with the poor and oppressed and those who care or show concern for them. To the rich young man who desired eternal life, he says: "If you want to be perfect, go sell what you possess and give to the poor, and you will have treasures in heaven, then come follow me" (Matthew 19:21; Mark 10:21; Luke 18:22). In the parable of the last judgement (Matthew 25:31-46), we see how Jesus identifies himself with the hungry, the naked, the sick, the stranger, and the prisoner, and concludes emphatically, "As you did it to the least of my brethren you did it to me."

Jesus' revolutionary teaching is that we cannot claim any measure of godliness or Christian piety if we oppress or marginalise the poor, the weak, and the lowly; if we do nothing in the face of injustice and oppression; and if we are not engaged in promoting human dignity and better quality of life for the poor, the weak, and the sick. With his life and teaching, Jesus demonstrated that true, authentic religion consists in defending the widow, coming to the aid of the orphan, and befriending the poor. He teaches that even if we could keep all the commandments, we would still not achieve perfection until we genuinely identify with and do something about the situation of the poor!

The 1971 Synod of Bishops declared that "action on behalf of justice and participation in the transformation of the world fully appears to us as a constitutive dimension of the preaching of the Gospel or, in other words, of the Church's mission for the redemption of the human race and its liberation from every oppressive situation" (*Justice in the World*, no. 6). The Church as an institution, and individual Christians as well have indeed been commissioned, by virtue of their baptism, to be engaged in social transformation, to defend the poor and promote human dignity, to fight for justice and equity where there is social injustices; to promote and defend the truth where there is widespread falsehood and corruption; and to work towards reconciliation, unity and peace, where there is disunity, division and violent conflict.

Conclusion

Christians are challenged today to be like Christ in every way: freeing those held captive, lifting up the poor and downtrodden, educating the ignorant, feeding the hungry, clothing the naked, welcoming the stranger, sheltering the homeless, visiting the sick and the prisoners, and supporting the widow and orphan, because as we do it to the least of Christ's brethren, we do it to him.

Questions to Ponder

1. In our 1st Reading (Nehemiah 8:2-10), after Ezra finished reading the Word of God to the people, they all started crying. What do you think made them burst into tears?
2. What is the key point of the 2nd Reading (1 Corinthians 12:12-30)? And how does it apply to us in the Church today?
3. What is the link (if any) between the 2nd Reading and the Gospel of today (Luke 4:14-21)?
4. How does the Gospel message challenge our own Christian witnessing today?

Additional Readings:
Ezra 10:23; Acts 1:8ff; Romans 12:4-5; 1 Corinthians 15:3

4th Sunday of the Year

Jesus and the Prophetic Burden

Readings: Jeremiah 1:4-5, 17-19 | Psalm 71 | 1 Corinthians 12:31-13:13 | Luke 4:21-30

Summary:

The prophetic vocation is a difficult one, because the message of true prophets often makes people uncomfortable. It is the false prophets who will say what the people want to hear. The truth of God which genuine prophets preach, will often unsettle many of the hearers, because human beings often have little appetite for truth. The truth bearer himself or herself is often hated, maligned, persecuted and sometimes even killed for daring to speak the truth of God. But God has promised to always be with the bearer of his truth, such that at the end of the day, he or she will be vindicated.

The Burden of a Prophet

In the biblical sense, a prophet is one who speaks for God. He is one who is called and commissioned by God to stand in the Temple, to go to the town square, to use the traditional and social media, to use his or her position in government or the corporate boardroom, to speak the truth of God or declare God's plans to the people. Prophets are servants of the word of God. While living in the material world, prophets are always very sensitive to the spiritual realm. They have a critical relationship with the future because the truth of God which they proclaim today naturally illuminates the future. Living out the truth of God or rejecting such truth today will inevitably impact on future events.

Because they are in close contact with God who is the Defender of the widow, the Father of orphans and the Friend of the poor, prophets are called not only to proclaim the truth of God, but also to live out God's mercy and compassion for the broken-hearted.

The word of the prophet often convicts those who are comfortable with the unjust status quo and at the same time their word comforts the unfortunate victims of the evil status quo. This is what the author of the letter to the Hebrews means when he says, "The word of God is sharper than any double-edged sword…" (Hebrews 4:12).

Prophets hate sin, injustice, and immorality. They often live lives of simplicity, frugality and purity. They are often willing to stand alone and to suffer for righteousness' sake. They know how to run back to God (in prayer) when things go wrong. The prophet is a man (or woman) on a dangerous mission because his or her life will often be at risk. But the prophet is not to take any weapons to defend himself or herself. This is one reason why no one on his or her own would choose to be a prophet in the classical sense. The prophetic task is such an arduous one that at a point Jeremiah cried out: "You have seduced me Lord and I have allowed myself to be seduced. You are the stronger and I am the weaker" (Jeremiah 20:7).

The Prophet Will Not Be Crushed
The Lord promises to make his prophets a fortified city, a pillar of iron, and a wall of bronze. The Lord supplies the graces necessary for his prophets. That is why the prophets must always be close to God. They recognise that they are doing the work of God, not their own. The prophets are however assured of ultimate vindication, because of the presence of God in their lives, as we read in Jeremiah 1:19, "They will fight against you but they shall not overcome you, for I am with you to deliver you."

The prophet is a messenger of truth. We know that truth may suffer only temporary setbacks, but both truth and the messenger of truth cannot be destroyed. The mighty and powerful of this world, those benefitting from the status quo, those living lives of falsehood and corruption, and those presiding over unjust and evil systems, often seek to silence the truth and to kill the truth bearer, but no one can destroy the truth and the truth bearer because the Lord promises to take care of his own.

Jesus and his Prophetic Mission

In Jesus, the prophecies of Jeremiah, Isaiah, Baruch, Daniel, Zachariah, and John the Baptist find fulfilment. Jesus is the Messiah to whom all the major prophets point. He is Jeremiah's "Appointee over nations and kingdoms" (Jeremiah 1:10). He is Isaiah's "Wonderful Counsellor and Prince of Peace" and "Suffering Servant" (Isaiah 9:6 and Isaiah 53). He is John the Baptist's "Powerful one who will baptise with the Holy Spirit and with fire" (Matthew 3:11). And when Jesus appeared at the Synagogue in Nazareth, after reading the text of Isaiah 61:1-2, he says, "This prophesy is being fulfilled today, even as you listen" (Luke 4:21).

Reaction to Jesus' Proclamation

Following this spectacular declaration of Jesus in the Synagogue of Nazareth, we find three levels of reaction among the listeners:

(i). Admiration and astonishment. We are told that "all spoke well of him and were amazed at the gracious words that came from his mouth" (Luke 4:22);

(ii). Questioning, doubt, and suspicion. They asked, "Is this not Joseph's son?" They told him, "We heard that you performed many miracles elsewhere, why not perform such miracles here?" (Luke 4:23);

(iii). Rejection, condemnation, and an attempt at execution.

The admiration of the listeners in the Synagogue soon turned to anger and hostility. Jesus' admirers soon got into a murderous rage. They took him out of the city, meaning to silence him forever, but Jesus slipped out from their midst (Luke 4:28-30).

Jesus came on a mission to set humanity free from sin and damnation, to show the way to those who are lost, to shed his powerful light into the darkness of the world, to heal the broken-hearted, and to give humanity abundant life. Yet he had to contend with the doubts, suspicion, prejudices, presumptions, gossip, and character assassination of the local people. He was not immune to any of these. Jesus recognised that prophets are not accepted among their own people. The people of Nazareth complained that Jesus performed no miracles among them. They told him that charity should begin at home. Yet they showed disbelief in him.

Jesus demonstrated to the people of his hometown of Nazareth that he was not part of their narrow nationalism. He refused to be part of the madding crowd with their narrow clannish idea of salvation. He showed them that God is always much more than people's expectation. And when he used two classic examples from their own history - the stories of the Widow of Zarephath and Naaman the Syrian - to tell them that his mission is universal, the people became enraged and turned on him. The crowd of admirers quickly turned into a violent mob.

They wanted to put him to death, but since it was not yet his time, he successfully slipped away and never returned to Nazareth. The people of Nazareth rejected him because he pointed out their lack of faith. They were not prepared to hear the truth that the Gentiles were more open to the message of God's salvation than his own people. The truth of the universality of salvation, that many Gentiles will come and obtain the benefits of salvation even before the Jews, was one that his people were not prepared to hear. They did not take kindly to Jesus' affirmation that the group that one belongs to does not really matter, that God's salvation is meant for all, and that the only condition for membership of God's new family is repentance and faith the good news he brings (see Acts 10:34).

Speaking God's Truth in Love

God's truth should be told wholly and entirely, yet it must always be spoken in love. Love was the greatest motivation of Jesus Christ in his prophetic mission and as such, love should be the greatest motivation of all who *'speak for God.'* Those who speak for God should live like God. Love should be the driving force for all who live by Jesus' mission statement: freeing captives, healing the broken-hearted, opening the eyes of the blind, preaching the good news to the poor, and declaring the Lord's year of favour (Isaiah 61:1-2, Luke 4:18-19). Even in the face of aggression and hostility, the prophet must carry out God's command and deliver God's message in love. There should be no bitterness, no brooding over injury, and no thought of revenge in the prophet.

All Christians have a prophetic calling, since we were baptised as prophets, priests, and kings. Part of this prophetic calling is to listen to God's word and witness to it with our very lives. We are to do this by speaking for God in all circumstances and shining God's light on the darkness of our societies. Speaking God's truth in an environment of falsehood and being the conscience of society – denouncing sin and immorality in all their manifestations, condemning social injustice, oppressive customs, corrupt practices, racial and ethnic bigotry, defending the poor, and being the voice of the voiceless in society, etc., are all duties associated with the Christian's prophetic vocation.

Conclusion
Speaking the truth without love leads to frustration because love is the prophet's source of energy. It is the driving force for all who speak for God. To effectively perform this task, Christians must not allow self-indulgence to get the upper hand of them. Ardent faith in God, love, humility, fortitude and perseverance, are necessary virtues for a successful prophetic ministry. Without these virtues, those who attempt to speak the truth of God in an environment dominated by evil will often end up in frustration.

Questions to Ponder
1. Who is a Prophet in the Biblical tradition? And what is the true role of the Prophet as reflected in today's readings?
2. What prompted St. Paul to admonish the Corinthians (in 1 Corinthians 12:31) to earnestly desire the higher gifts? And what are these higher gifts?
3. Why did the people of Nazareth suddenly turn against Jesus? And how do we sometimes reject the prophets of our own day?
4. At Baptism you were anointed Priest, Prophet & King: In what ways are you being called today to play the role of a prophet in your society?

Additional Reading
Exodus 3:1-12; Isaiah 6:1-10; Jeremiah 1:1-10; Amos 3:1-8; Matthew 10:16

5 Sunday of the Year

Come Follow Me
Readings: Isaiah 6:1-2a, 3-8 | Psalm 138 | 1 Corinthians 15:1-11 | Luke 5:1-11

Summary:
Jesus enters the lives of people with a purpose. He entertains sinners, goes to their homes, meets with their families, eats at their table, and listens to their stories - all in a bid to call them to a new way of life. If we respond to his call, he welcomes us just the way we are. But as soon as we truly encounter Jesus, we never remain the same, because his saving power transforms us and empowers us to live new lives.

Coping With Failure and Defeat
Failure comes with a feeling of distress, a sense of limitation, helplessness, vulnerability, shame and embarrassment. Now and again individual human beings as well as groups experience failure or defeat. It could be failure in school, in marriage and family life, in business or career, and failure to live out one's moral and spiritual values. A sense of failure or defeat could also come with the onset of a terminal illness or the loss of a loved one in the prime of life. When this happens, many unanswerable questions are raised.

Peter: From Failure to Victory
Peter was a professional fisherman who had family members and staff whom he took care of from the business. Night is the time when fishermen make the most catch, because that is when the fishes come up to the surface. But there are times when the fishermen would toil all night and catch nothing. These are nights of failure.

Our Gospel story today starts after one of those nights of failure with Peter and his companions. Tired, dispirited, and disillusioned, they were washing their nets and preparing to go home in shame and embarrassment. But Jesus found them at that very point in time, and he told Peter to throw in the net for a catch.

Peter may have hesitated for a moment, but he obeyed, and the result was a miracle – a great haul of fish was caught. Peter recognised immediately that this was not an ordinary event, and that no human skill could bring this about. He knew that whatever turned the night of failure around had something supernatural about it. He recognised there and then in the person of Christ, the presence of the all-holy God. Peter also recognised immediately his own utter sinfulness and unworthiness before this all-holy presence. So, he shouted, "Depart from me, for I am a sinful man!" But Jesus did not go away. Instead, he demonstrated that the Son of Man has come to seek out and to save the lost, just as he told Zacchaeus and his household (in Luke 19:10).

Once Jesus saw that Peter had acknowledged his sinfulness and unworthiness, he moved the discussion to another level – about Peter becoming a fisher of men, leading other people to God. Jesus brought out the best in Peter and challenged him to go out and do the same for people. He made him the head of the apostles, the rock on which the Church is built. Jesus thus transformed Peter's failure into a spectacular victory.

Jesus did for Peter and his companions what we all need in our moments of failure and defeat. Jesus believed in the endless possibilities and potential that reside in his weak followers. So, he encouraged them, and he challenged them to bring out the best that is yet hidden within them. He challenged them to plunge into the deep waters for a catch; to reach out beyond what they thought they were capable of, and what they had settled for, to ever greater heights.

On his part, Peter demonstrated absolute trust in Jesus. He was prepared to attempt the impossible, and he was rewarded for it. This is what we all are called to do – to attempt the impossible. Like Isaiah and Paul, Peter acknowledged his sinful state before the all-holy and all-powerful one, and he was well rewarded for it. When people truly encounter the Lord, the results are evident. After Isaiah had experienced God in the temple, his life did not remain the same. He got a new career; he became a prophet. In the same way, on meeting

Jesus, Peter and his companions got a new job – they became fishers of men.

The Service of Others

Until each of us has a cause to which we dedicate our lives, a cause that is greater and higher than ourselves, our lives will often be devoid of meaning and true fulfilment. A life that is dedicated solely to just taking care of oneself is often an unfulfilled life. Such a life becomes rather frustrating, because, as St Augustine notes, "God has created us for himself, and our hearts are restless until they rest in Him."

Jesus can see beyond our sinfulness to the God-given dignity of the sinner and the endless possibilities that lie ahead. St. Paul corroborates this in the 2nd Reading when he says: "I believe that nothing can happen that will outweigh the supreme advantage of knowing Christ Jesus... All I can say is that I forget the past and strain ahead for what is to come" (Phil 3:8,13).

The God who did it with Isaiah, Peter, and Paul, can do the same with us even today! Jesus never writes us off because we have sinned. He does not define us by our sins, because he knows that we have more possibilities than our past weaknesses show. So, for Jesus, sinners have a future, not just the sinful past, and our future calling is to sainthood!

Come Follow Me

Jesus therefore addresses us today as he addressed Peter. He says:

- Come follow me, all you who are lost, confused, distressed and frightened in a world of false prophets and fake preachers that are simply wolves in sheep's clothing. Come follow me, for I am the Way, the Truth and the Life.
- Come follow me, all you who are groping in the dark or are entangled with the works of darkness. Come follow me, for I am the Light that dispels the darkness of the world.

- Come follow me all you who have lived in sin and have had the agonising experience of alienation from God. Come follow me for I am the Lamb of God who takes away sin.
- Come follow me all who are experiencing hunger and thirst in the depths of your being for ultimate meaning. Come follow me, for I am the Bread of life, the Water of life, and the Spring of living water.
- Come follow me all you who are suffering the debilitation of illness and disease.
  Come follow me for I am the Prime Healer by whose wounds you have been healed and by whose stripes you have been made whole.
- Come follow me all you who are tired of the bad news of terrorist violence, suicides, accidents, man-made and natural disasters, and the scandalous behaviour of political and religious leaders. Come follow me, for I am the Resurrection and the Life, and I bring the good news of abundant life to everyone.
- Come follow me all you who have been frustrated by the widespread selfish manipulation that camouflages as love in our society; yes, all who are searching for authentic love; come follow me, for I am the image of God who is love.
- Come follow me all you who are suffering loneliness, rejection, and abandonment, and all you who have been betrayed by those you thought were your best friends. Come follow me, for I am the faithful one who lays down his life for his friends.
- Come follow me, abandon the old life of selfishness and greed; abandon your old life devoted to the cult of power, wealth, and pleasure, which has brought upon you so much pain and frustration. Come follow me in a life of service and sacrificial love, a life of meaning and purpose; and you will experience the abundant life which I give freely. Come follow me and receive the tremendous gift of eternal life which I offer you graciously.

- Come follow me, be my companion in a life of holiness and peace; be salt of the earth and light of the world; and be co-heirs with me in the kingdom of God the Father.
- Come follow me and seek out with me your brothers and sisters who are still lost in the world of darkness and corruption. Yes, come follow me, and become fishers of men and women with me.

Conclusion

Humility and trust are the key Christian virtues put before us in today's readings. Thus, the starting point for growth and development in the Christian life is acknowledging our sinfulness and our utter unworthiness in the presence of God, as well as trusting that with God all things are possible. It is true that we have often failed; that we are weak, sinful, vulnerable, and handicapped creatures. But God can strengthen us and transform our circumstances unto good. All we need do is trust and surrender our lives to his transforming Spirit.

Questions to Ponder

1. Today's readings show Isaiah, St. Paul, and St. Peter as having at least one thing in common. What is it?
2. In the Gospel story (Luke 5:1-11), Peter demonstrated two core Christian virtues. Name them.
3. How does each one of today's readings treat the issue of sin and human encounter with God?
4. Jesus called fishermen to become fishers of people. What is your own profession? How are you being called to use your training and your talents, skills, and resources to advance the Kingdom?

Additional Reading

1 Samuel 3:3-19; Luke 9:1-19, 19:1-10; John 1:35-42; 2 Corinthians 12:7-10.

6th Sunday of the Year

Blessed Are You Who Are Poor

Readings: Jeremiah 17:5-8 | Psalm 1:1-6 |
1 Corinthians 15:12, 16-20 | Luke 6:17, 20-26

Summary:

In today's first reading, the Prophet Jeremiah sets out the two paths that are available to the people of Israel – to trust in God or to trust in their human abilities. The Psalmist also emphasises the benefits of trusting in God and the consequences of trusting in our human abilities. In St Paul's letter to the Corinthians, he explains an important issue at the heart of our Christian enterprise. It is belief in the risen Christ, and why this belief is so necessary. The Gospel reading is Luke's version of the Beatitudes, where Jesus proclaims not only the blessings that come with living the Beatitudes, but also the woes that accompany living a life that is contrary to it.

The Cursed and the Blessed

Prophet Jeremiah puts side by side two kinds of people: Those who are CURSED, and those who are BLESSED. Those who put their trust in human beings are cursed. They are compared to a shrub in the dry, arid desert. Those who put their trust in the Lord are blessed. They are like a tree planted by the waterside. Psalm 1 does the same comparison, using slightly different words. It says:

> "How blessed is the man who follows not the counsel of the wicked nor stands in the path with sinners…who delights in the law of the Lord and who ponders his law, day and night. He is like a tree that is planted beside the flowing waters that yields its fruit in due season and whose leaves never fade and all that he does prospers. Not so are the wicked, for they, like winnowed chaff shall

be driven away by the wind, for the Lord knows the way of the just, but the way of the wicked perish."

The two passages (Jeremiah 17 and Psalm 1) have the same message: "Cursed is the man who trusts in man," and "Blessed is the man who trusts in the Lord". They contrast the WICKED who trusts in man and the RIGHTEOUS who trusts in the Lord. The one who does not trust in the Lord is considered a wicked man.

The Two Ways
The Scriptures are full of this kind of comparison between two opposite ways that we see in today's readings. For example, we hear Moses say to the people in Deuteronomy 11:26-28,

> "See, I have set before you today a BLESSING and a CURSE: a blessing, if you obey the commandments of Yahweh our God that I enjoin on you today; a curse if you disobey the commandments of Yahweh your God and leave the way I have marked out for you today, by going after other gods you have not known."

In Deuteronomy 30:15-20, he says, "See, I have set before you today LIFE and PROSPERITY, DEATH and DISASTER." Constantly we are being admonished to make a choice, whether we like it or not. If you obey the commandments of the Lord your God, by loving the Lord your God, then you shall live and prosper. But if your heart turns away and you do not hear but are led astray to bow down to other gods and serve them, then you shall perish.

In Ecclesiasticus 15:16-17, we read: "The Lord has set fire and water before you; put out your hand to whichever you prefer." In Jeremiah 21:8 the Prophet says, "Thus says the Lord: See, I am setting before you the way of life and the way of death," and in Proverbs 8:34-36, we read: "Happy is the one who listens to me, watching daily at my gates and waiting beside my door. For whoever finds me finds LIFE and obtains favour from the Lord. But those who miss me injure themselves; all who hate me love DEATH."

In his letter to the Romans 6:21-23, Paul says: "So what advantage did you then get from the things of which you now are ashamed? Every act of sin brings regret. The end of those things is DEATH, but now that you have been freed from sin and enslaved to God, the advantage you get is sanctification." In Galatians 6:7-8 he says, "Do not be deceived; God is not mocked, for you reap whatever you sow. If you sow to your own flesh, you will reap corruption from the flesh."

Blessed Are You Who Are Poor; Woe to You Who Are Rich
In Luke's version of the Beatitudes that we read today, Jesus speaks directly to his disciples in the presence of the crowds and says:

> "Blessed are you who are poor, for yours is the kingdom of God. Blessed are you who are hungry now, for you will be filled. Blessed are you who weep now, for you will laugh. Blessed are you who are hated now, rejoice and exalt for joy for your reward is great in heaven."

Jesus did not stop there. To press home this strange logic, he reversed the blessings for the rich and powerful. He says,

> "But woe to you who are rich, for you have received your consolation. Woe to you who are full now, for you will be hungry. Woe to you who are laughing now, for you will mourn and weep. Woe to you when all speak well of you, for that is what their ancestors did to the false prophet."

This puzzling message of Jesus was addressed specifically to his disciples but in the presence of the crowds. It was addressed to those who had been presented with the TWO WAYS: the Way of Life and the Way of Death, the Way of the Spirit and the Way of the Flesh. The disciples had made the radical choice for Jesus Christ, the Way of Life. He was now presenting to them the logic and the ethos of his Kingdom. It must be emphasised that the blessedness of which Jesus speaks is reserved for only those who have made the radical choice to live "IN CHRIST," and therefore St. Paul says in Philippians 3:8-10 that they count everything this world can offer as vanity, as loss, and only count their relationship with Christ as GAIN.

With all of St. Paul's qualification as a lawyer, a Roman citizen, and a Pharisee, etc., once he encountered Jesus Christ, he considered all these qualifications as rubbish. Thus, the blessedness that Jesus speaks of will only make sense to those who, like St. Paul have truly encountered him, and fallen in love with Him and His Kingdom. For others, it will be like a parable.

We can connect the Beatitudes to the other readings from Jeremiah 17 and Psalm 1. They summarise what the Gospel message is about, that trust in human beings is often the attitude of the rich, those who are full, those who laugh, and those of whom people speak well. Trust in the Lord on the other hand is often the attitude of the poor, the hungry, those who weep and mourn, and of those who are hated, reviled, and rejected.

In this puzzling passage, the Lord demonstrates that he came to overturn the status quo of power, wealth and pleasure, which has been the cause of so much evil in the world. In the new logic of the Kingdom, Jesus speaks of the happiness or blessedness of the poor, little ones who have no one to trust in but God. He speaks of the melancholy of the rich who trust in their wealth, power and privileged connections, and are often pre-occupied solely with "this-worldly ultimate goals."

In the logic of the Beatitudes, the rich are often seen as belonging to the same class as the wicked, whom the Old Testament writers likened to "barren desert shrubs," while the poor often belong to the same class as the righteous, that are like fruitful trees planted beside flowing waters. In the eyes of the world, the rich seem to be the ones who are blessed by God, while the poor seem be cursed. But Jesus speaks of the strange poverty of those who live for the wealth of this world, and the strange wealth of those who trust in, or rely on, God. He speaks of the strange hunger of those whose only food is the food of this world, and the strange nourishment of those who seek the food that only God can give.

He speaks of the strange sadness of those who laugh, and the strange joy of those who know how to weep. He speaks of the strange happiness of those who are persecuted for righteousness' sake; the strange weakness of the strong who rely on their strength, and the strange strength of the weak who put their trust in God. This is known as the MESSIANIC INVERSION! Jesus turns upside down everything the world ordinarily celebrates as success or achievement.

In and of itself however, there is nothing wrong with riches or material resources. To acquire sufficient resources to live decently and be guaranteed good food, decent housing, and a measure of comfortable life, is good and even desirable. Also, abject poverty and all forms of human degradation that come with it, are not at all to be desired. Jesus did not sanctify abject poverty and human degradation. Such poverty is evil and should not be desired. It is for this reason that the Church constantly sets up institutions to fight poverty and promote human development. It is the reason why the Church establishes schools, hospitals, and vocational centres, etc., to help take people out of poverty and other conditions that degrade the human person.

Yet, it is the truth of human nature well demonstrated through the course of history, that the rich tend to rely on their riches and forget the God of all riches; that the rich tend to abuse the enormous power and privilege that riches bestow, and become arrogant, presumptuous, insensitive, and oppressive of the poor; and that the rich tend to occupy their lives with the pursuit of ever greater material wealth, power and pleasure, often to the neglect of spiritual and transcendental goals. Whereas the rich often think they possess riches, these riches however have a way of "possessing" the rich. Riches have a way of preventing those who have them from looking beyond this world to the life after death, to the Kingdom of God.

The poor and oppressed on the other hand often tend to look more towards life beyond this world, because of the precarious situation they must cope with in this world. This is why Jesus says, "Blessed are the poor for the Kingdom of God is theirs." So, the poverty that is blessed is the poverty of those who put their trust in God, rather than simply poverty in material things. It is the poverty of those who recognize that only God can assuage the profound hunger and the distressing void in the human heart and soul.

Conclusion

Jesus confronted his disciples, and he confronts us today with a radical choice: To live either by the values of the world, which include money, pleasure, power, popularity, and prestige, or by the values of the kingdom, which include fear of God, poverty of spirit, purity of heart, mercy and forgiveness, modesty and frugality, service, sacrificial love and detachment, submission to god's will, and the ability to suffer for the cause of right. Attachment is one of our greatest problems that come with riches. Once we learn what it means to be detached, then we are on the way to the kingdom of God.

The Church has always taught the virtues of frugality, modesty and simplicity, by which Christians are admonished to live simply, even when they are exposed to enormous riches. This is part of the reason why in the course of time the Christian Church developed and promoted the concept of willful poverty. The Church does not desire that people be forced into poverty. Such will amount to impoverishment. But willful poverty is a free choice which many Christians have made in the course of time, with many attendant spiritual benefits. At the end of the day, fear of God, poverty of spirit, purity of heart, mercy and forgiveness, modesty and frugality, service, sacrificial love and detachment, submission to God's will and ability to suffer for the cause of right, etc., are among the values of the Kingdom of God which Jesus came to inaugurate.

Questions To Ponder

1. What is the matter of contention that Paul was responding to in the 2nd Reading of today (1 Cor. 15:12-20)? And what is the connection, if any, with the rest of the readings?
2. Discuss in brief your understanding of Jesus' saying: "Blessed are you who are poor…" and "Woe to you who are rich…"
3. As a Christian, in what ways have you attempted to live by the values of the Kingdom as enunciated in the Beatitudes?

Additional Reading

Proverbs 8:34-36; Deuteronomy 11:26-28; Romans 6:21-23; Galatians 6:7-8

7th Sunday of the Year

Be Merciful as Your Heavenly Father

Readings: 1 Samuel 26:2, 7-13, 22-23 | Psalm 103 | 1 Corinthians 15:45-49 | Luke 6:27-38

Summary:

Our first reading shows how David demonstrated his fear of the Lord and his godly character to a heroic degree, when he refused to kill Saul who was pursuing him with the intention of killing him, declaring that he dared not lay his hands on the Lord's anointed! David conquered the natural man's inclination to revenge. His exceptional conduct on this occasion can be described as "heavenly conduct," and not earthly conduct (to use the words of St. Paul in our second reading). The Gospel is part of the Sermon on the Mount, where Jesus calls on his followers to be merciful as their heavenly father is merciful. This is exactly what David did when the life of Saul was put into his hands.

The Way of the Kingdom

The ethos of the kingdom as laid down by Jesus often contradicts some of the established norms in the human society. Jesus says that we are to love our enemies, to do good to those who hate us, to bless those who curse us, and to pray for those who treat us badly (Luke 6:27-28). Jesus also says that the new order of happiness and fulfilment is achieved via poverty of spirit and suffering for the cause of right (Luke 6:20-26). Humility and meekness as well as mercy and compassion are critical to happiness in the new kingdom dispensation.

Nearly 2000 years before Jesus came, King David already demonstrated the godly character of tender mercy and compassion in a very spectacular manner, in the story presented to us in today's 1st Reading (1 Samuel 26:2-23).

The Example of David

Saul was the first king anointed over Israel. He was a simple shepherd and a countryman who never dreamt of becoming king and had no experience of any sort in leadership or in the art of waging wars. His reign was afflicted by multiple wars and internal strife. He had to fight against the Philistines, the Moabites, the Ammonites, and the Edomites. His army was defeated and humiliated on many occasions.

They suffered exceptional humiliation at the hands of the Philistines who had a giant called Goliath. King Saul was tormented by these defeats, and he even suffered regular bouts of depression and melancholy. Young David, who had in the meantime been secretly anointed by Samuel to eventually rule over Israel and Judah after Saul, was gifted in music and often played the harp and sang for King Saul to get him off the blues.

Whereas Saul enjoyed David's music, he was, however, provoked to murderous jealousy when David was praised more than himself for killing Goliath who had tormented the people for a long time. David was unusually brave on the field of battle and led many successful expeditions, which earned him praise and admiration from the women, but it provoked Saul to jealousy. Saul's jealousy turned to anger. His anger turned to bitterness, and his bitterness degenerated to malice.

Saul resolved to kill David for no other reason except that David appeared to be stealing the show. He mobilised his entire army to hunt David down. But in a twist of fate, while Saul was in pursuit of David to kill him, David was presented with an opportunity to pay him back in his own coin. But he did not. When David's companion, Abishai, said to him: "God has given your enemy into your hands today; now therefore let me pin him to the ground with one stroke of the spear; I will not strike him twice." David reprimanded him, urging him never to touch the Lord's anointed.

David still recognised Saul as the anointed of God, even though Saul set out to kill him. He believed that though the Lord put Saul in his power, he nevertheless had no right to raise his hands against him, because Saul was the Lord's anointed. The temptation to kill Saul was one he was able to overcome. This is what godliness entails. No wonder that David came to be known as a friend of God, notwithstanding his sins.

David's godly character of tender mercy and compassion was also shown very powerfully in his reaction on hearing of the death of King Saul and his son Jonathan. The tribute he made to Saul and Jonathan in 2 Samuel 1:1-27 is generally recognised as a literary classic!

God of Love, Mercy, and Compassion

The commandment to love, which encompasses being merciful, forgiving, and compassionate, is so central to the Christian faith because the God we serve has revealed himself in Christ Jesus as a God of love, who is slow to anger and abundant in graciousness. He is not a vengeful or capricious God! (See Exodus 33:19, 34:6-7; Psalm 111:4; Hosea 11:1-3).

Our God is one who, from the abundance of his graciousness, bestows upon his children "grace upon grace" (John 1:14,16-17). At the birth of John the Baptist, we hear in Zachariah's Benedictus:

> "As for you little child, you shall be called a Prophet of the Most High…to give his people knowledge of salvation through forgiveness of their sins…By the tender mercy of our God the rising sun will visit us from on high, to give light to those who live in darkness and the shadow of death, and to guide our feet into the way of peace" (Luke 1:76-79).

Jesus himself was a personification of divine mercy and compassion. His entire life, teaching, miracles, and suffering and death, gave loud witness to the tender mercy and compassion of our God.

Be Merciful as Your Heavenly Father is Merciful

Love is the central commandment in Christianity because our God is love. Also, mercy, forgiveness and compassion (even towards a sworn enemy), are a Christian imperative because the God we serve is merciful, forgiving, and compassionate. The Christian vocation is understood as a journey or process of becoming like God. It is a calling to transcend our natural human inclinations and our societal value orientations, and begin to live out the values of the kingdom of heaven. We are called to continually subvert the established order and live by a radically new set of values. Jesus insists that it is only in this way that we will be sons and daughters of the Most High God, for he himself is kind to the ungrateful and the wicked" (Luke 6:35).

Jesus demands that we live true to our nature as Christians. So, when a Christian shows mercy to the wicked, he or she brings light into darkness, and he or she gives life where there was death. When a Christian unilaterally forgives an offending party, he or she breaks the cycle of violence that destroys the human society. When the Lord says we should be merciful as our Heavenly Father is merciful, he reminds us that we are beneficiaries of God's mercy ourselves. We should simply share with others what we have received.

Love is Hardly True Love Until It Hurts
Jesus has taught us that hatred can only be defeated by love, injury can only be healed by forgiveness, and evil can only be controlled by goodness. He has taught us how to make a habit of confusing our enemies with love. The process of transforming hatred with love and healing injury with forgiveness is always a painful and bloody affair. It cost Jesus everything. It will also cost each one of us who loves genuinely a lot. Christian love is not a sweet sensation. It involves suffering and pain, and often even martyrdom! We will never build a better world until we embrace the pain and sacrifice that inevitably go with Christian love, since we cannot make an omelette without breaking eggs.

Note that love for our friends and family is good, but it is not enough, because we will be paid back in some way. The love which can heal and redeem our broken world is the sacrificial love which Jesus modelled for us with his very life and death. The pains we bear and the sacrifices we make, in loving the most troublesome persons around us will not go in vain, for the Lord rewards every man for his righteousness and faithfulness. Yet we must bear it in mind that the reward does not always follow immediately, and we may not even see it in our lifetime. We can only bank on Jesus' promise that "the measure you give is the measure you will get back" (Luke 6:38). So, the good we do will come back to us.

Conclusion

Jesus once again confronted his disciples and confronts us with a radical choice: to live by the values of the world or the values of the kingdom, which include the fear of God, sacrificial love and forgiveness, mercy and compassion, kindness and generosity, as well as humility and non-violence. Jesus' admonition is simple and straightforward, namely, that we be merciful as our Heavenly Father is merciful.

Questions to Ponder

1. What will you say is the theme of today's readings?
2. What is the key point of St. Paul in the 2nd Reading (1 Corinthians 15:45-49), and what is the link (if any) with the Gospel message?
3. Why is the command to love so important in the Christian tradition?

Additional Reading

Isaiah 43:1-5; John 16:33; Philippians 4:6-7

8th Sunday of the Year

By Their Fruits Ye Shall Know Them

Readings: Sirach 27:4-7 | Psalm 92 | 1 Corinthians 15:54-58 | Luke 6:39-45

Summary:

We Christians are sent out as witnesses of Jesus (Matthew 28:19-20). We are called to live daily in accordance with the faith we profess and teach. Our conduct must be consistent with what we say we believe. As we proclaim our belief in the God of love, we cannot live by hate. As we proclaim our belief in the God of purity, we cannot engage in lives of impurity and unchastity. And as we proclaim our belief in the God of truth, we cannot be living a lie! Our practical lives must be consistent with all that we say we believe.

Synchronising Words and Actions

Our first reading reflects on human behaviour and the kind of hearts from which such behaviour emerges. The state of our hearts can be assessed by our words and actions, in the same way as one can assess a tree by its fruits. Jesus challenges his disciples and followers to live lives of integrity, and to produce the fruits of the new life which they have received, since it is the inner reality of a tree that is reflected in its fruits.

Bearing Fruit

Occasions of joy and satisfaction, provocation and frustration, disappointment and betrayal, and failure and loss, often bring out who we really are on the inside. Our readiness or otherwise to forgive hurts and let go of offences for example, or our excessive attachment to material possessions, will easily show the kind of persons we are. Our reluctance, and often our failure to defer gratification, does speak volumes about the quality of our Christian conversion, no matter what claims we make to the contrary.

The Place of Reflection and Meditation

It is important for us to spend time to reflect and to regularly look at ourselves, and to correct whatever needs to be corrected, because we cannot guide others if we are blind ourselves. This is why the Church recommends that we develop a habit of regular examination of conscience, especially before the close of each day, before we approach the Lord in the Eucharist, and as we prepare for the sacrament of reconciliation. Such self-examination is very critical, for as Socrates says, "An unexamined life is not worth living."

From the Abundance of the Heart...

Just as a good tree produces good fruit so does a good heart produce goodness. From a kind, loving heart we find kind words and kind deeds. From a humble heart we find words of truth, not self-adulation, self-flattery, or vainglory. On the other hand, violent and bitter words often reveal a heart full of bitterness or one poisoned with hate, for from the abundance of the heart the mouth speaks.

The Christian who lives like Jesus will reflect St. Paul's teaching that: When the perishable puts on *imperishability*, and the mortal puts on immortality, then "death is swallowed up in victory" (1 Corinthians 15:54-55). Jesus died and rose from the dead to give us abundant life: a life of selfless love, mercy, and compassion; goodness, kindness, and generosity; humility, obedience, and surrender; service and sacrifice for others; justice, peace, and non-violence; as well as brotherly concern, and human solidarity. To live in this way is to bear the good fruits of the resurrected life of the kingdom.

The moral authority to proclaim the Gospel comes from the truth we profess and the consistency of our words with our attitudes and our actions. Such consistency is a compelling testimony. This is what is required of Christians every time and everywhere. Such transparent reflection of gospel values in our conduct is what makes the gospel "believable" in every generation. Unfortunately, on account of the "sting of sin" which St. Paul refers to in the second reading, we fail now and again to reflect this consistency and transparency before the world.

"The wages of sin is death," says St. Paul, but Jesus has conquered this death for us. We are therefore admonished to "be steadfast, immovable, always excelling in the work of the Lord." Putting our faith into practice even in difficult and disconcerting times will be a powerful testimony before unbelievers. This is the way to build up the moral authority which Jesus demonstrates so abundantly. We are challenged today to emulate Jesus our teacher, and to be men and women of integrity with Jesus as our master and model.

Jesus' love is true, authentic, and selfless. We cannot claim to be his followers if our love is often selfish, self-serving, and exploitative. No disciple of Christ can be preaching conversion to others who is not himself or herself is not engaged in an ongoing process of self-examination, self-criticism, and conversion. We cannot criticize or judge others until we have done a good dose of self-assessment and self-criticism; until we have set for ourselves much higher standards than we set for others. We must ensure that we have taken the log from our own eyes before we become preoccupied with the speck in our neighbour's eyes.

To exact high standards on others while turning a blind eye on our own faults or readily finding excuses for our own poor performance is condemnable. Self-criticism is an essential part of genuine relations with other people. People will pay more attention to what we have to say when they can see that we are aware of our own shortcoming and that our criticism does not emerge from any sense of self-righteousness.

Conclusion

Jesus teaches us today that criticism must come from the store of goodness in our hearts. If such goodness is absent, then we are better off keeping silent, because sharing a bad heart will not lead to the conversion of anyone. Our vocation is not to be professional faultfinders and critics, because critics are hardly ever the ones who reform the world. We should put our houses in order first, before attempting to put someone else's house in order.

Questions to Ponder
1. Explain this text from our 1st Reading: "The fruit discloses the cultivation of a tree; so the expression of a thought discloses the cultivation of a man's mind."
2. What is the resurrection as believed by us Christians? Distinguish between "resurrection" and "resuscitation."
3. What do you understand by hypocrisy? In what ways could you be guilty of hypocrisy without knowing it?
4. How would you as a Christian tell the truth to people around you without taking away their dignity or leaving them humiliated?

Additional Reading
Galatians 5:19-23; James 2:14-17; 1 John 4:20

9th Sunday of the Year

The Exemplary Faith of a "Foreigner"

Readings: 1 Kings 8:41-43 | Psalm 117 | Galatians 1:1-2, 6-10 | Luke 7:1-10

Summary:

In the first reading King Solomon asks God to hear and answer the prayers of "foreigners" who come to believe in the God of Israel and pray to him for their needs. In the reading, Paul showed how astonished he was that the Galatians could so quickly succumb to the false teaching of the Judaizers who were insisting on circumcision for gentile converts. He then reasserts his authority as an apostle, and the authenticity of his message. The Gospel reading is an account of the spectacular demonstration of faith by a Roman Centurion, considered by the Jews as a "foreigner!" Jesus marvelled at the immensity of the Centurion's faith and presents him to all as a model of faith.

The Exemplary Faith of a "Foreigner"

In our first reading of today from the first book of Kings, Solomon presents one of the earliest indications of God's plan to extend his salvation to people of all nations. At the solemn dedication of the newly built Temple of Jerusalem, Solomon prayed that the God of Abraham, Isaac, and Jacob, will hear and answer the prayers of "foreigners" who from far and near will hear of the glory of the God of Israel, and come to believe in him.

At the beginning, the Israelites thought that God's promised salvation through the coming Messiah was only meant for Jews, and perhaps proselytes - those who converted to Judaism, who got themselves circumcised, and who kept strictly to all the laws and ritual prescriptions of the Jewish religion. However, towards the end of the Old Testament period, we begin to see the Psalmist and several prophets proclaiming the universality of the salvation to be wrought in the coming Messiah. Psalm 71:11 says that "all nations shall fall prostrate before you O Lord."

Among the prophets, Isaiah stands out as in several passages he speaks of all nations and all peoples coming to acknowledge and worship the God of Israel and sharing in the light that God sheds to enlighten all the people who had walked in darkness. In Isaiah 9:2 we read, "The people that walked in darkness have seen a great light." In Isaiah 2:2-4 he says, "In the days to come the mountain of the Lord's house shall be established as the highest of the mountains, and shall be raised above the hills; and all the nations shall stream to it…" And in Isaiah 56:6-7 he says, "And the foreigners who join themselves to the Lord…their burnt offerings and their sacrifices will be accepted on my altar; for my house shall be called a house of prayer for all peoples."

Thus, by the close of the Old Testament period, it had been made clear to many holy men and women that God's salvation is not limited to the Jews alone, but open to people of all nations, languages, and cultures. This is why in Luke 2:29-31, on beholding the child Jesus, the old man Simeon declared: "Master, now you may dismiss your servant in peace, according to your word; for my eyes have seen your salvation, which you have prepared in the presence of all peoples, a light to enlighten the Gentiles, and for glory to your people Israel."

Soon after Paul's dramatic conversion, he understood this all-inclusive dimension of Christian salvation, and the critical role he was to play in bringing the message to the Gentiles. This is why he got really upset when he discovered that the members of the Church he only recently established with the authentic message of Christ, were now listening to some hard core Judaizers who came in from Jerusalem, telling them that one could not benefit from Christian salvation unless he first gets circumcised and abides by all the customs and ritual practices of the Jews. Peter himself who was originally hesitant about admitting Gentiles into the Church got convinced by the events leading up to the conversion and baptism of Cornelius and his household. He declared in Acts 10:34-35 that "The truth I have come to recognise is that God shows no partiality, but that anyone of any nationality who fears him and does what is right, is acceptable to him."

The Gospel of today presents one such person, the Roman Centurion, who is supposed to be a "foreigner," but who fears God, and who does what is right, and whom Jesus presents as model of a person of faith. At a time when the Roman emperor conquered and occupied the entire Jewish territory, they stationed their army in companies of 100 soldiers (then known as *Century*) in each town, under a Commander that was known as a *Centurion*." The central character in today's story is one such Roman Centurion. He was a high official or representative of a regime that the Jews generally hated. So, he belonged to a group that was outside the Judeo-Christian tradition. But this Centurion was loved and trusted by the Jews. When his servant was critically ill and at the point of death, he sent Jewish elders to come plead with Jesus to heal his servant. And they did.

The emissaries told Jesus that he was a good and generous man who loved the Jewish people; and that he even built their synagogue for them. Jesus was on his way, when, close to the house the Centurion sent his friends to tell him: "Lord, do not trouble yourself, for I am not worthy to have you come under my roof; that is why I did not presume to come to you. But speak the word, and my servant shall be healed..." (Luke 7:6-7). When Jesus heard this, he was amazed at him, and turning to the crowd that followed him, he said, "I tell you, not even in Israel have I found such faith." And when those who had been sent returned to the house, they found the servant in good health. The Roman Centurion is the kind of person that King Solomon had in mind when he prayed that God's house will be open to foreigners who fear God and requested that God hear and answer them when they come and pray for their needs.

The central message of today is the universality of the saving mission of Christ. We are challenged to abandon our close-mindedness and narrow vision against "others," and adopt the disposition of "openness" to the good that is present in every race and culture. We are called upon to abandon our prejudices and biases about others whom we often do not know sufficiently and reach out to embrace all children of God – Jews and Gentiles, black and white, rich and poor, slum inhabitants and palace dwellers. When Jesus spoke the word to heal the servant of the Roman Centurion, he confirmed God's plan already indicated in the prayer of Solomon centuries earlier, that he would offer healing and salvation to all people.

God's vision of humanity is not an exclusivist or isolationist vision. It is an open vision. God's vision is one of universal acceptance. In offering salvation, God treats all human beings equally. The Gospel of Christ transcends all cultures. All human beings are offered the opportunity to be saved in Christ, irrespective of what their past has been. Jesus demonstrated this universality of God's love in his very life and his daily engagements. He loved public sinners who were considered outcasts (see the story of the call of Matthew the Tax Collector and the conversion of Zacchaeus in Matthew 9:9-13 and Luke 19:1-10 respectively). He loved people across ethno-racial and religious barriers (see the story of the Samaritan woman at the well in John 4:1-42). For the God revealed in Christ, there are no outsiders.

In Jesus' life and teaching, we see a very clear rejection of any form of ethno-religious bigotry and the illusions of racial superiority as were dominant among many Jewish contemporaries of Jesus and the Apostle Paul, and as we still witness today. Instead, Christians are people of universal salvation, a salvation that is destined for men and women of all times and places. Respect for the "other," who is different from us, as well as openness to the good that could be found in the foreigner, are core imperatives of Christian universalism. There is indeed the seed of the gospel in every person, and in every culture. There are good, loving, kind-hearted, God-fearing people, such as the Roman Centurion or *the Good Samaritan* in every culture. What is required of the Christian is openness of mind, and above all, openness of heart, to see God at work in those that our own cultural or religious group may consider "foreigners."

It is part of Jesus' civilisation of love, to bring together the scattered children of God, to reconcile warring parties, to pull down walls of division and build bridges across the rivers that block our loving acceptance of others. It is a Christian imperative to recognise and give witness to the fact that all human beings are children of the one God and Father of all. Christians must be the champions of this civilisation of love, which embraces everyone, and constantly rejects the learned prejudices of our families or our cultural and religious groups, which often lead to discrimination, multiple injustices, violence, and war.

The Roman Centurion in today's Gospel demonstrated such spectacular act of faith that Jesus was astonished, because "not even in Israel" did he find such faith. The Centurion's unusual faith and spirituality were not an abstract enterprise. They were expressed in humility and vulnerability before the person of Jesus; in openness to what he needed but did not deserve; in sensitivity to Jewish ritual customs; in love, kindness and compassion for his servant who was critically ill, and towards whom he showed the same concern as he would show a son; and finally, in generosity towards the Jews of Capernaum for whom he built a Synagogue.

Conclusion
Today, the Lord praises the Centurion and presents him as a model or an example of faith to his Jewish followers. The Church has since taken the Centurion's words of faith and put them on the lips of all who at every Eucharistic celebration approach the Lord in communion: *"Lord I am not worthy that Thou should come under my roof. But speak the word, and my servant shall be healed."* True, we are all unworthy. Yet the Lord in his mercy and compassion invites us all to communion with him. The God of Jesus Christ has no favourites. But anyone of any nationality or cultural group who fears God and does what is right, is acceptable to him.

Questions to Ponder
1. Attempt a one sentence summary of all the readings today.
2. What can we learn from the faith of the Centurion in the gospel passage?
3. What was Paul's complaint about the Galatians? Are today's Christians any better than the Galatians?

Additional Reading
Matthew 8:5-13; Mark 7:24-30; Acts 10:1-2; Romans 12:16.

10th Sunday of the Year

God's Compassionate Visitation

Readings: 1 Kings 17:17-24 | Psalm 30 | Galatians 1:11-19 | Luke 7:11-17

Summary:

We deal today with God's merciful and compassionate visitation to his people in times of intense suffering and pain. Ours is not a God who is incapable of feeling the suffering of his people. Our God is not "an un-moved mover." Instead, we have an affectionate God who is often "moved" or deeply affected by human suffering. He is a God who does not pass by in the face of suffering, but he intervenes directly or through the prophets.

God Visits to Save

The Old Testament is replete with accounts of God's visitation to save his people when they repented of their sins and cried out for help. Instances include:

- Exodus 3:7-10 - God saw their misery, heard their cry, and sent Moses with a charge to liberate them from their Egyptian taskmasters.
- Judges 3:9-11 – God sent Othniel to save his people from the Edomites into whose power they were given as punishment for their sins.
- Judges 3:15-30 - God sent Ehud to save the Israelites from the Moabites who enslaved, pillaged, and dealt ruthlessly with them.
- Judges 4-5 – God sent Deborah to deliver his people from the Canaanites.
- Judges 6-8 – God sent Gideon to help deliver his people from the Midianites.

- Judges 10-12 – God sent Jephthah to deliver his people from the Ammonites.
- Judges 13 -16 – God sent Samson to deliver his people from the Philistines.
- 1 Samuel 17 – God sent young David to deliver his people from the Philistines.
- Tobit 3 – God sent the Archangel Raphael to deliver his people from blindness and demonic possession.
- Daniel 13 – God sent Daniel to deliver innocent Susanna from unjust execution.

Many other accounts of how God constantly saved his people with power and compassion abound all through the Scriptures.

Today we are presented with the stories of Elijah and the widow of Zarephath, as well as Jesus and the Widow of Nain. A key lesson from these two stories is that only God has power to overcome death. Elijah was able to raise the son of the widow of Zarephath, and restore life to him, because he had access to divine power on account of his special relationship with God. Jesus on his part demonstrated that he is the lord of life, and has power over death, as he raised the son of the widow back to life.

Compassion and Jesus' Miracles

Jesus did not perform any of his miracles to show off his power. His miracles were always on account of compassion. He was out to do something to help suffering people. He was always roused to action and provoked to do something. Stirred inside by compassion, he moved physically to do something to alleviate the suffering he saw around him. The same thing should happen with us believers. If we are ever going to do some great compassionate act, we would first be stirred up on the inside. All the kind acts of godly men and women through the ages were often a result of this inner stirring. They were often spurred to action by some passion within, and then some action would take place on the outside.

Every miracle performed by Jesus emanated from the well of goodness, mercy and compassion inside him. He was full of sensitivity, empathy and consideration, and he was committed to wiping away tears from the faces of sufferers. He achieved this in today's Gospel by raising the widow's dead son back to life, bringing joy to her and to the mourners around her. It was Jesus' compassion that made the young man in the gospel story to rise and begin to speak. His compassion was not merely a feeling. It had concrete life-giving and life-affirming effects.

A Christian Challenge

The stories of Jesus' compassion should spur Christians into action. These stories should call us to true conversion, to become children of the God of compassion, and to be merciful as our heavenly father is merciful (Luke 6:36). We should seek to have the compassion which leads to concrete commitment to bring light where there is darkness, joy where there is sadness, relief where there is distress, and hope where there is despair.

Today's stories are about godly people who bothered about other people's sufferings and pains. The widow bothered about Elijah's hunger and offered the little she had. Elijah bothered about the widow's grief when her son died, and did something about it, to bring her comfort. Jesus bothered about the pain of the widow, and he did something about it.

This is a challenge for us Christians today. What do we do when we encounter people in concrete situations of need? What is our level of engagement in alleviating the suffering of the poor, the sick, the handicapped, and the victims of injustice? This Sunday's readings present us an opportunity to reflect on these critical questions.

Conclusion

The God of Abraham, Isaac, and Jacob is a God who visits his people in their time of need, to deliver them, to comfort them, to save them. In Jesus Christ, he is "Emmanuel," God with us. Jesus says, I will not leave you as orphans. Before ascending to the Father he told his disciples, "I am with you always, to the end of time." We should constantly comfort ourselves at times of distress that in Jesus Christ, the God of love who has always intervened to save his people, is always with us, ready to enlighten us when we find ourselves in the valley of darkness, ready to heal us when we are sick, and ready to raise us up when we slip into death.

Questions to Ponder
1. The widow of Zarephath learnt at least two lessons following the raising up of her son by Prophet Elijah. What are these lessons?
2. What point does St. Paul make in the 2nd Reading (Galatians 1:11-17)?
3. Think of a single word or a short phrase that captures the content of the 1st Reading and the Gospel.
4. What can you do to make those around you experience more of the love, mercy, and compassion of Christ Jesus?

Additional Readings
2 Kings 4:33-36; Acts 9:37; Hebrews 11:35-38

11th Sunday of the Year

Christ's Loving Forgiveness

Readings: 2 Samuel 12:7-10, 13 | Psalm 32 | Galatians 2:16, 19-21 | Luke 7:36-8:3

Summary:

Sin is the action of a person. But the person is much more than the sin. Sin does not define anyone. The sinner who is created in the image and likeness of God can always change or be transformed, to become holy. When a sinner hears the good news and he or she repents and turns to Christ, everything about him or her changes. He or she can now live the new life of Christ, in the Spirit.

Sin and the Challenge of Repentance

David was a privileged friend of God. God gave him victory over all his enemies. In a very dramatic way, God saved him from King Saul who went all out to kill him. God secured the entire kingdom under him, and David lived in peace. But once David became powerful, successful and prosperous, self-indulgence set in. He gave free reign to his lustful passions, and he became guilty of the most wicked and shameful acts of adultery and murder.

In a bid to cover the sin of adultery, David committed murder. But when confronted by the Prophet Nathan, David quickly acknowledged his sins and repented with all his heart (see Psalm 51). In response, the Prophet said to him: "The Lord on his part forgives your sins; you are not to die" (2 Samuel 12:13). Following his repentance and God's loving forgiveness, David retained his position, not only as king of Israel, but also as a man after God's heart. This is a graphic demonstration of the graciousness of our God.

The sinful woman in the Gospel showed her own repentance by passionate gestures of loving affection for Jesus. She was not ashamed to repent publicly, because she had encountered Jesus Christ and had been forgiven much. So she came back to thank him, and though she never uttered a word, her gestures said it all: She used her tears to wash Jesus' feet and wiped them with her hair. She covered his feet with kisses and anointed them with ointment. It was an extravagant public display of loving affection which touched Jesus profoundly, but it shocked Simon the host terribly. To her show of repentance, Jesus responded with those gracious words: "Your sins are forgiven" (Luke 7:48).

Jesus knew what kind of woman she was, but he graciously accepted her loving service. While others looked at the woman and saw sin and filth, Jesus looked at her and saw a wounded child of God in need of healing and forgiveness. The lesson for us is that with God the sinner has a future and not just a past. This is good news for all of us and a challenge for us who treat our neighbours as if they only have a past and not a future.

Jesus saw that the woman had already been sufficiently judged, condemned, humiliated, and punished by life. Even the eyes that were looking at her in derision already constituted enough humiliation. Jesus saw that what she needed at that moment was healing and not further condemnation.

When the Lord says that we should not judge so we may not to be judged, it is because he sees through us like an X-ray or scan machine. He knows us more than we know ourselves. We often just see the terrible act that a person has committed, and we confuse the act with the person, condemning the person along with the act. But while God hates sin, he continues to love the sinner.

What is Repentance?

Repentance, like faith, is a basic prerequisite for receiving salvation in Christ. Repentance is brokenness of heart which results from sincerely recognising that we have sinned, and a readiness to change, to turn around, and take the path of rectitude. True Christian repentance does not result simply out of fear of punishment, but a recognition that we have been unjust and unfaithful to one who loves us immeasurably and desires our utmost good. David was brought to repentance when Nathan skilfully reminded him of the horror of his sin against God. And following his sincere repentance, David's friendship with God was restored.

For true repentance to occur, there must be absolute sincerity on the part of the sinner. We need to own up to, and take responsibility for our sins, because we recognise that we are called to a life of holiness and wholeness, even as we make our way through this world of sin to our heavenly homeland. Both David and the sinful woman in the Gospel had to own up to and take responsibility for their sins, before friendship with God could be re-established. Acceptance of our responsibility for the sins we have committed, is the first stage in the process of repentance. It is only then that we can say with David: "Have mercy on me for I have sinned."

Love: The Most Subtle Form of Exorcism
By treating the sinful woman with kindness, Jesus helped her to believe in her own hidden goodness. Jesus' goodness towards her made her want to be like Jesus. It made her to recognise the inherent goodness in herself. By graciously accepting her humble gifts, Jesus put wind in her sails. If he had judged and condemned her, perhaps she could have sunk back deeper into darkness. But following the encounter with Jesus, she rediscovered her real potential for greatness, and began to live a new and a better life. She travelled further down the road with Jesus than any of those who had judged her.

Jesus tells his host (Simon) that he prefers the extravagant love of this public sinner to his own "cold welcome," and using the parable of the debtors, Jesus declares that this sinful woman is nearer to the heart of God than the self-righteous people around, for "the man who is forgiven little shows little love." It is much easier for us to label sinners, condemn them, and cast them away, than to help them out of their miserable state. To Simon's mind, the woman was beyond redemption; she was a sinner and would remain so forever.

Like Simon, many people today are not ready to give those who are seen as public sinners a second chance. Yet, a culture that does not give people a second chance is a callous culture that will see to the destruction of many. When we reject sinners, it is often because we are under the illusion that we are righteous ourselves, and we presume that we have been accepted into the privileged circle of those acceptable to Jesus. We fail to realise that we never help people to improve when we isolate them socially; but that instead social isolation is among the worst things that anyone can suffer.

With Jesus, however, it was different. He saw in the woman a sinner who could become a saint. He saw the woman's sincere repentance expressed in her humility, in her courage, in her love, in her service, and in her thirst for acceptance. He saw another side, a better side to her, and he affirmed that better side. Jesus dwelt not on the shame of the woman's past life, but on her future possibilities. He not only forgave her of her sins, but he also loved her. Thus, the encounter with Jesus would have become the most profound experience of her life. It is in the same way that Jesus relates to us. He sees our potential for the future, and not just our past.

After encountering Jesus' gratuitous mercy, the woman's joy and happiness knew no bounds. So, she poured out her gratitude in loving service. Her tears were tears of gratitude, not tears of repentance. What Jesus did with her highlights the truth that, indeed, love is the most subtle form of exorcism. Jesus has taught us that to love is to be light which dispels darkness. We must learn therefore to see and affirm the goodness in people. A lot of broken people can be healed with love and acceptance. Jesus has given us an example in today's gospel.

Love Expressed in Forgiveness
Forgiveness is a soothing balm to the troubled spirit. It is at the very heart of the mystery of the incarnation. The reason the Son of God came into the world is to forgive sins. So, forgiveness is at the heart of the Christian religion. If we do not forgive, we are simply saying that we do not accept that Jesus should come into our lives. God became man so that we may not perish, but that (through forgiveness) we may gain eternal life (see John 3:16; Romans 5:8 and Philippians 2:6-11). The new commandment of Jesus is for us to love one another (John 13:35). He taught us not to judge that we may not be judged, and to forgive so that we may be forgiven (Luke 6:37).

Jesus' teaching on forgiveness was so radically opposed to the status quo that Peter was completely confounded, coming as he was from a culture of "an eye for an eye, and a tooth for a tooth." So, Peter asked: "If a brother sins against me, how often must I forgive? As many as seven times?" Jesus responded: "Not seven but seventy-seven times" (Matthew 18:21-22). Jesus Christ did not just teach about forgiveness; he went about forgiving people. He forgave the woman caught in adultery (John 8:10-11). He forgave Peter who denied him (Luke 22:61). He forgave those who crucified him on the cross of Calvary (Luke 23:34).

Conclusion
We cannot make anyone change, unless we first accept them as they are and assure them that there is room for growth. Condemnation does not liberate people; it destroys them. Forgiveness on the other hand, heals, liberates, promotes positive change, brings out the best in people, and equips them for a new future.

Questions to Ponder
1. What is the overriding theme of today's readings?
2. Why do you think David remained a man after God's heart in spite of his heinous crimes?
3. What is the primary reason for which the Sinful Woman desperately wanted to meet Jesus?
   To seek salvation; To ask forgiveness of her sins; To show gratitude?
4. What does St. Paul mean when he says (in Galatians 2:20) "I live now, not my own life but the life of Christ who lives in me…" And how does this challenge your Christian life today?

Additional Reading
Micah 6:8; Matthew 7:1-5, 9:9-13; Luke 15:11-31, 19:1-10

12th Sunday of Year

Who Do You Say I Am?

Readings: Zechariah 12:10-11, 13:1 | Psalm 63 | Galatians 3:26-29 | Luke 9:18-24

Summary:

Every Christian ought to answer this question of who Jesus Christ is to him or her. In doing so we need to ask the Holy Spirit for inspiration, to be able to answer accurately, just as it happened with Peter. Such response should stem from what we know through our experiences of Jesus as opposed to what we have read or heard about him.

You are the Christ

Jesus Christ had been with his disciples for nearly three years. He was on his way to Jerusalem to suffer and to die. He went up to Mount Tabor where he was transfigured and was now at Caesarea Philippi. He turned and asked his disciples: "Who do people say the Son of Man is?" After hearing their responses about what people say of him – that he was John the Baptist, or Elijah, or one of the ancient prophets come back to life, Jesus directed the question to the disciples: But who do you say I am? Then Simon Peter spoke up and said: "You are the Christ."

By this response, Peter professes that Jesus is the Messiah, the promised one, the redeemer. He reveals that Jesus is the one about whom so much has been written. From the correctness of the response, Jesus knew that Peter did not come to this realization on his own accord. So, Jesus tells Peter that the answer was revealed to him from above.

The Person of Jesus

The question of who Jesus is to us personally is a very critical question because if we do not have a personal appreciation of Jesus' identity, we will not be able to live his life. We can only truly come to know Jesus through personal encounters and not solely by what we read and hear. It is critical to ask this question because who Jesus is to us will determine our relationship with him, which in turn will influence the way we live our lives and what choices we make.

It is interesting to note that after Peter's profound response to the question, he soon began to rebuke Jesus for announcing his impending passion and death. Peter reacted the way he did, because he did not fully understand the implications of the response he had given. In his very finite mind, he could not relate how the messiah, the promised one, could suffer so grievously and be killed. In fact, Peter was so focused on what he reasoned as "irrational" coming out of the mouth of Jesus, that perhaps he never heard the latter part of Jesus' statement, namely, that he will rise on the third day.

The answers the disciples gave showed that the people understood that Jesus belonged to the line of prophets. But the disciples on their part, knew that Jesus was much more than a prophet, though they did not fully understand what to make of his identity. And when Peter confessed that Jesus was the Messiah, the Christ of God, he must have held the traditional belief that the Messiah would be a great worldly king, a warrior who would save the Jews from Roman occupation, a powerful conqueror who would not be touched by suffering or defeat, and God's anointed who cannot be humiliated. There are Christians who even today still think of the Messiah in this manner of power and prosperity, and they often repudiate the cross. Yet, without a proper understanding of who the Messiah really is, people will never believe in Jesus beyond healing miracles and material prosperity.

The Cross of Jesus and the Cost of Discipleship
It is in order to help the disciples and ourselves to see our salvation in the crucified Christ that Jesus began to announce to them that the Messiah must suffer, that they must be prepared to share in his suffering, but that his suffering and theirs will ultimately lead to glory. Sadly, many Christians live as though they do not believe in the ultimate glory that comes after the cross. Like Peter who had to be

rebuked in very harsh terms by Jesus when he rejected the cross, many Christians still find the idea of the cross a very difficult one.

Jesus made it clear that we cannot be his followers if we refuse to understand the logic of the cross from which true victory comes, and if we refuse to take up our cross daily and follow him. And St Paul says that the cross represents the foolishness of God that is wiser than human wisdom, and the weakness of God that is greater than human strength (see 1 Corinthians 1:25).

It is the core teaching of Jesus that:
>To find your life – you must first lose it (Luke 17:33).
>To bear fruit – you must first die (John 12:24).
>To be exalted – you must humble yourself (Matthew 23:12).
>To be great – you must make yourself the least (Luke 9:48).
>To be first – you must be last and servant of all (Mark 9:35).

He demonstrated that suffering is inevitable. For committed Christians, suffering is not a probability, but a certitude. It is guaranteed, especially if we want to live godly lives in a corrupt, sinful world such as ours. We recall the statement in the book of Sirach (2:1) which says, "My child, if you aspire to serve the Lord, prepare for an ordeal." To live a consistent life of love and compassion, purity and humility, service and sacrifice, mercy and forgiveness, as well as peace and non-violence, in an evil society such as ours, will often amount to an ordeal, a cross. Yet Jesus does not compel anyone to carry this cross. It is for those who freely accept to follow him. That is why he says, "If anyone wants to be a follower of mine, he must deny himself, take up his cross and follow me" (Matthew 16:24; Mark 8:34 and Luke 9:23).

Conclusion
To love is to be prepared to suffer for the beloved. To be faithful to the values of Christ is to share his suffering, and it is only in this way that we will share his glory. It is in taking up our crosses as Jesus did that we live up to our true name as Christians. The Lord however does not ask that we submit to any pain in a fatalistic manner. We

must take all legitimate steps to remove pain and prevent unnecessary suffering. But when despite all efforts we are still faced with pain, then we must embrace it with Christian fortitude. This is what it means to carry our cross!

Questions to Ponder
1. What does St. Paul say is the basis of our unity and equal dignity as Christians?
   And what are the implications of this for us?
2. What are the virtues that make one a true hero?
   Identify your Christian heroes and the virtues that make them Christian heroes.
3. List three titles of Jesus Christ and explain your understanding of each one.
4. Who is Jesus for you?
   Whatever you believe Jesus to be, what difference does that make in the conduct of your life?

Additional Readings
Amos 8:10; Matthew 24:30; John 3:14ff, 17:21ff, 19:37; Romans 6:4; 13:14ff; Colossians 1:15, 18

13th Sunday of Year

No Turning Back

Readings: 1 Kings 19:16, 19-21 | Psalm 16 | Galatians 5:1, 13-18 | Luke 9:51-62

Summary:

Jesus Christ calls Christians the salt of the earth. The potency of salt in any dish is such that you do not require a handful of it to season the food. Just a pinch can make the difference. This is how potent Jesus Christ wants us to be, and we truly can if we decide to quit mediocrity and half-hearted commitment and take our faith seriously. We can transform anything and everything for Christ if we take our Christian conversion seriously and resolve to be in the world but not of the world.

Elisha's Call and His Response

Elisha was a successful farmer. He was happy with his life and career and never needed another. He was farming with his oxen when Elijah passed by, removed his cloak, and threw it over him. Elisha recognised immediately that he was being called by God to be a prophet and he answered the call readily and wholeheartedly. He ran after Elijah and bid goodbye to his past life.

As a pledge of his irrevocable decision, total acceptance, and whole-hearted commitment, he slaughtered his oxen and made a bonfire of his plough, using it to cook a meal for a send-off feast. This signifies that he had no intention whatsoever of going back to his former life. For Elisha, it meant no turning back!

The Road to Jerusalem

According to Luke 9:51, "When the days drew near for him to be taken up, Jesus set his face resolutely on the road to Jerusalem." Though aware that persecution and rejection, betrayal and condemnation, torture and violent death awaited him there. He was nevertheless determined to go up there to fulfil the mission for which he was sent into the world by his Father. He will not let anything distract him from seeing his purpose through.

Roads can be very important; they take us either to our destination or away from it. When we come out from our houses each time, we often decide which way to take, depending on where we are headed. This is very important because we are either on the right road, or we find ourselves on the wrong road. If we take the wrong road, we will not get to the right place.

Jesus was constantly on the right road. If he had listened to James and John, he would be on the wrong road. He was constantly heading in the right direction towards his destination. His road map was the will of his Father. He followed it faithfully, and he admonishes us to make the will of the Father our own road map too.

Jesus' Resolute Commitment
Jesus had to be focused and resolute as he headed for Jerusalem, because along the way there would be many distractions and temptations. For instance, what happened in that Samaritan village was a temptation and a distraction. Jesus could have stopped his journey momentarily and focused on dealing with these people or attending to the provocations. But he did not fall for any of the distractions. The Father gave him the task of bringing salvation to the world and he would not opt out until he accomplished it. His commitment was total. His 'Yes' to the Father was irrevocable. And like Jesus, we too are faced with temptations and distractions. Every day, we are tempted to take our gaze off where we are headed and focus on the distractions. Like Jesus, we should never allow ourselves to be distracted from our goal.

The Three Would-be Followers
Along the road to Jerusalem, Jesus meets three would-be followers. The first voluntarily offered to follow him, but Jesus saw the shallowness in him and simply laid the cost of discipleship bare before him: "Foxes have holes and birds of the air have nests, but the son of man has nowhere to lay his head."

In other words, he was saying that he had no home, or rather that his life is to be constantly on the road, and so the fellow should not nurse any illusions of material success, comfort, security or prosperity as possible benefits of being his disciple. We are not told if the man followed Jesus or not, but he most probably did not follow him.

The second fellow was called by Jesus, but he was reluctant to trust God and let go of the things he was attached to. By asking him to let the dead to bury their dead and giving him a new mission to go and spread the news of the Kingdom of God, Jesus resets his priorities.

Just like the first, the third fellow offered to follow Jesus but, like the second fellow, he had other things that were important to him, which he would rather do first, before coming to Jesus. Jesus' response that, "once the hand is laid on the plough, no one who looks back is fit for the kingdom of God," was a sound warning that following him requires total commitment and allows no room for other considerations.

Reading this passage should help us come to the realisation that the cost of Christian discipleship is very high indeed. Many Christians are yet to come to grips with this reality. We have often been part of a cultural Christianity that makes little demands on followers. We have often carried on with our numerous this-worldly attachments and addictions, while claiming to be Christians. We have often remained lustful, unforgiving, self-centred, proud and sometimes even vengeful and hateful, and yet we call ourselves disciples of Christ.

But following Jesus demands much more than going to Church regularly and engaging in some routine devotional activities. The decision to follow Jesus is a radical, life-transforming one. We cannot embrace Christianity on our own terms or by our own human standards. Jesus demands a radical discipleship that recognises the cost, and yet is determined to go the whole way and not look back.

The Challenge of Radical Discipleship

There is a dramatic urgency in the message of Jesus. For those who accept him, it cannot be business as usual. The disciple must place the values of the kingdom as a matter of the highest priority. In following

Christ, nothing should be allowed to distract us, not even such matter of high value in the human society as attachment to wife, husband, parents and children. Thus, to follow Jesus is to die to self and all the cravings of the flesh, including such legitimate cravings as the love of parents and children. The Lord says, "What shall it profit a man to gain the whole world and lose his soul?" Jesus does not accept half-hearted followership. Christian disciples must be fully available and must give the new commitment their all.

Conclusion

Part of the reason why many people changed their names or took up new names when they became Christians, was to indicate or highlight their totally new identities in Christ. Thus, answering the call to Christian discipleship requires whole-hearted commitment, total fidelity, intense focus, undivided attention, and immense discipline. It requires that all our resources be channelled towards the task of living out and promoting the values of the kingdom of God. Such radical discipleship however promises to be very rewarding and fulfilling, notwithstanding the hardship it entails.

Questions to Ponder

1. When St. Paul says in Galatians 5:1, 13-18, "It is for freedom that Christ set us free..." What does he mean? Free from what? Free for what?
2. The 2nd Reading urges us to walk by the Spirit and not to gratify the desires of the flesh.
   What is "the Flesh?" What is "the Spirit?"
3. How do the following statements of Jesus challenge your Christian commitment: "Foxes have holes... Leave the dead to bury... No one who puts his hands on the plough...?"
4. From today's Gospel story what can we learn about the true Christian attitude in the face of aggression and provocation?

Additional Reading

Matthew 6:33, 13:44-46, 19:16-22; Mark 1:16-20; Galatians 2:20; Philippians 1:21

14th Sunday of Year

Be Ambassadors of Peace

Readings: Isaiah 66:10-14 | Psalm 66 | Galatians 6:14-18 | Luke 10:1-12, 17-20

Summary:

In the first reading, Isaiah prophesied about the prosperity of Jerusalem and the good times that lie ahead for God's people. In his letter to the Galatians, St Paul explains that he is a new creation in Christ. And the Gospel reading from Luke is about Jesus sending out the 70 disciples on a mission to preach and bring tidings of peace to all the people they meet.

Isaiah: Messenger of Peace and Glad Tidings

At a time of great suffering and tribulation, Prophet Isaiah gives the very cheering prophesy we come across in our first reading. Isaiah did not live at a time when Israel was flourishing, and everything was going well. He lived at the time when Israel was suffering and undergoing great tribulation, and he proclaimed: "All who have cried and mourned for Jerusalem, rejoice, for your time has come; You will be held in the laps of your mother and cuddled like a baby" (Isaiah 66:10-14).

In fulfilment of that prophesy, Jesus emerged on the scene and announced in Luke 4:18-19, that the Spirit of the Lord was upon him and that he has come to open the eyes of the blind, to bring good news to the afflicted, to heal the broken-hearted, to set the oppressed free, and to proclaim the Lord's year of favour. He went about instructing the ignorant, healing the sick, and freeing people from the bondage of Satan, and from oppressive social structures. He announced that he has come that we may have life in abundance (John 10:10).

Sending of the Seventy Disciples

Having stayed with the disciples for a while, it was now time to send them out to proclaim to others the good news of the Kingdom which they have heard. Note that it is not the twelve apostles that were sent, but 70 disciples, who belong to the generality of his followers. All those who receive the good news of Jesus immediately become missionaries. To receive Jesus is to be sent on a mission, to proclaim the truth of salvation that one has received. As Christians, we receive the light of Christ and we feed at his table. To receive the Light of Christ is to become light to others. This is why Jesus says in Mathew 5:14, "You are the light of the world." And to feed at the Lord's table, to eat the bread of life, is to become bread broken for others.

For their missionary journey, the disciples were to carry no purse, haversack, or spare tunics. They were to salute no one on the road, so that they will not be distracted by the exchange of greetings and pleasantries. They were to eat whatever was set before them. They were to stay in whichever house welcomed them (and not move from house to house). To carry no purse and no haversack means that they were to travel light. They were not to put their trust in any worldly securities and possessions, but to rely completely on what providence will provide, including the hospitality of total strangers that the Lord himself will arrange.

Lessons from the Missionary Task

In addition to travelling light, we also learn that the missionary task is a very urgent one. Jesus told them to start off now, to go quickly, to waste no time saluting people and surveying different menus. All that will be time-wasting! Jesus knew that he didn't have much time. He knew that he must rely on the talents and the understanding of his followers. He also knew that the territory out there is rough and tough. That is why he said: "I send you like lambs among wolves." To survive, one must lead the radical lifestyle of the wandering preacher with the right discipline and focus, staying committed to the cause.

Upon their return the disciples rejoiced that the people welcomed the message of salvation which they bore. They rejoiced that they never lacked anything, that the devil submitted to them when they used the name of Jesus, and that their mission was very successful.

The Harvest is Rich, but the Labourers are Few
Our God is the God of all goodness, yet, today's world is torn apart by human greed and selfishness, wickedness and vengeance, violence and crime, as well as multiple tragedies. The moral fabric of the human society is ripped asunder by social injustice, indiscipline, and promiscuity. Religion, for many, is no more than a series of empty rituals. Many carry on without the fear of God. Others are devoted to the cult of mammon, pursuing worldly power and sensual pleasure without restraint. Unfortunately, the Christian virtues of love, forgiveness, compassion, humility, frugality, and purity of heart seem no longer to have a place in the life of many. While some have never really heard the good news of salvation, others unfortunately are being fed with chaff by rogue preachers.

Many have no sense of purpose and meaning, and they are losing their way. Others are dwelling in darkness and living destructive lives. We are witnesses to human suffering on a large scale in many societies: the sick are often unattended, the handicapped are often neglected, poor children are often abandoned to the streets, widows and orphans often have no social security, there is widespread youth unemployment, the urban poor are condemned to the slums in many of our cities, and the suffering victims of the growing criminality in many societies often find little or no support. The harvest is indeed rich, but the labourers are few.

We are all called to be labourers in the Lord's Vineyard: gatherers and harvesters, witnesses of God's love amid selfishness and hate, peacemakers amidst violent conflicts, truth bearers amidst falsehood and deceit, bridge-builders amidst widespread division and dissensions, and healers and comforters amidst sick and distressed people.

All who have truly encountered Jesus must get involved in the urgent task of saving the world from sin, corruption, violence and death. The Lord wants us to share with others what we have received from him. Those Christ sent out in today's gospel were the simple followers, not the apostles or the "specialists." So, work in the Lord's vineyard cannot be left to those that may be called "specialists" – the Priests and Pastors. A real relationship with Christ must bear fruit in evangelisation. It must impact positively on others, and lead to the dissemination of Kingdom values.

Ambassadors of Peace

Jesus says, "When you enter any house let your first words be 'Peace to this house'." As disciples we are meant to be ambassadors of peace and reconciliation in a world of conflict and division, promoters of love and forgiveness in a world of hatred and vengeance, champions of human dignity and non-violence in a world of violence and human degradation, agents of truth and justice in a world of widespread falsehood and injustice, and messengers of healing and restoration in a world of sickness and pain. We must realise that there are things which will remain undone if we don't do them, and so we must now and again ask ourselves what we are doing in the world and in the Church for Christ's sake.

Conclusion

We have reflected upon the cheering prophecy of Isaiah at a time of great distress in Israel. Jesus came to fulfil this prophecy and sends out his disciples to go spread the message of salvation – to heal the sick, to liberate captives, to cast out demons, to preach the good news to the poor, and to declare the Lord's year of favour. If we follow the disciples' example who, in their missionary journey, obeyed Jesus' instructions, our own missionary enterprise will be equally successful.

Questions To Ponder

1. St Paul says: *"Far be it from me to glory, except in the Cross of our Lord Jesus Christ."* What does he mean? And how does this statement challenge you?
2. Identify 2 or 3 elements that link today's Gospel very closely with last Sunday's Gospel passage.
3. What do you think Jesus meant when he said: *"Do not rejoice that the (evil) spirits are subject to you, but rejoice that your names are written in heaven"*?

4. List some of the ways in which we Christians are being called to be messengers of Christ's peace to the men and women of our country today.

Additional Reading
Matthew 16:24-26, 28:19-20; Mark 16:14-20; John 14:27

15th Sunday of Year

The Good Samaritan

Readings: Deuteronomy 30:10-14 | Psalm 19 | Colossians 1:15-20 | Luke 10:25-37

Summary:

Religion is supposed to be a way of life, and religious values are supposed to inspire the whole of one's life. But there is always the great danger of separating the love of God from the love of neighbour, and of disconnecting religion from life, prayer from active love of neighbour, and Sunday worship from life during the rest of the week. Such religiosity is a distortion, and such worship is worthless. For Jesus Christ, meeting critical human needs is an integral part of honouring God and fulfilling the law.

The Priest, the Levite and the Despised Samaritan

The Samaritans were at the very bottom of the Jewish social classification. They were the outcasts, seen by the Jews as impure, and as people who are never to be mixed with. Relating closely with Samaritans was thought to defile practicing Jews. Yet, it is one of these despised people that did what was right for the man who was robbed, wounded, and left to die on the side of the road between Jerusalem and Jericho.

When the Samaritan came along and saw the wounded man, his heart went out to the wounded man. The Samaritan did not bother to find out who the man was. All he saw was a wounded man, a man in pain, and he knew he just could not walk away. He momentarily forgot that he was of a despised race, and he forgot his destination, and he gave his all to save the wounded man. Before him, two highly respected individuals had come across the wounded man. The first of the two, a priest who may not necessarily be a bad man, saw the dying man and passed by on the other side, for fear of getting defiled. He decided not to risk being contaminated by blood, because that would have rendered him ritually unclean and therefore unfit to offer sacrifices, until he goes through a rite of purification.

The second, a Levite, reacted in the same way as the priest, because Levites belong to the priestly clan also. So, these two categories of people who belong to the highest levels in the social hierarchy of the Jews, quickly walked away from a man who was badly injured and needed help, because of the consequences of stopping and rendering help. But the Samaritan who was the next person to come along on the way recognised that it is not possible to live a good life without taking any risk. And Jesus told the lawyer who asked the question about neighbourliness to "go and do likewise."

Means to Eternal Life

Jesus must have shocked his listeners when he projected the despised Samaritan as the more truly religious person in the scenario presented. He demonstrated that the Samaritan was the one who was more certainly on the path to eternal life, and this would have been highly provocative to his Jewish adversaries.

What Jesus is saying with this story is that eternal life is not guaranteed by mere adherence to ritual prescriptions, but by godly conduct. Godliness is in the heart and the state of our heart is often reflected in our behaviour. Godliness is best expressed in concrete acts of love, mercy, and compassion. So, Jesus is teaching us that the way to eternal life is to love as God loves, to show compassion as God shows compassion, and to have mercy as God has mercy.

Our various devotional and ritual engagements as Christians, such as regular prayer, participating in the sacraments and other devotional activities, etc., are all supposed to help us become more loving, more merciful, and more compassionate. They are not ends in themselves. Unfortunately, these ritual activities often appear to become ends in themselves, when those actively involved in them do display sufficient evidence of the godliness that is supposed to result.

The Samaritan was not known to be religious. But he had a heart full of mercy and compassion. His conduct was godly, and so according to Jesus, he was squarely on the path of eternal life. It is his merciful and compassionate heart that earned him the title, "Good Samaritan," especially when compared to the Jewish religious elite, as represented by the priest and the Levite in the story. Jesus uses this parable to highlight the self-righteousness and hypocrisy of the Jewish religious elite.

Love of God and Love of Neighbour: Two Faces of Same Coin

It is not possible to love the God that we cannot see when we do not love the neighbour that we can see. In his new commandment of love, Jesus brings together two Old Testament injunctions (Deuteronomy 6:5 and Leviticus 19:18) that sum up the entire law. Thus, for Jesus, there are only two commandments: to love God and to love those that are dear to God. The two are so closely linked that one cannot exist without the other and one cannot be fulfilled without the other.

The Pharisees and Scribes often laid too much emphasis on the external observance of the law, including their elaborate ritual prescriptions, but they were often very deficient in what Jesus called the weightier matters of the law, which include the fear of God, as well as love and compassion towards the neighbour (see Matthew 23:23). Loving God is not only to be expressed in rituals but more importantly in loving those whom God loves, making people who are important to God equally important to us.

Vertical and Horizontal Dimensions of the Law

The Judeo-Christian religion presents both vertical and horizontal dimensions of what should be the believer's faith practice. The vertical dimension is represented in faith and trust in the one true God, union with him through prayer and meditation, community worship, the practice of the sacraments, as well as the discipline of fasting and abstinence. The first three commandments of the old law could be said to sum up these requirements.

The horizontal dimension is about our relationship with others. It entails loving solidarity with our neighbour, expressed in care, concern and sensitivity; truth, fairness, and justice; mercy, forgiveness, and compassion; generosity, kindness, and patience; humility, meekness, and selflessness; purity, chastity, and modesty; peacefulness, mellowness of spirit, and working for peace and non-violence, etc. The last seven commandments of the old law do contain several prescriptions covering these areas. The two dimensions are so closely linked that it is impossible to be truly faithful in one area, while being negligent in the other area. To love God is to love those that God loves, and to love and care for those that God loves, is to love God.

Conclusion
Ritual observances are critical elements of religious practice. They often demonstrate our love for, and submission to God. Yet with the Good Samaritan story, Jesus teaches that now and again some urgent human needs may take precedence over those ritual observances, because the Sabbath was made for man and not the other way round. Coming to the aid of a neighbour in distress, showing love, care and compassion, etc., should often be given priority over the observance of ritual prescriptions (See Luke 10:25-37 and Mark 2:23-27). Loving our neighbour as ourselves is not an additional commandment. It is not an optional extra. It is part and parcel of loving God!

Questions to Ponder
1. What is it that makes the commandment to love God and neighbour a new commandment, when the two elements were already in the Old Testament? What is really new about it?
2. What is neighbourliness and who is a neighbour according to Jesus? To whom are you being a neighbour today? And how?
3. "Every Good Samaritan is contributing to the realisation of Jesus' kingdom in the world." Discuss.
4. Our country today presents numerous opportunities for us to show Christian love, care, and compassion. List some of these opportunities.

Additional Reading
Exodus 20:1-17; Deuteronomy 6:5; Leviticus 19:18;
Acts 10 :34-35 ; 1 John 4:16.

16th Sunday of the Year

Welcoming Jesus in Contemplative Silence
Readings: Genesis 18:1-10a | Psalm 15 | Colossians 1:24-28 | Luke 10:38-42

Summary:

Our first reading shows how Abraham was hospitable to three strangers, not knowing that he was entertaining God himself! His generosity was rewarded with the good news that his wife will conceive and have a son. In the second reading St. Paul tells us that he rejoices in his many sufferings for the sake of the Gentiles to whom he has been sent as steward of the great mysteries of salvation. The gospel story contrasts the attitude of the two sisters who hosted Jesus at Bethany - Martha and Mary. While Martha was engrossed in activities that are aimed at entertaining Jesus, Mary was engaged in quiet devotion. And when Martha complained that Mary was not helping her to do the chores, Jesus responded that "Mary has chosen the better part and it will not be taken from her."

Welcoming Jesus in Contemplative Silence
The Christian Scriptures teach us with several stories what it means to welcome the Lord. Often the Lord appears in the form of a weary stranger or traveler. When such a stranger is welcomed with generosity, kindness, and utmost attention, abundant blessings follow. One of such episodes in the Old Testament is the encounter between Abraham and the three angels in Genesis 18:1-10. Another episode is the visitation of the widow of Zarephath by Prophet Elijah in I Kings 17:7-24. In both cases the stranger was given a warm welcome and generously entertained. The result in the case of Abraham is the promise of a son from his wife Sarah, and in the case of the poor widow of Zarephath, it was an end to the prolonged draught that had devastated the land, and the raising back to life of the widow's son.

Following immediately after the story of the Good Samaritan, the Evangelist Luke records the visit of Jesus to the house of his friends Martha and Mary in Bethany, just three miles away from Jerusalem, where he was going to face utmost rejection and eventually a brutal death. At the time of his visit to Bethany, Jesus had become a "persona non grata" for Jewish officials and many individuals who did not want to run into trouble. More and more people would rather not associate with him because of his unconventional ways and what they see as unorthodox teaching. He had become a security risk, his life constantly threatened.

Martha and Mary however welcomed Jesus into their home with all excitement. The young women demonstrated their love for Jesus in different ways. Mary just sat at the feet of Jesus, like a disciple in the presence of a Rabbi, listening attentively to what the teacher is saying, watching the expressions on his face, and contemplating his words. Martha on the other hand was active, very active. She was running up and down between the kitchen and the store and the living room where Jesus was. She was reaching out for warm water to wash his feet and cold water for him to drink. She was all over the kitchen making sure that in no time food will be ready for their honoured guest. She was running breathless, fussing and fretting, and becoming overwhelmed with the chores, such that she was getting irritated about her sister Mary, who just sat there with Jesus, letting her alone do all these chores.

Martha eventually complained to Jesus, who, to her astonishment said that "Mary has chosen the better part," after reproaching her for worrying and fretting over many things, when only few are needed. He told her that in all her fret and fuss, she had forgotten the one thing that was necessary, which is listening to what the Lord had to say. For Jesus, Mary exemplifies the true disciple, hearing the word and pondering upon it, while in Martha the word faced the risk of being choked by the cares and worries of the world.

From Contemplation to Social Activism

The Martha-Mary comparison in this gospel story has a powerful lesson to teach us: That service or social activism must spring from contemplating the face of God, hearing His word, and reflecting upon it. This episode in the Gospel of Luke comes immediately after the

Good Samaritan story, as if to balance the teaching on service. Referring to the Good Samaritan who stretched himself to help an unknown victim, Jesus says, "Do this and you will live." Indeed, the love of neighbour as oneself flows from and is inspired by the love of God with all one's heart, soul and might. Social activism can become empty and devoid of meaning if the Christian loses focus on the essential element of Christianity, which is the practice of the presence of God, otherwise called prayer. To serve in a manner that one becomes distracted by one's service, is to lose touch with the "better part."

Jesus appreciated the role of both Martha and Mary. The running around of Martha was surely a sign of her love for Jesus, of her faith in him, and of her hope in the salvation that comes through him. Martha was contributing immensely to the great task of "welcoming" Jesus. In her own way, she was being the "Good Samaritan" to Jesus who was at this time facing rejection on many fronts. But when she started condemning her sister for not joining her in her activism, Jesus had to speak out in defense of Mary.

We need many *Marthas* in our world today. But we need even more *Marys* who know how to be in the presence of God, and how to listen to his word and be guided by it. Too many people today are anxious and troubled about many things, but as Jesus says, only few are important. Jesus does not want his disciples to be troubled. He wants them to live lives of serenity, contentment and quiet submission to his word and his will. He warns his disciples against allowing the cares of this world to stifle the word (Luke 8:14). He says they should not be anxious about what they will eat or put on (Luke 21:34ff). He says they should remember that man does not live on bread alone (Luke 4:4). On one occasion when he had not eaten for a long time, and his disciples were worried about him, he answered them: "My food is to do the will of the One who sent me" (John 4:34).

Disciples of Jesus are challenged today to slow down a little. We need quality time to be in touch with ourselves and with our God. But the men and women of the 21st Century often find it difficult to slow down, to stop and to pray. This is perhaps because we are often so preoccupied with achievement, so busy acquiring goods and techniques, and so distracted by the objects of our adventure that we hardly have time to be in touch with the depth of our being, where alone we could connect with God who is our Creator and ultimate Sustainer. Many of us today live very empty and restless lives. Urged on by the profit motive, and sustained by an aggressively competitive and consumerist culture, we often fill our day with too many appointments and engagements, leaving no room for wholesome relaxation and reflection. We rush from one appointment to the other and we do not seem to know when to stop, except when we are suddenly halted down by a major illness.

We find all sorts of excuses for not praying: our appointments, our jobs, our studies, etc. Even Sundays have become difficult to observe as days of rest. We rush into Church a minute or two before Mass starts and dash away as quickly as possible once the priest says, "The Mass is ended," as if all the while we were in prison. Sundays are filled up with so many activities that for many of us, they are like any other day of the week. In this way we are increasingly alienated from the source and centre of our being. No wonder the widespread sense of emptiness, futility and despair among some of the most successful men and women in our day. No wonder the increasing phenomenon of depression in the population.

It is clear that human beings have an inner hunger and thirst that only God can quench, and this can only happen when we find time to rest in him. As St. Augustine says, "You have made us for yourself O Lord, and our hearts are restless until they rest in you." Thus, to pray is to desire intimacy with God. To pray is to rest in the presence of the Lord. To pray is to contemplate the face of God. To pray is to listen to God. Therefore, the men and women of our generation who desire meaning, fulfilment and peace, must learn how to slow down, how to stop, how to listen, and how to pray.

Conclusion

From the story of Mary and Martha, the Lord teaches today, that the one thing necessary in our lives is love, love shown both in contemplation and in action. It must be the kind of love that springs from contemplation and expresses itself, foremost, in outgoing hospitality. It is our love for God that should inform our love for others.

Questions to Ponder
1. What is the dominant theme in today's readings?
2. What is the link (if any) between the 1st Reading and the Gospel passage?
3. Paul rejoices in his many sufferings for the sake of the Gospel (Colossians 1:24-28). In what way can the pains and sorrows I suffer today be turned unto good?

Additional Reading
Proverbs 19:17; Luke 19:1-10; Acts 28:7-8; Philippians 2:14-15; Hebrews 13:1-2

17th Sunday of the Year

Teach Me to Pray

Readings: Genesis 18:20-32 | Psalm 138 | Colossians 2:12-14 | Luke 11:1-13

Summary:

The Lord's Prayer is the first and greatest of all Christian prayers. It contains the basic elements of Christian prayer – worship and petition. It also highlights the basic dispositions of submission and surrender, and the child-like trust and confidence required of a praying Christian. It is important to note that the whole prayer is couched in plural terms. Thus, it is not "my" father but "our" father, and this implies that we are children of the same father.

Abraham Haggles with God

Genesis 18 portrays Abraham as an intimate friend of God with whom the Lord could share his thoughts and plans. The reading portrays Abraham as a shrewd negotiator engaged in some kind of "Dutch auction" with God over Sodom and Gomorrah, something one can only do with a very familiar person, not with someone you have only a formal relationship with. Abraham proved himself a persistent and an untiring intercessor who will not give up easily. He took advantage of his relationship with God and, by sheer persistence and near blackmail, he got his generous friend – God – to agree that if there existed even as few as ten righteous people in the city of Sodom and Gomorrah, the city will not be destroyed.

A God Who Hears and Responds

In this passage, God is portrayed as a listening friend, a patient dealer, and a merciful and compassionate judge. This is a radically different image of God than people were used to, and it is quite close to the image of God the Father painted for us by Jesus Christ. He is a God who can be moved by a friend's pleading to change his cause of action. He heard the cry of the Israelites, saw their miserable plight, and took action to deliver them (Exodus 3:7-10); he sent Isaiah to King Hezekiah and before Isaiah finished delivering his message, Hezekiah pleaded, and God changed his mind and made him well (2 Kings 20:1-6). Paul and Silas prayed and sang, then the Holy Ghost came down, and they were miraculously freed from prison (Acts 16:25-28). Many other examples abound in the Scriptures where God was moved to action in the face of suffering and pain. We are constantly being saved by a generous God.

Lord Teach Us to Pray

The disciples noticed how close Jesus was to God the Father. They often saw him withdraw to pray, usually very early in the morning, long before dawn (see Mark 1:35). The disciples did not know the content of his prayer because he often prayed in silence, but they suspected that his unique power could be linked to those moments spent in prayer. So, they said to him, "Lord, teach us to pray as John taught his disciples." Jesus then taught them the Lord's Prayer. Also known as the 'Our Father,' the Lord's Prayer is a model prayer, a perfect and complete prayer.

No one knows how to pray very well, because none of us can be an expert in the presence of God. Jesus asks that we do not be like the Scribes and the Pharisees who use many words, but that we lock ourselves up in our rooms as we talk to our Father who hears in secret. Prayer is about aligning our wills to the will of God, and our hearts to the heart of God, believing that those who leave everything in God's hands will eventually see God's hand in everything, recognising with St. Paul that, "All things work together unto good for those who love God."

Trust in a Loving Father

Jesus wants his disciples to see prayer as a filial experience. He wants us to relate with God as "father" with the confidence of children who know that they have a loving father. Jesus wants Christians to be bold, courageous, and audacious as they approach their loving Father in prayer. His model of a smart Christian is one who keeps knocking at God's door and never quits. Jesus maintained a close loving relationship with the father, and he wants us to have the same quality of relationship with our God. The God revealed to us by Jesus is the God of love. He is One who loves to hear us and who loves to speak to us. We must, therefore, keep on asking, keep on seeking, and keep on knocking. He will answer us. He will give us the best things at the right time. The example of Abraham and the lesson of Jesus should make us to pray with trust, knowing that our loving God has a plan for us and is leading us by the hand.

The Art of Listening in Prayer
Christian prayer should be a conversation with God which flows from a relationship of love with him and submission to his will. The praying Christian is one who knows how to pour out his or her heart to God, listen to hear God respond, and rise up from prayer, comfortable with God's will. This is what happened at the garden of Gethsemane. Jesus poured out his heart: "If it is possible let this cup pass from me…" But after shedding tears, he surrendered to, and he was comfortable with God's will. He then declared, "…let your will, not mine, be done." Whatever time we spend in prayer should leave us feeling better off than before we began, having been in the presence of God.

Conclusion
At the heart of Christian prayer lies the preparedness of the Christian to accept his or her lowly state. The acknowledgement that we are only handmaids of the Lord, and that we often do not know what is best for us, is key to successful prayer life. So, we must rely on him to give us our daily bread, whatever that daily bread will be. The praying Christian must acknowledge that God is all-powerful, all-loving, and all-caring, and that God knows best.

Questions to Ponder
1. Make a brief summary of last Sunday's message on Jesus' visit to Martha and Mary.
2. After reflecting on all we discussed last Sunday, how would you now define Christian Prayer?

3. What does Abraham's prayer and God's response in today's 1st Reading reveal to you about Abraham's relationship with God, and how does this challenge your faith?
4. When we say in the Lord's Prayer: "Your Kingdom come. Your will be done…" What do we really mean? What are the implications of this part of the prayer for your daily life?

Additional Reading
Exodus 3:7-10, 32:7-14; 1 Samuel 3:1-14; 2 Kings 20:1-6; Matthew 6:5-8; Philippians 4:6-7

18th Sunday of the Year

Vanity of Vanities

Readings: Ecclesiastes 1:2; 2:21-23 | Psalm 90 | 9-11 | Luke 12:13-21   Colossians 3:1-5,

Summary:

Wise people of all ages have constantly grappled with the fundamental question of the meaning of life and the puzzling reality or mystery of death. Men and women of thought have constantly asked: Why are we alive? Why do we have to die? Is death the end of everything? If we are born only to die, then why be born at all? What is the meaning of life? What is the purpose of human existence? These are fundamental questions highlighted in the first reading, and on which Jesus throws some light in today's gospel, when he encountered a man who had a dispute with his brother over the sharing of their father's estate, and the parable of the rich fool which Jesus told.

The Purpose of Life

Quoheleth, the author of Ecclesiastes, a wise man who lived for a long time, deals with the fundamental question of the meaning of life and the purpose of human existence with all its toil, sweat, and eventual death. With us humans, the certainty of death is ever present. Philosophers of all ages and creeds have spent a lot of time reflecting on the meaning of life and the mystery of death.

For Quoheleth, all of life's ambition, preoccupations and accomplishments, do not make sense. It all amounts to vanity, futility, and emptiness. Unless there is some purpose to life which transcends death, then life itself is meaningless. Quoheleth was not sure what this purpose was. The human mind abhors mortality and annihilation, hence the enormous efforts people invest in the attempt to perpetuate themselves. There is a profound longing deep within each one of us for immortality – to live forever. In the face of the inscrutable reality and certainty of death, we instinctively work towards living on, either through procreation or through some spectacular achievements or legacy building.

Greed and Avarice Amount to Idolatry

Jesus had just finished one of his teaching sessions when a man from the crowd came up and asked him to intervene in an inheritance dispute with his brother. But Jesus refused to be dragged into any controversy over material goods. The man had a legitimate complaint and he saw this big Rabbi who could authoritatively speak to his brother and get the matter sorted out. But the man got a reaction he least expected from Jesus, who started cautioning him about not putting his trust in material goods or seeking meaning in worldly possessions. Then he turned and warned the crowd around him (and ourselves too), to beware of becoming prisoners of greed and slaves of acquisitiveness as well as inordinate ambition for worldly power and security, which often amount to idolatry (see Colossians 3:5; Ephesians 5:5).

The Rich Fool in today's parable did not only put his trust in his possessions but he was also determined to use them exclusively for his own benefit. He was a very selfish man who cared only for himself alone and saw no link between his fortune and the fortunes of others. He saw no link between his bumper harvest and the plight of others.

Greed and Avarice Amount to Death

Not to care about others is to be a living dead. The Rich Fool, though alive was already dead. All that God did at the end of the story was simply to pronounce the reality. He was a walking corpse just like the Prodigal Son whom the father said was dead when he was wasting away with greed and self-centredness. He only came back to life when he returned home to his father.

The cause of the dispute between the two brothers is greed for possessions. This divided the two brothers, and such greed continues to wreak havoc between brothers and sisters, parents and children, husbands and wives, and one group against the other, even today. Stories abound of many rich people, whose families have been torn apart by the wealth left behind at their demise, because of greed and avarice.

The sin of the Rich Fool was not that he had a bumper harvest, but that he thought only of himself. Rather than share, he hoarded his goods and forgot his obligations to the poor. He forgot that there is always an obligation that goes with all blessings. He forgot that from him to whom much has been given, much is expected. He forgot that we are expected to bless others in the same proportion as God has blessed us.

The Rich Fool put his trust and had his security in material wealth. He failed to recognise that no one celebrates alone and that we find meaning in life only by reaching out. His life was limited to what he owned. His thoughts were all about himself, his grains, his barns, his possessions. He was too preoccupied with the comfort and security which he thought bumper harvest could provide him.

In his search for happiness and security, he forgot the more important things in life: he forgot the God who makes all things possible. He forgot the poor. He forgot that death could strike any time, and he forgot to prepare for what lies beyond this world. He was simply a fool who did not understand life's ultimate purpose and therefore got his priorities wrong. The Rich Fool lived a life that was an exercise in vanity and futility.

Being Rich in God's Sight

We were created by a God who shares his life, his creativity and his abundance with us. In contrast with the Rich Fool, Jesus came and spent his whole life for others – his love, his wisdom, his energy, his spirit, his body and his blood, etc. He kept nothing to himself and did nothing for himself, because he recognised that all things come from the Father. Jesus modelled for his disciples and followers a life of detachment because he does not want them to live purposeless lives, buried as it were in the false security of wealth and possessions, while real life passes them by. The wealth that Jesus bestows does not separate brother from brother. The wealth of Jesus is one that we must constantly give away so that we may become rich in the sight of God.

Conclusion

Greed is like fire. The more wood you pile on it, the hungrier the fire gets. In 1 Timothy 6:10 St. Paul observes that "The love of money is the root of all evil, and there are many who pursuing it have wandered away from the faith and given their souls a number of fatal wounds!" Many people do not know the extraordinary freedom and peace that come from living simply and with contentment. Many do not know that living with few material goods enables the human spirit to soar, which is why Jesus calls us all to be detached, to be free of any material encumbrances. The only possessions worth striving for are those that death cannot take away, those that endure to eternity

Questions to Ponder

1. The first reading raises a fundamental question. What is this question? And as a Christian what answer can you provide for this question?
2. Why do you think greed and avarice are considered in Christian thought to be equivalent to idolatry, worship of false gods?
3. The successful farmer in today's Gospel was condemned by God. But why? What did he do wrong?
4. The Gospel challenges Christians to adopt a certain attitude towards our physical life, material wealth, and worldly power and fame. What is this attitude?

Additional Reading

Matthew 13:44-47, 19:16-26; John 11:25

19th Sunday of the Year

Living By Faith

Readings: Wisdom 18:6-9 | Psalm 33 | Hebrews 11:1-2, 8-19 | Luke 12:32-48

Summary:

Obedience is the first and most critical element of the life of faith. The heroes and heroines of our faith obeyed God and therefore did the most impossible things. The next elements are hope and trust, by which they took God at his word. They trusted that God was faithful to his promises and looked forward in hope to the realisation of those promises, even when there was nothing in the horizon to show that what they hoped for will be realised. They often set out on a journey not knowing where they were headed, but simply trusting that the God who has called them knows best and will lead them to the land of promise.

Faith: What it is

The letter to the Hebrews offers us the classic Christian definition of faith as "...the confident assurance of things hoped for, the evidence of things not seen..." There is a relationship therefore between faith and hope. Faith is the conviction of things not seen. Once those things can be seen or touched, it is no longer a matter of faith. Faith for us Christians is not knowing what the future holds but knowing who holds the future. It is being able to see light with our heart when all our eyes can see is darkness. It is believing that it shall soon be dawn, and that all shall be well, even when we are stuck in the midnight of distress. Faith does not make things easy, rather it makes them possible (Luke 1:37).

Faith means trusting in advance what will only make sense in reverse. It is taking the first step even when you cannot see the whole stairway. In the words of the Lebanese American writer and poet,

Khalil Gibran, Faith is "a knowledge within the heart beyond the reach of proof."

Our Ancestors in Faith

By faith, Abraham obeyed and went out, not knowing where he was going, because he considered the One who called him faithful. By faith he offered up Isaac, even though Isaac was his only child, because he considered that God was able to raise men even from the dead. Abraham's deep faith in God gave him the courage to dare, and it was reckoned to him as righteousness.

By faith Sarah received the power to conceive though she was past the age. She considered Him faithful who made the promise. It was by faith that Moses with only a staff in hand, took on an all-powerful Pharaoh with his immense army and his chariots, and he got the Israelites out of Egypt. By faith Moses persevered as though he saw Him who is invisible.

By faith Joshua got the Israelites to march round Jericho seven times while blowing trumpets, and the city walls fell flat. Isaac, Jacob, Gideon, Deborah, Jephthah, Barak, Samuel, David, Elijah, Elisha, Isaiah, Hezekiah, Daniel, Tobit, Tobias, Susana, Ruth, Mordechai, the Virgin Mary, John the Baptist, and numerous others did incredible exploits by faith. They did the impossible because they saw the invisible. They lived by faith and died in hope.

All these heroes of faith conquered kingdoms, lived upright lives through trying times, emerged unscathed from battle, embraced torture and violent death rather than let themselves be defiled, conceived and bore the saviour of the world, and did many other astounding things by faith. They all died in faith, not having received all that was promised, but they held on to a vision of these promises.

Spiritual Descendants of Abraham

We Christians identify ourselves as spiritual descendants of Abraham. Yet we prove ourselves true children of Abraham only by imitating his faith. Like Abraham, we are journeying into the unknown; we do not know what lies after the next bend on the road of life, but we simply trust and rely on the One who has called us. Life is full of challenges and uncertainties and the older we get, the more confounded we become about life. As we face many trials and tribulations, disappointment and frustrations along the way, faith gives us the required strength to live in fidelity through the dark and difficult moments, while keeping hope alive.

At the time of his death, Abraham was only the father of Isaac, not of many nations, neither did he witness the land of Canaan becoming the heritage of the Israelites. He died without seeing God's promises in this regard fulfilled. Abraham's faith enabled him to see the promise fulfilled, not as part of his experience now but in the far distant future. What Abraham valued the most was his friendship with God. He worked all his life in order not to lose anything of this friendship; rather he built on it, making it stronger and better. He treasured it as the source of meaning for his life. Abraham went everywhere with this friendship and would not be separated from it even in times of trial. Abraham's heart was in the same place where his treasure was (see Matthew 6:21).

Like Abraham, we Christians travel in faith and die in hope. We believe for example that Jesus the second person of the Trinity took flesh and became man; that he died and rose from the dead on the third day; that he is present in the gathering of believers; that he is present in his word; that he is really and truly present in the Eucharistic species; that he loves us immensely; that he will return in glory; and that we will live with him forever in glory. These are not a verifiable quantity. We simply know them by faith.

Living by Faith

Jesus said that he will appear unexpectedly. Now while he seems to be absent from history, he calls us to be vigilant, to stay awake, to be prepared, and to be obedient to his word. This is our task in the time in-between. There is a treasure awaiting us. We must be vigilant so that when we are called to take possession of our treasure, we will be ready.

The Christian faith is more than a personal declaration that, "I believe" or that, "I am born again." Believing is an action-packed verb. Believing is a series of actions, such as daily walking in the presence of the Lord, being attentive to the Lord's voice, obeying the word of the Lord, witnessing to God's kingdom, waiting on God in prayer, and being busy with faith-filled actions (Luke 12:43), for faith without works is dead! (James 2:14-26).

If like Abraham our treasure is our faith in God, if we consider ourselves beneficiaries of the promise of eternal happiness in God's presence, then we would spend our lives seeking God's kingdom and its righteousness above all things, providing for ourselves treasures in heaven where no thief can steal, nor moth consume.

Conclusion

Believing in God means living the life of God and cherishing the things that are important to God. The life of faith must bear fruit in the godly life of love and compassion, mercy and forgiveness, discipline and self-control, service and self-sacrifice, passion for justice and peace, commitment to the welfare of the poor and the lowly, as well as persevering through suffering. As Jesus says, "By their fruits, you shall know them" (Matthew 7:20).

Questions to Ponder

1. Give a short definition of faith (in your own words). And what does it mean to live by faith?
2. For us Christians there is something positive about the unexpected manner in which death often comes. What is it?
3. Jesus says: "Where your treasure is there will your heart be also." As a Christian what do you consider your ultimate treasure? And how much of your heart is in it?
4. Like Abraham, Christians are called to travel in faith and to die in hope. Explain.

Additional Reading

Genesis 22:1-14, 23:4, 26:3, 35:12; Matthew 24:45-51; Romans 4:19-21; Revelation 21:10-12

20th Sunday of the Year

Standing For or Against Christ

Readings: Jeremiah 38:4-6, 8-10 | Psalm 40 | Hebrews 12:1-4 | Luke 12:49-53

Summary:

At our baptism we were anointed priests, prophets, and kings even though we have often shied away from our prophetic mission to live out and proclaim God's undiluted truth like Jeremiah, Jesus Christ, and the cloud of witnesses all through history. We are challenged today to make a choice for or against Jesus while bearing in mind that standing with him will often bring conflicts and division.

The Prophet as Troublemaker

Jeremiah loved his people very dearly. But he loved God and the truth even more. At a time of moral decay and political turmoil, he predicted an upcoming catastrophe. He warned that if they do not immediately repent, the people will soon be defeated and humiliated by their enemies. He accused the false prophets of appealing to popular sentiments, preaching prosperity, and prophesying peace when there was no basis for such peace.

The leaders of his society, including the king, the princes, the army, the hired or false prophets, the political and economic elite, and the religious authorities, were all enraged, and they were fed up with Jeremiah on account of his prophesies of doom and gloom. They conspired to get rid of him. They threw him into prison at the first instance, but even in prison he did not keep his mouth shut. He continued to harass the leaders with his message. Then they threw him into a well full of mud, so that he may drown and die a miserable death. But he was saved following the intervention of an Ethiopian friend of the king.

As a Prophet Jeremiah was an utter failure. He met a stone wall in the people. Nobody listened to him or gave a thought to his prophetic word. He got to a point where he conflicted with God, with the people, and even with himself. He questioned God who sent him on this mission, and the people who refused to listen, and he wondered whether he was in his right senses. He was hated and isolated because of his fidelity to God and his commitment to the truth. His powerful message and his values unsettled a lot of people and brought conflict and division.

Jeremiah did not do violence to anyone, but because he proclaimed godly values, those who were comfortable with the status quo of evil, saw him as a dangerous fellow. He so irritated the people that they eventually got rid of him. Thus, he paid the ultimate price for truth with his life. Jeremiah prefigured Jesus, the Suffering Servant, who at the beginning of his ministry brought the good news of God's kingdom but was condemned and executed because he was a thorn in the flesh of those who were determined to sustain the evil status quo.

I Have Come to Bring "Fire" and "Division"

Jesus' words in today's Gospel appear to contradict all we know about him as Isaiah's Prince of Peace (Isaiah 9:6). They appear inconsistent with the message of the Beatitudes, "Blessed are the peacemakers..." (Matthew 5:9). Rather than peace, Jesus says in today's gospel that he has come to bring fire, and how he wished it were already blazing! The fire Jesus talks about however is the fire of God's presence, the fire of God's love, that sets aflame the hearts of the faithful. Jesus' fire is that which makes the faithful passionate for the things of God. Jesus' fire does not do violence to anyone. His fire promotes love, forgiveness, compassion, harmony, unity, and lasting peace.

Jesus' message rebukes all those engaged in the idolatry of money, power, pleasure, and inordinate ambition. The message of Jesus unsettles those guilty of corruption, racial and ethnic bigotry, and all forms of social injustice. His message chastises the powerful who oppress the weak and lowly, and the rich who are insensitive to the plight of the poor. The message of Jesus is meant to unsettle those with vested interests, those who are beneficiaries of a corrupt status quo, who would stoutly resist any change in the system.

Conflict appears to be an inevitable part of the prophetic mission. Even though the prophet hardly ever desires to bring about conflict, conflict inevitably results from his message. There will be conflict when anyone strives to live out courageously the values of the Gospel in a corrupt, promiscuous, wicked, violent, exploitative, and idolatrous society. In defending truth, justice, human dignity, and freedom, the Christian message will inevitably be met with opposition. As he strives to preach the undiluted truth of God, the faithful Christian disciple like Jeremiah will often be isolated and persecuted, discredited and maligned, abused and calumniated, mocked and derided. The opposition or persecution could even come from the truth bearer's immediate family or group. Yet we recall that Jesus said that those persecuted for the sake of the Gospel are blessed, and that they shall be handsomely rewarded in heaven (see Matthew 5:9-12).

The message of Jesus was not always palatable or crowd friendly. Listening to Jesus therefore was not always a sweet experience. This is why on a number of occasions, after listening to him, some people reached out for stones to throw at him. Though he was gentle, meek, and humble of heart, when it came to denouncing evil, speaking against the oppression of the least of his brethren, and proclaiming the truth of God, Jesus was always firm, decisive, and uncompromising. He did not seek to make himself popular with some sugarcoated message, nor was he any kind of crowd puller. His message was strong and uncompromising.

He cared so much about people that he disturbed them because they needed to be disturbed. He shocked some and infuriated others. What he taught brought him in conflict with the religious, political, and economic elite, the Scribes and Pharisees, whom he called blind guides, hypocrites, and whitewashed sepulchers. Jesus' justice brought him in conflict with those who exploited the poor and the weak. His integrity brought him in conflict with the dishonest and corrupt people. His sense of universal brotherhood and inclusiveness brought him in conflict with the narrow-minded, racial bigots of his day. He, like Jeremiah before him, stirred up so much hatred that he ended up being crucified. Jesus ended up the way he did because he was a prophet, and every true prophet is almost always a persona non grata.

The Gospel: A Force for Transformation

The gospel of Christ is the most potent force for individual and societal transformation. It is a fire that warms and comforts, but it also burns up what is useless and refines what is impure. Prophets and true bearers of the gospel are troublemakers in the real sense of the word. If a preacher of the gospel is not causing trouble in a corrupt world, perhaps it is not the gospel of Christ that is being preached. There is no greater disturber of peace than the one who preaches justice and truth, because people often prefer to live in falsehood and have the peace of the graveyard, which is no peace at all. A lot of what our societies consider normal, are often an affront to the gospel of Christ and the values of the kingdom.

For children of God, the widespread indiscipline in our world, the level of corruption, the rampant immorality, the degree of violence, the abuse of power, the often-scandalous gap between the rich and the poor, etc., are far from normal, and should be considered an aberration. Christians cannot keep quiet where such evils thrive. There is a tendency today to want to make the gospel of Christ palatable or acceptable to everybody, robbing the gospel of some of its transforming influence and reducing the Christian enterprise to some feel-good experience. When this happens, the leaven loses its power, the salt loses its taste, and the fire goes out as it were.

Committing to the Gospel of Jesus Christ

Believers in Christ must constantly choose to stand for Jesus. This means standing against many structures and practices that run counter to the values of the kingdom. Standing up for Jesus is not a superficial enterprise. It often means martyrdom. Standing up for Jesus requires the courage to speak the truth and to live out this truth in an environment of widespread falsehood and debauchery, the courage when necessary to stand alone, and the courage to patiently endure the inevitable suffering that such witnessing entails.

Conclusion

A life of fidelity to Christ and his message of salvation is sure to rock the boat. It is sure to cause division and conflict now and again in the family, at work and even in the Church community. The committed Christian living in the world of today is in trouble, and he or she is a troublemaker, to the extent that his or her life of truth and daily witnessing to the light of Christ constitute a sign of contradiction to the world of darkness and the prevailing falsehood and debauchery.

Questions to Ponder
1. What is the overriding theme that runs through all of today's readings?
2. Identify the sentence in our 2nd Reading (Hebrew 2:1-4) that urges us to embrace "Deferred Gratification."
3. Jesus says: "I have come to bring fire on earth…" What kind of fire has Jesus brought to the world? And how do we reconcile Jesus the Prince of Peace with the Jesus who brings Fire and Division?

Additional Reading
Exodus 3:1-12; Jeremiah 1:1-10; Amos 3:1-8; Matthew 10:16

21st Sunday of the Year

Enter by the Narrow Door

Readings: Isaiah 66: 18-21 | Psalm 117 | Hebrews: 12:5-7, 11-13 | Luke 13: 22-30

Summary:

The first reading is from the Prophet Isaiah who speaks about the universality of our religion and worship. In the second reading, we are encouraged to remember that as disciples we will have to endure certain hardships and face certain challenges. In the Gospel reading from Luke, Jesus explains that it is the narrow door that leads to salvation.

God's Salvation is for All Peoples

Isaiah and several other Old Testament Prophets often presented a picture of the Messianic times as when God will gather all his children together from the East and West and from the North and South. This means that from the nations where they were scattered (in exile) they would all move towards Zion, the city of God, and worship the Lord with one voice.

Christians see this prophesy fulfilled partly at Pentecost, and in the gathering of the Church that is universal or Catholic. The God of Abraham, Isaac, and Jacob is the God of the whole universe. With the coming of the Messiah, it will be clearly demonstrated that God's salvation is for all peoples. He desires to save everyone, and not a privileged few, as Jesus confirms in Luke 13:29.

Who Will Be Saved?

Questions regarding who will be saved have engaged many believers through the course of the centuries. Many of the ancient Jews believed that salvation is for only those who are privileged descendants of Abraham by blood, and those who converted to Judaism, and subjected themselves to circumcision and other Jewish rituals. They often considered Gentiles as lost or damned! Even after Jesus' life and ministry and the experience of Pentecost that brought people from different places to speak with one voice, many among the early Jewish Christians still had difficulty accepting the truth of the universality of God's salvation in Christ. The first major conflict in the Church arose over this matter and it necessitated the calling of the first Synod of the Church in Jerusalem (see Acts 10 and 11; 15:1-35).

Because of Peter's mission to Cornelius' house, the other apostles who were not privileged to have the kind of encounter he had with Jesus, were furious that Peter was fraternizing with Gentiles. They accused him of getting himself defiled by the "impure" gentiles, until he narrated his encounter with the Lord. Then in Acts 15, at the Council at Jerusalem, through the inspiration of the Holy Spirit, they resolved not to place unnecessary burdens on the gentiles.

It was this kind of preoccupation that prompted someone (most probably a Jew) to ask how many people will be saved in today's gospel. This fellow probably wanted to know if there's a limited number that would be saved, and if any non-Jews would be among the saved. Jesus did not answer the question but gave the fellow the formula to attaining heaven. He warns the man, and all of us, that the door to God's kingdom is narrow and that only few find it; and that it will not remain open indefinitely. There is a time when the door will be closed, after which excuses will not be entertained.

In today's account, the Lord encourage the questioner not to get bogged down with speculations about who will be saved or the whereabout of another person's soul. Instead, he was to try hard to see that his own soul is saved while there is still the chance to do so. The Lord never wasted his time answering speculative questions. So, the questions that should bother us are questions like how can I be saved? What must I do to inherit eternal life? What can I contribute to God's mission of saving the world? These are some personally relevant questions that should engage believers.

Striving to Enter by the Narrow Door

Jesus warned the Jews who are presumptuous of their privileged place in God's kingdom, and all who think that they have a divine right, to repent, produce the fruits of repentance, and strive hard, or face the risk of being locked out. To strive indicates effort, and effort involves some pain, like denying ourselves some benefits and pleasure in order to advance God's work or to meet our neighbour's need.

We cannot presume that our place in heaven is guaranteed simply because we are Christians. Rather, each one must strive hard to do God's will. This explains why St. Paul says that those who think they are standing firm should be careful, lest they fall (1 Corinthians 10:12). The door to the kingdom is quite narrow and many are struggling to get in. Each one of us must strive to squeeze through this narrow door.

We would even have to bend low, because that narrow door is likely to be short as well. So, to enter, not only are we going to have to squeeze ourselves in, we must also we must make ourselves small to enter. No wonder Jesus Christ said that only the humble, the little ones, have ready access to the Kingdom of God (Luke 18:16). This is particularly so because little children often do not hesitate to do whatever they are asked to.

Our second reading is on how God sometimes uses discipline to prepares us for the Kingdom. Sickness appears to be a terrible thing, but some people are prepared for the kingdom by it. Sometimes God allows sickness, so that the person who has been living in an illusion can begin to see the reality about 'the smallness and fragility of the human person in the grand scheme of things.

God's Peculiar Heritage

Jesus demonstrates that the Jews had completely misunderstood the concept of "the chosen people." He teaches that God does not choose a particular people to the exclusion of others. If God chooses a group at all, it is so that they may be of service to others and lead others to God. Thus, being a priest is not a privilege because the priest is chosen to serve others and in doing so lead to them to God. In the same way, all Christians are chosen, and our status as the children of God comes with a corresponding responsibility. We are chosen for service and so must drop all claims to any entitlement. When God chooses anyone, it is a call to service, a call to lead others to God.

Peter expresses this truth in Acts 10:34-35. God has no favourites. No one should be tempted to think that God operates in the same manner as the world which is so rife with exclusion and exclusivism. No one should think they can bribe their way to heaven because God does not operate along the parameters of the world that we are used to. Jesus advises us all to strive to enter by the narrow door.

Accessing the Narrow Door

The Kingdom of God is a gift, but we must struggle to keep and nurture this gift. Striving for the Kingdom does not mean that it is no longer a gift. It means that we must be ready to make the required sacrifices to receive to embrace this gift. We must be willing to accept the cross and endure the sufferings and pains that come in the cause of living out the values of the Kingdom.

Jesus shocks his self-righteous listeners (the Pharisees and Scribes) who believed that their place in heaven was guaranteed when he told them that the last shall be the first and the first last (Luke 13:30). He told them that many shall come from the east and west and will eat with Abraham…in the kingdom of heaven (Matthew 8:11); and that tax collectors and prostitutes are entering the kingdom of God before them (Matthew 21:31). In this way he demonstrates that biological relationship or some superficial acquaintance with him, will not grant anyone entry into the kingdom. Only with the fruits of true repentance and conversion can the gift of the kingdom be properly embraced.

In fact, he says the only grounds for claiming closeness with him is obeying the word of God when we hear it. This informs his response to those who told him of the presence of his mother and brothers at the venue of one of his teachings (Luke 8:21, 11:28). The Blessed Virgin Mary, we believe, is sitting at the right hand of the Father, not only because she is the mother of Jesus, but also because she did the will of God. She answered God's call and remained faithful to the end.

Conclusion

To possess the Kingdom of God, it is not enough to simply declare that one is born again. One must demonstrate it clearly in one's practical life and be known by the fruits produced. Christians must be seen to be producing the fruits of the spirit listed by St. Paul in Galatians 5:22-23, as love, joy, peace, patience, kindness, goodness, faithfulness, gentleness, and self-control. These fruits are proof that we are living up to our calling and our name, for by our fruits shall we be known.

Questions to Ponder
1. What is the overriding theme of today's readings?
2. Why, according to our 2nd Reading (Hebrews 12:5-13), does God sometimes allow Christians to suffer?
3. Jesus says, "Strive to enter by the narrow door." What is this narrow door? And what does the striving entail for us?
4. What category of people according to the readings of today will be saved?

Additional Reading
Isaiah 55:8 | Matthew 7:21 | Luke 9:23 | John 16:33

22nd Sunday of the Year

The Virtue of Humility

Readings: Sirach 3:17-20, 28-29 | Psalm 68 |
Hebrews 12:18-19, 22-24 | Luke 14:1, 7-14

Summary:

Jesus identified himself so closely with the suffering poor that he declared in Matthew 25:31-46 that what we do to the hungry, the naked, the stranger, the sick, and the prisoner, we do to him. He was always very gentle and kind with the poor but often very hard on the rich and the powerful. Like the prophets of old, he comforts the afflicted, and afflicts the comfortable as it were. This is what is known as "Jesus' preferential option for the poor."

Jesus' Life of Humility

Jesus Christ was born in a manger in Bethlehem and raised in the small town of Nazareth. When he began his ministry, he surrounded himself with poor fishermen as disciples. There were doctors of the law, people who trained under the renowned Rabbi Gamaliel, and there were other highly educated as well as rich people at the time, but Jesus chose to surround himself with poor fishermen, tax collectors, and prostitutes. He fraternised with the poor and despised people, he had nowhere to lay his head, and he rejected the devil's temptation to demonstrate power and glory (Matthew 4:1-11). He washed the feet of his disciples and submitted himself to a humiliating death on the cross. These are powerful lessons in humility.

Jesus calls all those who have been beaten by the travails of life, all who have laboured and are over-burdened by unemployment and poverty, disease and bereavement, loneliness and abandonment, discrimination and persecution, physical and mental handicap, etc., to come to him and find their rest, because he is meek and humble of heart. In this way Jesus reveals the face of Yahweh who is known as the Father of orphans, Defender of the widow, and Friend of the poor.

Jesus' Teaching on Humility
With his spectacular life of humility, and the manner in which he treated the poor and the lowly, Jesus reverses all established social norms, standards, and conventions. While the champions of this world urge people to go for it, to conquer the world, to blow their own trumpet, to fight their way to the top, to be aggressive, and to be assertive, Jesus teaches that the greatest among us is the one who serves. While everyone is struggling for more wealth, more power, more prestige, and more celebrity status, Jesus urges his followers to seek the lowest place! Christian humility is indeed a sign of contradiction to a world that promotes the proud and celebrates the arrogant.

Materialism and Consumerism
Today's world is plagued by vanity and vainglory, immodesty and showmanship, as well as ignorance and presumption. Many young people are caught up with what has come to be known as "Acute Celebrity Syndrome," by which popular entertainment and sports personalities and extremely wealthy people are adored and celebrated almost to the point of idolatry. Such a world makes little or no room for the poor and the weak, the blind and the lame, the widow and the orphan. Yet it is in their company that Jesus was found most of the time. Our world makes little or no room for a successful person who is frugal, humble, and modest. But it is the way of Jesus.

The Virtue of Humility
Jesus' paradoxical teaching on humility can be summarised as follows:

> Do you want to find your life? Lose it!
> Do you want to be first? Be last of all!
> Do want to be the greatest? Be servant of everyone!
> Do you want the crown of glory? Take up your cross!
> Do you want to be exalted? Be humble!

He does not try to water them down, couch them in such a way as to make them more easily acceptable, or apologise for them. He states things the way they are, and you take them, or you leave them.

Humility is the most characteristic Christian virtue, the mother and guardian of all virtues, the solid foundation of the virtuous life, the doorway to genuine Christian life, the pathway to true greatness, and the first step to salvation. According to D. L. Moody, the American evangelist, "To begin the life of greatness, be little; to increase the life of greatness, be less; and to perfect the life of greatness, be nothing." Jesus exemplified this for us. Rabindranath Tagore, the Indian mystic and writer, says of humility: "We come nearest to the great when we are great in humility."

On Ash Wednesday each year, we hear it drummed into our ears that we are dust and shall return to dust. This is the truth of who we really are. Humility is not thinking less of ourselves, but thinking of ourselves less.

Conclusion

Sin came through the pride of Lucifer, but salvation came through the humility of Jesus. Whereas pride constitutes a barrier between us and God and between us and our neighbour, humility facilitates in us the conditions for the closest possible intimacy with God, and the greatest possible relationship with our neighbour. Humility is living up to the truth of who we really are before God, and nothing sets us so much out of the devil's reach as humility.

Questions to Ponder
1. What is the relationship, if any, between humility and wisdom on the one hand and between pride and folly on the other?
2. Describe briefly how you would begin to teach your little child lessons on the Christian virtue of humility.
3. What do you understand by "Jesus' preferential option for the poor?" And how does this challenge the conduct of your life as a Christian?

Additional Reading
Proverbs 29:23; Matthew 18:1-4; Luke 18:9-14; John 12:24-25, 13:1-15

23rd Sunday of the Year

Renouncing All for Christ

Readings: Wisdom 9:13-18 | Psalm 90 | Philemon 9-10, 12-17 | Luke 14:25-33

Summary:

Choosing to follow Jesus is like a young man or woman finding the love of his or her dream and abandoning his or her family, relations, and all other attachments to cling to this new love. Jesus insists that we have a choice. He does not force anyone into discipleship. We can choose to follow him or not to follow him. But once we decide to follow Jesus, he must be the number one priority in our lives.

The Wisdom of God

The book of Wisdom declares that whereas God is all-wise and all-knowing, human beings are ignorant and often foolish. To understand earthly realities is difficult enough for us, how much more difficult it is to grasp heavenly realities - the mysteries of the universe, the meaning of life and death, and the inner workings of God. These are realities we cannot fathom on our own.

It is folly to try to understand life without seeking the wisdom of God. We need God to grant us his wisdom and his Spirit to begin to figure out some earthly realities so as to make wise choices in our lives. More so, we need the illumination of the Spirit of God and divine understanding to make sense of some realities beyond us, such as, "Why do bad things happen to good people" or "why some criminal lives up to 90 years while many saintly people die very young?" Such realities do not make sense when considered from limited human perspectives. But as St. Paul tells us in 1 Corinthians 1:25, "The foolishness of God is wiser than human wisdom." It is with the wisdom of God and the enablement of his Holy Spirit that we begin to make sense of some of these realities and to see and reason as God does.

Choosing Christ Above All Else

As Jesus journeyed towards Jerusalem many of his followers and admirers thought he was going to establish a worldly, political, kingdom, where they themselves will occupy privileged positions. They also thought that Jesus' movement presented an easier alternative to the rigorous demands of the Jewish law. But Jesus disappoints them all. With his call for total renunciation (of one's family ties, one's material possessions and even one's very life) and carrying one's cross to follow him (Luke 14:25-33), Jesus sets the tone for his elaborate teaching on what high cost and sacrifice Christian discipleship will entail.

In Matthew 10:37-39, Jesus says that if we love anyone or anything more than him, we are not worthy of him. In other words, if we say that we are Christians, the only thing that we cannot do without is our relationship with God in Christ. We can let go of every other thing, including our very life itself, for as he says, "What does it profit a man if he gains the whole world and loses his soul?" (Mark 8:36).

Following Jesus

The option for Jesus must be total and radical. He does not accept a second place in our lives. He allows for no competition. Even our closest relationships must be subordinated to Christ, and all our dealings must be conducted in the light of our commitment to Christ. Jesus says that no one who puts his hands on the plough and looks back is worthy of him (Luke 9:62) and we must take that seriously. He told the would-be disciple who wanted to go and bury his parent to let the dead bury their own dead (Luke 9:60). He told the rich young man who desired eternal life to go and sell all his possessions and give the proceeds to the poor and then come follow him (Mark 10:17-21). No one, and nothing at all should be allowed to interfere with our commitment to follow Jesus.

Be Warned: It's Not an Easy Road

Jesus destroys all illusions of material power, glory, prosperity, abundance, comfort, and security, when we choose to follow him. The reality Jesus presents is that the life of a Christian disciple will be difficult, harsh, painful, and often punctuated by persecution. He urges his disciples to be prepared because it is not an easy road. There will often be difficult decisions to make; we will often find ourselves in conflict with family members and friends, on account of our uncompromising commitment to Christ and his values. There will be occasions when we will have to choose between speaking the truth of Jesus and remaining silent in the face of evil, and between standing up for Jesus and embracing the cross of suffering and joining the crowd in a life of sin and debauchery.

The words of Jesus in today's gospel are a major assault on the growing phenomenon known as the "Prosperity Gospel." Many people in our day would indeed prefer a Christianity of power and privilege, and one that makes no serious demands on them, but there is no such thing as a "cross-less Christianity." After outlining the conditions of Christian discipleship, Jesus then gives us two parables to emphasise that Christian discipleship is serious business that requires a radically new commitment, and one that will cost us everything.

The central paradox on which the Christian faith stands is that if there is no cross there will be no crown; if there is no suffering, there will be no glory; if there no pain, there will be no gain; and if there is no death, there will be no new life. We learn that every trial has a triumph in it, and that great hearts are made by great troubles. We must first lose certain things to find better things, and none of us can attain the highest maturity without enduring some trials. The cross is at the heart of Christianity. Leave it out and you have killed the religion of Christ. Christianity does not exist without the cross.

Conclusion

What Jesus outlines in today's gospel are the tough conditions, the high cost, the harsh realities, and the radical demands of the gospel. The decision to follow Jesus is not a light one; the price to be paid is high. The commitment required of Christian disciples is total. We have to practically "hate" all that we used to hold dear before meeting Jesus, because we are now a new creation with a new purpose and new set of priorities.

Questions to Ponder
1. What is the overriding theme of today's readings?
2. What is the point being made by St. Paul in today's 2nd Reading from Philemon? And what is the link (if any) with the Gospel passage?
3. Jesus says, "Whoever wishes to be my disciple must hate his father, mother, wife, children…and even his own life too." What does this mean?
4. How much has the Christian faith affected your life? What hard choices have you had to make? What high costs have you had to pay for embracing Christ?

Additional Reading
Matthew 19:16-22; John 12:24; 1 Corinthians 1:25

24th Sunday of the Year

Sin and God's Loving Forgiveness

Readings: Exodus 32:7-11, 13-14 | Psalm 51 | 1 Timothy 1:12-17 | Luke 15:1-32

Summary:

Paul confesses that his own conversion and salvation is proof enough of God's abundant mercy. He sees himself as the lost but found sheep and identifies himself with the prodigal son who squandered the properties of his father. He is like the sinner on account of whom there is joy in heaven at repentance. He is a prime beneficiary of Jesus' mission to save sinners.

The Nature of Sin

To sin is to disobey God, to rebel against him, to challenge his authority and to question his justice and goodness (see Genesis 3:1-8). To sin is to stray far away from home and become a fugitive, to abandon the path of wisdom and dwell in folly, and to turn away from light and dwell in darkness. The sinful life is a life turned in on oneself.

To sin is to know the way but decide to take the wrong path. It is to choose death and adversity instead of life and prosperity (see Deuteronomy 30:15, Romans 6:23). Praying is a difficult enterprise when one is in a state of mortal sin for which one has yet to repent. Unrepentant sinners are often in a world of misery and pain, lost to God and lost to themselves, because they are living a life of internal contradiction. But for all penitent sinners, the face or presence of God is the greatest source of delight.

The Root of Sin

Sin is more than just an offence against God. It is the state of being lost, separated, and alienated from the One who loved us into being, and from our source of purpose and meaning. Sin is rooted in the three-fold concupiscence: the lust of the flesh, the lust of the eyes, and the pride of life. The seven capital sins of pride, covetousness, lust, anger, gluttony, envy, and slot, summarise the various ways that men and women rebel against God. These principal lusts of the human person give birth to arrogance and disobedience, idolatry and blasphemy, hatred and wickedness, anger and resentment, greed and selfishness, as well as sensuality and promiscuity.

To sin is to deny ourselves the joy and happiness of God's presence. This itself, is hell. There are all kinds of images about hell, but what our Church teaches us is that hell is "the state of being separated from God." This is worse than any image we can come up with on our own. Unrepentant sinners are people who have been hijacked and enslaved by evil. This is an anomalous condition, because as St. Augustine says, the Lord has created us for himself, and our hearts are restless until they rest in him. This thought is re-echoed by the American Trappist monk, Thomas Merton, who said that God has put some divine spark in human beings, which keeps nudging them to return to him, each time they wander away from his presence.

When sin takes people away from the presence of God and his garden of delight, they often have little to hold on to, beside their bodies. This explains why a godless society is often rife with immorality and promiscuity. When the authority of God is not sufficiently recognised in our lives, we often begin to experiment with the most ridiculous forms of sensual pervasion. It often turns out that the punishment for sin is the predilection to commit even more heinous sins. To get things right, we would need to find our way back and be at home with our Father.

The Nature of Repentance

To repent and be converted is to abandon the darkness of folly, to come to one's senses, to embrace the light of wisdom, to return to God, to get back home, and be reconciled with our Father. To repent and be converted is to recognise that our God is a tremendous lover who desires to have all his children in his peaceful and gracious presence. God does not force his love on anyone. He hates sin but he loves the sinner and goes after the sheep that is lost. The lost sheep are often more precious in God's eyes, so he gives them priority attention. He does not count the cost involved in saving a sinner but rejoices tremendously over the conversion of even one of them.

Every repentant sinner is a witness to the fact that our God is gracious in forgiveness. This is what St. Paul speaks about in his first letter to Timothy where he witnesses to God's graciousness towards sinners, himself being a beneficiary of this graciousness of God. Indeed, God's mysterious love expresses itself best in forgiveness. He is willing to forgive, no matter how great the offence, and he forgives unconditionally and restores the sinner to his or her original state.

Celebrating the Lost and Found
With the three parables in Luke 15:1-32, Jesus justifies his mercy and loving commitment to welcoming back and saving sinners. The parables of the Lost Sheep, the Lost Coin, and the Prodigal Son show God's tenderness towards sinners. Every person is precious in his eyes, but more so, if that person was lost. As God loves every sinner more, not less, he challenges every Christian to do likewise towards those that have lost their way.

The way the Pharisees understood it is that God loves the virtuous and hates sinners. This is still the dominant logic in the world, and even among many Christians. Jesus, however, was gentle and loving towards sinners. He knew that condemnation and rejection will not change any person. So, he made sinners feel loved and accepted enough, for them to look critically into themselves, and begin to consider the required change. This is what it means to say that God loves the sinner but hates the sin. St. Paul says that what shows God's love is that Christ died for us while we were yet sinners (Romans 5:8). It is not because we are good children that he loves us.

Our God loves us so much that he wants us to dwell in the peace of his presence, in the joy of his home, and in the company of the saints in eternity. That is God's desire for all of us. We need to be constantly reminded that this world is not our real destination. As we grow older, we should begin to look beyond this world and its attractions and prepare for eternity. God loves all his children so much that when anyone of us is lost in sin, God goes to all lengths in search of us; and when at last he finds us (in contrast to the disposition of the elder brother in the parable, who expected stiff sanctions for the younger brother's sin), there is great rejoicing over our return home.

Conclusion
Blessed are those who, when they have sinned, follow the example of the Prodigal Son, and find their way back home to seek forgiveness. They will cause heaven to ring with joy! The fact that our homecoming will cause heaven to ring with joy signifies our worth and eternal value before God. It shows that every soul is priceless to him. We are pearls of inestimable value to our God who loved us into being. He promises to throw the biggest party that heaven has never seen, when we sinners repent and return to his embrace.

Questions to Ponder
1. Jesus told the three parables in today's Gospel (Luke 15) to teach a particular lesson. What lesson is this?
2. What, according to the parables of today, does sin do:
   (a) To the children of God?
   (b) To God Himself?
3. Mention the one word or short phrase that best connects today's 2nd Reading with the Gospel message.
4. If today I allow the word of God to bear fruit in me, what is going to change in the conduct of my life and in the practice of my faith?

Additional Reading
Deuteronomy 30:15-20; Psalm 1; Matthew 5-7, 7:13-14, 18:23-35; Luke 19:1-10 Galatians 5:19-23

25th Sunday of the Year

You Cannot Serve God and Mammon

Readings: Amos 8:4-7 | Psalm 113 | 1 Timothy 2:1-8 | Luke 16:1-13

Summary:

Today's gospel story is told to teach Christians the wise use of money; to stress the fact that it is not possible to combine devotion to God with devotion to mammon; to emphasise that to use money wisely is to give it away for a good cause and thereby ensure one's salvation. The dishonest steward gave away some of the wealth at his disposal for the sake of the future. His consciousness of and planning for the future is presented as an example for us.

Amos: Great Champion of Social Justice

Every baptised Christian is by virtue of his or her baptism a priest, prophet, and king. We have a prophetic responsibility, to speak for God in situations of social injustice and the oppression of the poor. This is what Prophet Amos did with consummate passion. Amos was a farmer. He neither belonged to the brotherhood of prophets, nor did he have any training in the art of being a prophet. He was called directly by God to condemn the wide and scandalous disparity between the rich and the poor, as well as the widespread exploitation of the lowly poor.

Amos denounced the behaviour of the privileged men and women who often paid lip service to God on the Sabbath while exploiting the poor the rest of the week. In discharging his prophetic task, Amos had none of the polished diplomatic language of the official prophets of the time, the kind of language that people want to hear. Amos pointed out the social injustices of the day and denounced them bluntly, vigorously and even brutally. Amos was evidently hurting inside, and he screamed out in protest, as he mourned the loss of fidelity and the absence of true religion in Israel.

He saw that people were claiming to be religious while living lives of greed and avarice and trampling on the lowly poor of the land. He condemned such behaviour in the harshest manner and declared that under such circumstances, their religious devotion and ritual sacrifices were not only useless but constituted a sacrilege. Rather than giving any honour to God, their gestures of worship and their sacrifices were offensive in God's sight.

Amos was addressing people who claimed that they loved God and were serving him, while at the same time living off the misery of the poor. He reminded them that true religion cannot keep company with greed for money and lust for power; and that when religious celebration is carried on along with corruption and oppression, such celebration is nothing but empty ritual and meaningless drama. Such celebration neither honours God nor sanctifies the person. When those who pretend to be religious are allies of the oppressive class who have conspired to sell the poor for "a pair of sandals," and when they turn a blind eye on the atrocities of their powerful allies, then they are far from worshipping the true God. When religious practice is not sufficiently critical of social injustice, such practice is indeed an affront to God.

The dishonest but shrewd steward
In the gospel of today, Jesus tells the story of a dishonest but shrewd steward, and commends him, not for his dishonesty, but for his prudence and shrewdness, his resourcefulness and ingenuity, his imagination and foresight, as well as his creativity and industry. In a time of crisis, the steward takes firm and immediate action. He uses the resources available to him today to guarantee his own future. With the news of the imminent termination of his job, he took immediate action to ensure some soft landing.

The steward in the gospel decided to use his prerogative to show some kindness to other people who like him were in trouble due to their indebtedness to his master. The lesson is this: If a dishonest man can use his master's money to ensure that there will be friends to welcome him when he is out of job, how much more should honest people use their God-given resources in such a way that when this life is over, they will be welcomed into the kingdom of God? Jesus holds up the crafty steward as an example because the children of light can learn one or two lessons from the children of darkness. Evil people are often industrious, single-minded, strategic, determined and prepared to make sacrifices to achieve their evil ends. How much more should good people develop these traits and deploy them towards the realisation of their good objectives!

Between God and Mammon

Every Christian must make a fundamental choice between serving God (and neighbour) and serving wealth and possessions, as we cannot serve both at the same time. While we are quick to think or say that it is God that we serve, a serious look at what we are passionate about, what we spend our energies and resources pursuing, etc., will often reveal who or what we are truly serving. Money and material possessions should never be treated as an end in themselves, but as an instrument for a higher end. God gave some people the grace of intelligence, resourcefulness, and industry, as well as the privileged opportunity to accumulate a lot of money and material goods. It is so that they can use these resources to benefit others in their society who may not be so gifted.

Our admission into the kingdom will depend on how well we have utilised the resources entrusted to us in furtherance of God's purpose. Today's parable challenges us Christians to reflect on our attitude towards money and material possessions in general. God does not want any of his children to be destroyed by inordinate love for wealth and material possessions. If we cannot exercise restraint in the pursuit of wealth, and we lack any measure of healthy detachment from material goods, then we are in danger of losing our souls to these possessions, and of being alienated from the Creator, who will not accept a second place in our hearts.

The Challenge of the Parable

An important lesson from the parable is that our dealings with the material world and everything contained therein, and especially the way we relate to money and material possessions, must be in total submission to and loving service of God, the One who is responsible for all that we are, and all that we have. We should use the resources at our disposal with an abiding consciousness that we are not the owners, but only stewards, and that we should be generous in dispensing those resources, in such a way as to ensure a comfortable place for ourselves when eventually the resources are taken away.

Another lesson from the parable is that when people really want something, they often rise to the occasion, deploying all their ingenuity into achieving the objective. Now if we are so smart in things of the world, how come we often appear so dumb when it comes to pursuing our spiritual values and objectives? How come we often fail to understand that real success in this life is being able to constantly align our present efforts in the service of our future objective? If such shrewdness can be used in the administration of earthly goods, so to ensure the material well-being of a steward when he is out of office, how much more should we who have been called to share in the treasures of the kingdom, commit ourselves to the administration of these eternal treasures with utmost diligence?

Instead of being greedy, rapacious and covetous with our material resources, we are being challenged to seize every opportunity that comes our way to use these resources for the benefit of others and to the glory of God. We are being challenged to use our earthly resources freely to serve God's purpose and thereby prepare a place for ourselves in his kingdom.

Conclusion
No one truly encounters Jesus without being set aflame for him and for his kingdom values. Jesus either has all of you or he has nothing of you. He accepts no compromise. You cannot serve both God and mammon!

Questions to Ponder
1. Identify the link, if any, between the 1st Reading from Amos 8:4-7 and the Gospel (Luke 16:1-13).

2. What human qualities, attributes, or abilities did Jesus find commendable in the Dishonest Steward? And what lessons must we learn from the story?
3. "Of all the idols people worship in our society, money is probably the most common." Discuss briefly.
4. What would you say is the correct Christian attitude towards money and material possessions?

Additional Reading
Matthew 19:16-26; Luke 14:25-33, 16:19-31, 19:8; 1 Timothy 6:9-10

26th Sunday of the Year

Lazarus and the Rich Man

Readings: Amos 6:1, 4-7 | Psalm 146 | 1 Timothy 6:11-16 | Luke 16:19-31

Summary:

God blesses us so that we can be a blessing to others who do not have the resources to meet their needs. We are just meant to be channels through which his gifts get to the needy in our midst. Once we forget that and see ourselves as possessors rather than channels to distribute God's gift, then we get it all wrong and get ourselves destroyed.

Amos: Great Champion of Justice

Prophet Amos strongly indicts, condemns, and denounces the behaviour of the rich, powerful and influential people in the land, who are often ensconced in obscene opulence, while the rest of the people wallow in degrading poverty. He rose against those who live in palatial mansions, purchase expensive furniture, feast sumptuously and entertain themselves endlessly, and who remain insensitive to the plight of the poor. As a true prophet, he could not reconcile their behaviour with the nature of God who is recognised as the Friend of the poor; a God who does justice to those who are oppressed; a God who raises those who are bowed down, who upholds the orphan and the widow, who protects the stranger; and a God who thwarts the path of the wicked, and sets prisoners free (see Psalm 146:6-9).

The God of Abraham, Isaac, and Jacob is revealed fully and definitively in Jesus Christ. This means that whatever is to be known about God has been revealed in Christ Jesus. He is known through all the scriptures as the Father of the orphan, the Defender of the widow, and the Friend of the poor. All through his earthly ministry, Jesus consistently demonstrated his preferential option for the poor and the weak, the sick and the lowly, the oppressed, and the marginalised.

In today's parable of Lazarus and the Rich Man, Jesus contrasts the fortunes of the Rich Man and those of Lazarus. The rich man was always dressed like a king in expensive clothes. He feasted sumptuously every day, surrounded by his rich friends, and he had no place for poor people like Lazarus. On his part, Lazarus lay at the rich man's gate covered with sores, only asking to eat the crumbs that dropped from the master's table. And the rich man's dogs came and licked his wounds.

Lazarus and the rich man lived side by side, but they dwelt in two different worlds. One person lived in a garden of delight while the other lived in an arid desert. Lazarus died at the gate of the rich man. He was totally neglected, and not a mention was made of his burial. But at death, he was taken (by angels) to the bosom of Abraham. The Rich Man also died and we are told that he was buried. If the story of Lazarus and the Rich Man ended with their physical death, then how tragic it would have been! If indeed as St. Paul says in 1 Corinthians 15:19 our hope in Christ were for this world alone, then of all people, we are to be most pitied. But the story did not end with his physical death, just as the story of Christ did not end at Calvary.

A Reversal of Fortunes

The story of Lazarus and the Rich Man continued in the afterlife, where there was a reversal of fortunes. In that new dispensation, Lazarus is given a place of honour at the heavenly banquet in the bosom of Abraham. There he was received with joy and he found happiness, while the Rich Man was in pain and anguish. Separated from God and his fair-weather friends, the rich man experiences hell. But as he looks up, he sees Lazarus in the bosom of Abraham, and he calls for help. In his anguish, the Rich Man expresses regret over the way he lived his life, asks for mercy, and requests Abraham to send Lazarus to dip the tip of his finger in water, to cool his tongue.

The denial of this request evokes some compassion in him for his brothers. Wishing that they do not end up in such a place, he requests that Lazarus may be sent to them to warn them so they may not end up like him in hell. This request is also turned down, and he is reminded that they already have Moses (the Law) and the Prophets to guide them. He argues that if someone goes to them from the dead, they will repent, but he is told that if they do not listen to Moses and the prophets, they will not be convinced, even if someone should rise from the dead to preach to them!

The Sin of the Rich Man
The Rich Man was condemned because he lived in sin. He failed to do something good that ought to be done. He was very selfish and lived only for himself. He did not realise that God's gifts are meant to be shared, especially with the underprivileged. He was insensitive and indifferent to the plight of the poor. He shut his eyes, his mind, and his heart, to the plight of the needy person at his gate. He showed Lazarus no compassion. He just did not care.

Because he despised the poor who are close to the heart of God, the Rich Man had made himself unwelcome in God's glorious company in heaven. He was too worldly to be able to see beyond the good things he enjoyed in this world. The Rich Man equally failed to recognise that this world, with all its glory, is not all there is, for according to St. Paul, "The world as we know it, is passing away" (1 Corinthians 7:31). He was not wise enough to recognise that before God we are all beggars, and once we fail to recognise this fact, we tend to treat the poor, the vulnerable and the destitute shabbily. But if we recognise ourselves as beggars before God, then we begin to see a commonality which facilitates the building of a relationship (of solidarity) between ourselves and the beggarly poor.

Unlike the Crafty Steward, who spent his master's money to make friends, the Rich Man did not use the resources available to him in such a way as to ensure that he will be welcomed when his wealth fails him. He forgot, as St. Teresa of Calcutta said, that at the end of our lives, we will not be judged by our material possessions or how many great things we have done but by "I was hungry and you gave me to eat; I was thirsty and you gave me to drink; I was naked and you clothed me; I was homeless, and you took me in; and I was sick and in prison, and you visited me..." (Matthew 25:31-46).

God's Gifts are to be Shared

The Rich Man misused God's gift because he failed to realise that to be truly enjoyed, God's gifts are to be shared. Some of us have been given the gift of food and every other thing in plenty because someone somewhere is hungry and needs to be fed and taken care of, and perhaps only we can reach this person. Some have great intelligence and rhetorical skills because someone somewhere needs to hear the word and needs to be taught. Some people have the gift of leadership because many are out there like sheep without shepherd, and they need to be led to green pasture. So, there should be no rich man or woman without some concrete commitment to care for the poor.

Some of the harshest words of Christ, and of the entire scriptures, are directed at the rich who, rather than care for the poor, further take advantage of them and exploit them (see 2 Samuel 12:1-15; Amos 5:14-24; Matthew 19:23; Luke 6:24-26). Jesus did not mince words when speaking against the rich regarding their care or lack of care for the poor.

The Real Poverty

It is St. Teresa of Calcutta who said that the greatest evil in the world of today is the lack of love in the hearts of men and women, which is responsible for the widespread indifference among many toward the plight of the neighbour. We must begin to teach the world that real wealth is judged not by the amount one has accumulated for oneself, but by the amount given away, and that the only wealth that is worth having is the wealth of a compassionate and generous heart.

Lazarus was poor but the Rich Man was even poorer, because he suffered the worst kind of poverty, the poverty of the heart. The materially poor are wounded by their poverty. The materially rich are also often wounded and blinded by their riches. If poverty makes a person sub-human, excess wealth can make a person inhuman. Christians must be on their guard because the danger of becoming inhuman when we have been abundantly blessed, is a real one.

Riches have a way of making one self-preoccupied. Many individuals and societies tend to lose their souls as they accumulate ever greater riches. On the other hand, according to John Wesley,

"The richer one's inner life is, the simpler becomes the person's outer life – the less one needs or wants!" True, if one's interior religiosity is strong, the outer manifestation of the person will be simple, frugal and modest, because one begins to desire less and less of material things.

The Challenge of the Parable

When confronted with oppression, persecution, exploitation, or abuse, God always pitches his tent on the side of the victim. He is the Father of the orphan, the Defender of the widow, and the Friend of the poor (see Psalm 68:5). That is how He has made Himself known, and we who claim to be His children must do likewise. In the face of grave suffering in our world on account of social injustice, Christians cannot afford to be neutral. We are either with the victim or with the oppressor. There is no other option.

The ever-widening gap between the rich and the poor, and the ever-worsening plight of the poor in our society, are a major scandal that no Christian should tolerate. Not only should we be careful that we are not contributing to the scandalous situation, but we should also be seen working hard to change the situation. Our Christian commitment obliges us to work against such scandalous situation with all the resources at our disposal. We are the ones who must teach the world another way of looking at life: that the first shall be the last; that the despised poor are precious in the eyes of God; that those who ignore or maltreat the poor will be rejected by the Lord; and that the love of money is the root of all kinds of evil.

Conclusion

We are all called to be of service and to be generous to the many poor people around us. For every one of us, there are people begging for something. So, we must constantly ask ourselves: who is sitting at my gate today begging for attention or for some of my food? Who is there in need of my compassionate touch? Who is it that requires my listening ear? Who is calling for my attention? Who is asking for my forgiveness? Who requires my affirmation?

Questions to Ponder
1. What is the overriding theme of today's readings?
2. What is the link (if any) between the 2nd Reading (1 Timothy 6:11-16) and the Gospel?
3. Who do you suppose the following persons in the gospel story represent in our own day: (a) The Rich Man; (b) Lazarus; (c) The Brothers of the Rich Man?
4. What was the sin of the Rich Man? What did he do wrong? To what extent are privileged persons often guilty of the same sin?

Additional Reading
Matthew 19:16-26, 25:31-46; Luke 4:18-19; 1 Timothy 6:9-10

27th Sunday of the Year

The Power of Faith

Readings: Habakkuk 1:2-3, 2:2-4 | Psalm 95 | 2 Timothy 1:6-8, 13-14 | Luke 17:5-10

Summary:

Through faith, the impossible becomes possible. With faith we can live amidst the sufferings, trials, troubles, and temptations of this world and our hearts and souls will remain peaceful and calm, undisturbed, and unperturbed. In this way we would be free of the anxiety and irritability that plague many in our world today, robbing them of the much-desired peace. We can achieve this only by growing in faith and trust in a loving and caring God who is the overarching controller of the universe.

Habakkuk: Prophetic Boldness

Armed with bold, courageous, and audacious faith, the Prophet Habakkuk cries out to God over the injustices and violence his people have been subjected to by foreign conquerors. So, he sought to find out from the Lord how long he will let his people suffer without intervening to save them, and make his prophet see death and look upon destruction; how long he will look the other way or keep silent while tyranny and violence rage in the land; and how long he will remain silent when some people are living in stinking opulence while the majority of people are dying of dehumanising poverty.

The prophet was angry because he believed in the goodness of God. He knew that God is good and capable of intervening to help his people. He knew that it is not an evil power that oversees the world, but rather a Loving Father. What he could not understand is why it was taking so long for God to intervene. So, he cried, screamed, and refused to keep silent in the face of evil, until God acts to save his people. He exhibited the kind of prophetic boldness that is rooted in the belief that God is good, and that God remains in control, all appearances to the contrary notwithstanding.

The problem of evil has engaged the human mind for ages, and countless philosophers have tried to unravel why there is so much evil in the world, with many questioning if God is really good. If he is, they ask, then why is there so much evil in the world? Some have come to the conclusion that it is either that he is good but not powerful, or that he is not good at all. If he is powerful, why does he not intervene immediately to stamp out evil?

Habakkuk's cry was a cry rooted in faith and fuelled by hope. He believed that God would do something, and his faith was proven right. The Lord heard his cry of faith. The answer Habakkuk received was that God will intervene in his own good time! It may appear slow, but it will surely come. The Prophet got an assurance that better days are coming. All he had to do was wait for it!

Witnessing for Christ

St. Paul instructs Timothy in today's second reading to hold on faithfully to the tradition he had received and to give witness to it in his daily conduct. In other word, his life must be a witness to what he believed and professed. Such life of fidelity to the Gospel will bring hardship to the Christian. The good thing is that most of us will not have to physically shed our blood for Christ. Yet a dose of martyrdom is called for every time we choose to die to falsehood, lust, selfishness, pride, possessiveness, greed, ego, and the craving for power and prestige positions. A dose of martyrdom is involved in choosing to let go of our natural craving for acceptance, when it stands in the way of the gospel of Jesus Christ.

Standing up for Christ in all circumstances requires the kind of courage, wisdom, and boldness that is born out of love. St. Paul reminds Timothy that the spirit he has received is not a spirit of timidity or fear but a spirit of power and love. Like Timothy, we ought to exercise our faith with all boldness while bearing courageously the hardships that Christian witnessing brings. St. Paul once again says that our faith in God should be so strong that it cannot be silenced by any degree of suffering (see 2 Timothy 2:8-13). Once we understand and accept that suffering is an inevitable part of

Christian witnessing, we will be better able to bear such suffering as our cross and see it as the cost of discipleship.

Faith: Quality, Not Quantity

When after his transfiguration, on his way to Jerusalem, Jesus spoke about the inevitable passion and death he was soon to undergo, the disciples were utterly confused, because their concept of a Messiah was not the one who will suffer. So, in exasperation, they said to him: "Lord increase our faith." Jesus responds to their request by illustrating the power of faith with something as small as a grain of mustard seed. The distinguishing factor of the mustard seed is that it is many times smaller than other grains, yet the mustard tree is the biggest of shrubs. Jesus uses these images to make the point that it is not the size of faith that matters but the strength or quality of it. What counts is not having *more* or *less* faith, but having a strong faith and putting it into practice. And our faith will not grow unless we put it into practice.

Trusting God in Adversities

To have faith does not mean that we will get exactly what we want when we pray. So even with strong faith, we may not always receive physical healing when we fall ill, and we pray for healing. But above all else, the prayer of faith will ensure that God's will is done in all circumstances, and that we would be comfortable with whatever God's will turns out to be. Faith can remove the poison from every grief. It can take the sting from every loss and quench the fire of every pain. We know that it is often not those afflicted with the worst tragedy or misfortune that end up committing suicide or getting clinically depressed. Many people of faith who go through terribly traumatic experiences often bounce back, and some even witness (as a result of the traumatic experience) what is known as "post-traumatic growth."

With such faith, we can learn to leave the past to the mercy of God, as we have no control over it, surrender the present to the love of God, and leave the future to the providence of God. When we believe strongly that God is in control of all our affairs, calmness and peacefulness will be our fundamental disposition, even when our world is threatening to cave in on us.

We Are Only Unworthy Servants

The Jews of old thought that if they kept the commandments strictly, and kept themselves from being defiled, they had a right to God's blessings. They thought that one could actually "bribe" God with good behaviour to merit God's favours and be entitled to salvation. But Jesus destroyed all their sense of entitlement, pointing out that all the good works that they could ever do is what is the minimum expected of them. He says they ought to see themselves as unworthy servants, doing their duty and nothing more (Luke 17:10). In this way Jesus teaches his followers that God does not owe human beings salvation in return for their keeping the law, even if they could keep it perfectly. Instead, Jesus emphasises that it is through God's gratuitous love that we can obtain salvation.

Christianity is a religion of grace not of merit, and salvation in Christ cannot really be earned. Our faith in God does not establish any claim for reward. To be faithful, loyal, dedicated, truthful, chaste, prayerful, penitent, and humble does not give us any rights before God. We are simply unworthy servants doing our duty. With love and joy, the grateful servant serves the master who has given him so much.

The Dynamics of Faith

Faith is the greatest power in the world. It is an organic (living, dynamic, vital) relationship with God. Faith is not a static or stationary thing. Faith grows and matures. If it doesn't grow, it will die. Faith grows when it is nourished, exercised, or practiced. Our faith grows and is strengthened by believing. It grows through a daily life of trust, obedience, dependence on the master, daily prayers and devotion, regular study of God's word, and keeping the company of other believing people, especially when all is not going well with us. Indeed, the ideal time to exercise faith is the time of hardship and adversity, because it is through the fire of affliction that our faith is best tested.

Conclusion

Jesus came to show us the face of the God who is love. Faith in the God of Jesus Christ is a way of life as well as a love affair. The servant who does what he is supposed to do deserves no thanks. God wants us to behave honourably, not to get a reward from him someday, but out of love for him and zeal for his service.

Questions to Ponder

1. What is the central theme of today's readings?
2. How would you describe Prophet Habakkuk's words in our first reading (Habakkuk 1:2-3)?
   (a) The words of a discouraged man.
   (b) A cry of faith.
   (c) Prophetic boldness.
3. Name some of the fundamental realities upon which the Christian faith is based as outlined in today's readings.
4. What are the things that can make our faith grow today?

Additional Reading

Genesis 15:1-6; Romans 8:28-39; 1 Corinthians 2:3-5; Hebrews 11:1-13

28th Sunday of the Year

Finding Salvation Through Suffering

Readings: 2 Kings 5:14-17 | Psalm 98 | 2 Timothy 2:8-13 | Luke 17:11-19

Summary:

In the first reading, Naaman the Syrian General is healed of leprosy and goes back to offer thanks and gifts to Elisha, recognizing the glory of God who had healed him through Elisha. Jesus heals ten lepers in the Gospel reading and out of the ten, only one came back to thank him, and like Naaman, the grateful leper was a foreigner. In the second reading, Paul explains the suffering that he has endured and the glory that he looks forward to, thereby encouraging us to endure suffering for Christ's sake so that we too may reign with Christ in Heaven.

Naaman Plagued by Leprosy

Naaman was Commander-in-Chief of the Syrian Army. He had led many successful expeditions into Israel, pillaging and plundering the land. Among the spoils of war was a Jewish girl who became a slave to Naaman's wife. But Naaman the great army commander contracted leprosy, a humiliating and deadly disease.

The slave girl believed firmly that if contacted, the Prophet Elisha would heal Naaman. Although Naaman initially refused, he eventually obeyed, got healed, and was saved. His body became like that of a new-born, and he came back to the Prophet with lavish gifts, thinking he could pay for God's goodness and mercy. But the prophet rejected them all. With the healing of his flesh Naaman came to believe in the one true God of all the earth and eventually begged for some sand from the land so that he can go and create a temple in his homeland where he would be worshipping the one true God.

As Commander-in-Chief, Naaman was used to giving orders, not obeying orders. He was not used to listening to the suggestions of slaves and servants. He was not expected to bow to the God of such a conquered people as Israel. But, when he came down from his Olympian heights, listened to the slave girl, paid attention to his servants, and obeyed the Prophet of God, he was both healed and saved.

Ten Lepers Healed, One Saved

In the Gospel of Luke, ten suffering men came to Jesus. They were tortured, humiliated, and isolated by the terrible disease of leprosy. Just like the case of Naaman and Prophet Elisha, Jesus simply told them - "Go and show yourselves to the priests." They trusted and obeyed, and, on their way, they found they had been cured. One of them came back full of gratitude, and he threw himself at the feet of Jesus in thanksgiving. The other nine simply went on their way. The only one who came back was a Samaritan, whose people were despised and considered as worse than pagans by the self-righteous Jews. Yet, it was he who recognised the need to come back to the Lord in gratitude. Jesus was puzzled and perplexed, and in a lamenting tone he asked: "Were not all ten cleansed; where are the other nine?" Then he told the grateful Samaritan, "Stand up and go on your way, your faith has saved you."

Once again, in God's mysterious design, it is the man from the most despised group who finds total and ultimate healing and salvation through gratitude. He not only got cleansed physically, but his gratitude also brought him into an encounter with Christ and he found a new reason to live. Henceforth he experienced life in abundance. It turns out that the leprosy and the eventual curing of the leprosy constituted a providential opportunity for the man to meet Jesus. Jesus did not become man only to cure us of one disease or the other. No. He came for something immensely more. He came to give us eternal salvation. The meeting with Jesus marked a break with the old, shallow and superficial life the grateful leper was living before. His faith, expressed in gratitude, changed his life and his fortunes dramatically. He was now saved in Christ.

Whereas God has given human beings the knowledge and skills required to heal us of many physical illnesses and diseases, there is however something that no human being can do, and that is to forgive our sins and grant us salvation. That is what Jesus came down from Heaven to do, and that is what Naaman the Syrian and the Samaritan Leper in the gospel received today. What they received was much more important than the physical healing that was immediately manifest. Unfortunately, too many Christians, like the other nine lepers, could be so preoccupied with getting some material benefit, such as physical healing from Christ, that they miss out on the more profound gift that he wants to bestow, which is the gift of salvation.

Ingratitude: A Barrier to Salvation

The nine other lepers in the gospel story only experienced superficial healing. They only got physical healing, but they were not healed spiritually. They went away, returning to their old lives, and this was the cause of Jesus' lament, "Were not all ten cured?" Their lack of gratitude made them miss the real essence of an encounter with Christ, which is eternal salvation. Ingratitude robbed the nine lepers of the opportunity for a providential encounter with the author of life and the healer of souls. This same ingratitude continues today to rob men and women of happiness, joy, fulfilment, inner peace and contentment. Many people do not realise that as they say, "God has two dwelling places: one in heaven, and the other in grateful hearts!

Finding Salvation Through Suffering

By God's mysterious design Naaman was led to salvation through the painful and humiliating experience of leprosy. God knows how to use adverse events for the advantage of his children, as we read in Romans 8:28, "And we know that in all things God works for the good of those who love him, who have been called according to his purpose." Naaman the conqueror of nations had to experience weakness, vulnerability, and desperation. In the dramatic irony that ensued, the Jewish slave girl and the lowly servants of Naaman played a key role in his journey to healing and salvation. Thus, the things we despise or the things that hurt us the most may be the providential route to the realisation of our life's purpose in Christ. That which hurts, harasses, humiliates us the most, like Naaman's leprosy, may be the providential route to the realization of our life's purpose.

Jesus brought us glory through his suffering, and Judeo-Christian history is full of examples of people who only found life and salvation through the crucible of suffering and humiliation. Examples include Joseph, Daniel, Jeremiah, Job, Peter, and Paul. Over the two-thousand-year history of Christianity, there are numerous examples of people who found holiness, who discovered the Lord, who lived exemplary Christian lives only after going through some adversity.

During the times of adversity, we would often not understand what is going on, but we are challenged to trust and obey. After all, we know that not all blessings are wrapped in beautiful packages; some blessings come in rather rough containers. Sometimes, the beauty we pursue turns out to be the fool's gold, as not all that glitters is gold.

What often gives depth to life are the storms we go through. When you find someone who has never suffered, you will quickly see that they have very shallow and often self-centred perspectives on life. By our human nature, we think that prosperity is always a blessing. Sometimes it is, but suffering could also be a blessing, if we endure it with faith and godly submission. The suffering of a Christian patiently endured and humbly offered to God, is a form of prayer. Something critical is often missing in the life of a Christian who has never suffered!

Conclusion

Naaman was plagued with leprosy and suffered greatly. It was through his suffering and humiliation that he discovered a new and a more glorious purpose for his life. He met the Prophet of God, received healing, and began to worship the Almighty God. Jesus also healed ten lepers, but it was only one of the lepers who came back and received much more than physical healing. Like the case of Naaman and the leper in the gospel story, God wants to do much more than simply endow us with material benefits. He wants us to encounter Him, to build a relationship with Him, and to find our salvation in Him. As we go through life, we will face difficult, challenging and even humiliating circumstances like Naaman and the other lepers. We should begin to see such situations as possible opportunities for a providential encounter with God.

Questions To Ponder
1. What is the theme of today's readings?
2. What does St. Paul mean when he says in 2 Timothy 2:8-13 *"I endure every suffering for the sake of the elect that they also may obtain salvation…?"*
3. Discuss briefly how the leprosy that plagued both Naaman the Syrian and the grateful Samaritan could be seen as a blessing in disguise?
4. Why do you think Jesus was sad when 9 of the 10 lepers who were cured, did not return to give thanks?

Additional Reading
Leviticus 13 & 14; 2 Kings 5:1-19; Job 42:1-6; Matthew 11:25-27, 18:23-35

29th Sunday of the Year

Persistence in Prayer

Readings: Exodus 17:8-13 | Psalm 121 | 2 Timothy 3:14-4:2 | Luke 18:1-8

Summary:

To pray persistently and relentlessly requires faith. Jesus tells us not to be discouraged when we pray and do not receive what we ask. He assures us that our loving God cares for us, and that the prayers of the faithful are always answered, but in God's own way and at God's own time. If we give God a timetable and conditions with which to answer our prayers, then we will often be disappointed.

Moses: Model of Persistence in Prayer

The Israelites were at war with the Amalekites and in battle. With hands raised in prayer, Moses interceded ceaselessly while Joshua led the army in battle. For as long as the hands of Moses were raised (in prayer), the Israelites had the upper hand, but when he got weary and his hands dropped, their enemies had the upper hand. The Israelites quickly realised the power in the prayer of Moses. So, Aaron and Hur erected stones for Moses to sit on and they supported his hands to ensure that the hands were perpetually raised in prayer. This is how they won the war (see Exodus 17:8-13).

Reward of Persistence

With the story of the Widow and the Unjust Judge who fears neither God nor man (Luke 18), Jesus illustrates the reward of patience, persistence, and perseverance in prayer. Earlier in Luke 11:5-13, Jesus told his listeners the parable of the Importunate Friend who needed food from his friend to entertain a midnight guest, but whose friend was unwilling to comply. And Jesus says, "I tell you, if the man does not get up and give him for friendship's sake, persistence will make him get up and give his friend all he wants." In this instance as in the encounter between the unscrupulous judge and the widow, his "nuisance value" got him what he wanted at midnight from his friend.

By the illustration in today's Gospel passage, Jesus was not in any way suggesting that God is an unjust and uncaring judge who must be pestered for a prolonged period before he grants favours to his beloved. No. The point of the story is that if persistence prevails with an unjust judge who cares for only his own convenience and comfort, how much more will it prevail with a gracious God who loves us his children.

It is a lesson on the need to pray continually and never to lose heart. It shows that patience and perseverance are two wonderful virtues that can soften even the hardest of hearts like that of the Unjust Judge. With these stories Jesus assures us that unlike the selfish, unjust, unscrupulous, and cynical judge, our just and loving God will listen to and answer his people who cry to him day and night, and he will do so speedily and without delay.

It is an assurance that those who in their hour of need and weakness, failure and disappointment, darkness and confusion, loss and frustration, go to God in faith and trust, and they persevere in prayer day and night, do not return home empty-handed. Rather, God hears their cry, intervenes on their behalf, vindicates them, and defends their cause.

It is then up to believers to place their petitions continually and persistently before the loving God as, according to Jesus, the problem is with us and not with God. If that widow had given up on complaining to the judge, she would not have received the favourable response eventually. Jesus ended this gospel story by asking if he would still find faith when he comes back to the world.

Perseverance is Key

A lesson that comes out prominently in today's readings is that prayer is powerful, that it can influence the outcome of events, and that it can change the lives of people. With the example of his own life of prayer, Jesus demonstrates what pivotal place prayer should occupy in the life of Christians. The problem however is that we now live in a world of quick fixes and instant results, where desires are always to be satisfied instantly. We seem to have destroyed the glorious space between desire and satisfaction. We do not seem to know how to wait for anything anymore. Yet, there is great value in waiting and we must earnestly seek to rediscover the virtue of waiting, because prayer works with such waiting.

In our lives as Christians, there will be delays, failures, losses, disappointments, and frustrations. Jesus calls us today not to quit, not to lose heart, and not to be discouraged. He admonishes us to persevere, wait for God, keep on praying, keep on knocking at heaven's door. He shows us the way to do this as he is constantly waiting for us to come back home to him. He waits for the wicked to repent (see Matthew 13:24-30; Luke 15:11-31) and wants us to wait for the manifestation of his mercy and compassion like the servants awaiting their master's return. He wants us to trust in his love and goodness and, as we wait on him, our faith and trust will grow stronger.

A critical part of Christian prayer is laying oneself open to God's will and God's gifts, whatever they may be. God's response to our prayer often calls us to accept his ways rather than our own. From our human perspective God may appear to delay, but it is always for our good. The period of waiting may be used to purify our desires and motives, so that we may ask for what we really need rather than simply what we want. It may be used to reprove, to correct, and to train us in holiness (2 Timothy 3:16), so that our hearts may be prepared to receive his good gifts. The period of waiting in prayer may be a providential period of growth, when we may reach beyond what is desired in the first place, to the point of making God himself the ultimate object of our desire.

Prayer As Surrendering to God's Will
Jesus prayed passionately at Gethsemane that the cup should pass over him. God heard Jesus' prayer, but the prayer was answered in another way, not in the way he requested. He still had to die on the cross! But God raised him up and gave him a name above all names (Philippians 2:6-11). In Jesus we see that prayer is waiting on God, walking with God, and being in communion with God.

The assurance Jesus gives is that our loving God hears our prayers. Yet, we must acknowledge that God's answers are not limited to our questions. We cannot determine beforehand how God is going to answer our prayers. True prayer is not an attempt to manipulate God into granting us our requests but surrendering ourselves to his ways and experiencing his presence even without his presents!

The ultimate desire of the human being is God himself (Matthew 6:33). Hence, Christian prayer seeks the will of God over and above our own. If our prayer life lacks such continual and more intensive submission, then we are not really praying in the Christian way. Christian prayer is answering the call to be in our father's house (Luke 2:41-50). It is the communion of a child with his father in thought, word, and deed.

Will the Son of Man Find Faith When He Comes?
Jesus asked a critical question in the gospel: "When the Son of Man comes will he still find faith on earth?" There appears to be a major shortfall in Christian commitment in our day. People make superficial commitments, and they give up too easily when difficulties set in. But Christian discipleship requires a sustained effort. Dealing with evil is a difficult and long-lasting engagement. The project of Christian transformation requires a life-long commitment. So, when the Lord comes, will he find us at our duty post?

Conclusion
Christian prayer is much more than words. It is the conduct of a loving relationship that God wants to establish with us. It is the process of ongoing submission to God. In the context of such a relationship, Christian prayer should involve an ongoing transformation of the heart, and an ongoing purification of thought. The one who prays should become increasingly godlike. True, the praying Christian should, on account of the union with God facilitated through prayer, become increasingly "divinised!"

Questions to Ponder
1. Joshua led the army of Israel to victory against Amalek. As a "Soldier of Christ," what war are you fighting today? Who is your Commander? And who are your adversaries?
2. St. Paul says in 2 Timothy 3:17, "Let the man of God be complete, equipped for every good work." Who is the Man of God referred to here?
3. In today's Gospel, Jesus appears to be comparing God to the Unjust Judge who answered the poor widow only when he was being pestered to death. What is the point of the story?
4. What is the relationship (if any) between silence and prayer?

Additional Reading
Genesis 18:16-33; Habakkuk 1:1-3; 2:2-4; Matthew 18:19-20; Acts16:25-28; Philippians 4:6-7

30th Sunday of the Year

The Pharisee and the Tax Collector

Readings: Sirach 35:12-14, 16-18 | Psalm 34 |
2 Timothy 4:6-8, 16-18 | Luke 18:9-14

Summary:

God is not looking for perfection from us because we can never be perfect. St. Paul demonstrates that we can try our best, but we will never be perfect. What God is looking for is a humble acknowledgment of our limitations, and an unwavering trust in the grace of God which is often at its best in human weakness.

A Humble Prayer Pierces Heaven

Today's 1st Reading demonstrates God's special affinity with the poor, the widow, the orphan, and the lowly. It points out that God is close to and has a particular interest in people who are put down, imprisoned, or humiliated by poverty, and that he pitches his tent with the marginalised, disenfranchised, oppressed, condemned, and vulnerable.

The God we serve is close to the broken-hearted. There should, therefore, be a close connection between the lowly poor or the broken-hearted and the faithful servants of God. Jesus demonstrates that he did not come for the healthy and the righteous but the sick, and to call sinners to repentance. He reveals to us the face of a loving God, who will keep the ninety-nine sheep by the hillside and go after the one who is lost. Indeed, God's ways and thoughts are far from our own ways and thoughts (see Isaiah 55:8-9; Psalm 103:10-11).

The story of the Pharisee and the Tax Collector teaches us that God's salvation is only for those who acknowledge that they have sinned and fallen short of the glory of God; that all their good deeds are worthless before the all-holy God; and that we can never merit the salvation of God, but that it is a sheer act of God's mercy.

Grace – A Free Gift

A story is told of a man who deserted the army during the reign of Napoleon Bonaparte, and he was unfortunately caught. He was convicted for desertion and sentenced to death. But his mother pleaded with Napoleon for mercy and the emperor told her that her son did not deserve mercy. The woman's response was that if her son deserved it, then it would not be mercy! An excellent response, because indeed no one deserves mercy.

The Pharisee and the Tax Collector

The Pharisee in the gospel story was arrogant, self-righteous, and self-confident. He was blind to his own sins. He thought it was his prerogative to confess the sins of the Tax Collector to God. Considering himself upright, he looked upon the Tax Collector with utter contempt. On the other hand, the Tax Collector was humble, self-effacing, and fearful of God. He acknowledged the truth of his sinfulness and unworthiness before the all-holy God. So, he refrained from even raising his eye heavenwards. With a heavy burden of guilt, he bowed his head and beat his chest, saying, "Have mercy on me a sinner."

Though two people went to the Temple, only one, the Tax Collector, ended up praying. The Pharisee simply talked to himself, singing his own praises. His was an exercise in vainglory, self-aggrandisement, and presumptuous judgement of someone else. The Tax Collector pleaded God's mercy and graciousness, recognising that nothing else will help his hopeless condition. He saw no need to confess his sins for he knew his entire life has been a mess. So, he simply cried to God for mercy. The Tax Collector did what David did in Psalm 51 and was accepted back by God: He pleaded sincerely and passionately for mercy.

The Pharisee, on the other hand, was blinded by his self-righteousness. He thought that he had it all, but he was wrong. His heart was far away from God, but he congratulated himself for the superficial acts of goodness and religiosity that he believed rendered him justified. If he had looked closely into himself, he would have noticed, among other sins, that he was proud, arrogant, judgemental, and spiteful of others. His attitude towards God was completely wrong. Rather than approach God in emptiness and humility, he exalted himself before God, believing that he could justify himself with what he thought was his own righteous and pious deeds. The Pharisee was highly mistaken!

Conclusion

We must face the truth of who we are: sinful, fallen persons in need of redemption. Recognising that sin is not just the acts that we commit, but a condition in which we live, we must learn to come to God in our brokenness, trusting in his mercy. God deals with who we really are and wants us to come to him with our true selves. We must all recognise that contempt for sinners prevents us from cultivating any relationship with the God of mercy and compassion. We are all beloved children of God, and the loving God does not despise even the worst sinners among us.

Questions to Ponder

1. Name two attributes of God that feature prominently in today's 1st Reading (Sirach 35:12-18).
2. The Pharisee in the Gospel story kept all the commandments, and even made extra sacrifices for God. But he was condemned. Why?
3. What is the relationship (if any) between humility and righteousness on the one hand, and pride and sinfulness on the other?

Additional Reading

2 Chronicles 7:14; Psalm 51; 1 Timothy 1:15; Luke 18:14

31st Sunday of the Year

Zaccheus: A Call to Conversion

Readings: Wisdom 11:22-12:2 | Psalm 145 | 2 Thessalonians 1:11-2:2 | Luke 19:1-10

Summary:

We all have the potential to be saved and that is good news. We can plead with God not to allow his handiwork to be destroyed and God will hear us. The Lord is good to all, and he extends his compassion to all. Divine mercy is universal, and that is what Zacchaeus benefitted from in today's gospel.

The Love, Mercy, and Forgiveness of God

The 1st Reading reflects on God's immense greatness and transcendence. The reading also reflects on God's tremendous love and the universality of his mercy and forgiveness. God is so great, so beyond us, and yet he stoops down to relate with us. Though the whole world is like a speck before God, he still pays compassionate attention to human beings. Considering the immensity and transcendence of God, it is amazing how he can still pay attention to us little sinful creatures.

We have made such an awful mess of his creation, but we are still God's handiwork; his immortal spirit still dwells in us. He overlooks our sins, hoping that this generous gesture of his will lead sinners to repentance. No matter the sin we commit, each one of us still bears the image of God in us. Many do not recognize this truth, which is why public sinners and criminals can so often be humiliated, brutalized and dehumanized. Jesus constantly emphasized that he has come for sinners, not the righteous.

Zacchaeus: A Dramatic Encounter

Today's gospel presents us with the story of Zacchaeus, a senior tax collector, seen by the Jews as a corrupt dealer and public sinner. He was despised by his people who saw him as a betrayer of the Jewish cause. This is because he took up the job of collecting taxes from his own people for the Roman empire that had conquered and was exploiting his people. The wealth he made from the job alienated him thoroughly from his people who considered him a traitor. Jews who were nationalistic and who loved their people would not accept the job of a tax collector for the Roman empire.

A person like Zacchaeus was not to be seen in the company of holy men like Jesus. Zacchaeus knew it himself and would have stayed far off, yet he was anxious to see Jesus. He recognised that he was a very short man. With the crowds around Jesus, he knew there was no way he could see Jesus from a distance unless he did something dramatic. So, he resolved to climb the Sycamore tree located along the road where Jesus was to pass, to catch a glimpse of him.

Zacchaeus never imagined that Jesus would notice him on the tree, let alone talk with him. All he wanted to do was to catch a glimpse of him. He never dreamt that he would be eating with Jesus. But God gave him exceedingly more. On getting to that spot where Zacchaeus was, Jesus looked up, noticed him on top of the tree, recognised the effort the man had put in just to see him, and rewarded him immensely. At that moment, the barriers created by his sinful life and by the Jewish nationalist resentment against those among them serving the Roman empire, were broken down, and Jesus called him by name.

Zacchaeus came down hurriedly and welcomed him joyfully into his house. But for Jesus to go into the house of such a public sinner and eat with him was, for many of his adversaries, a major scandal. Jesus, on his part was looking at a son of Abraham who was ready to come back home. So, while they were outraged and complained that he has gone to be the guest of a sinner, Jesus was already celebrating the return of a sinner. At this point, realising that he had the attention of Jesus, Zacchaeus refused to be intimidated by the people, and he stood his ground. He was instantly transformed by the encounter with Jesus, and he made what could be called a public penitential declaration, as well as a public commitment to godly generosity.

In one moment of grace Zacchaeus the notorious public sinner received salvation along with his entire household. This is the purpose of Jesus' coming. He came "to seek out and to save the lost." This is what Jesus announced at the very onset of his ministry as recorded in Mark 1:15, that, "The time is fulfilled, and the kingdom of God is near; repent and believe the good news!"

Repentance is the reason for the coming of Jesus. This is why he ate with tax collectors and prostitutes. This is why he took the cross upon himself. This is the meaning of the Parables of the Lost Coin, the Lost Sheep, and the Lost Son (Luke 15:1-31). He came to seek out and save those who are lost due to sin. It needs to be constantly emphasised that Jesus is the Lamb of God who takes away sin (see John 1:29), that he came to preach repentance from sin, and that all his followers must be committed to preaching repentance from sin and combating the various consequences of sin.

Zacchaeus: Radical Conversion

Zacchaeus was touched by the profound and loving encounter with Jesus, and he experienced instant conversion and holistic transformation. He was surprised by Jesus' love, knowing how unworthy he was. He felt honoured that Jesus recognised and called him by name, and entered his house to share a meal, even before he repented of his sins. Rather than condemn Zacchaeus, Jesus loved him and brought out the best in him. Jesus recognised that Zacchaeus was not defined by his sins. As a result of that merciful heart of Jesus, Zacchaeus had the courage to stand before his adversaries and the goodness that was buried inside of him began to ooze out. His heart was moved to genuine repentance, and he opened his treasures in generosity. This experience is supported by the observation of Johann Wolfgang von Goethe that, "If you treat an individual as he is, he will remain how he is. But if you treat him as if he were what he ought to be and could be, he will become what he ought to be and could be."

Zacchaeus felt the magic of being loved in his sinfulness and his life was changed. To be loved in one's goodness and beauty is not a big deal. How wonderful it is to be loved in one's sinfulness and ugliness! This is what God did for us, as so well captured by St. Paul when in Romans 5:8 he says, "What shows God's tremendous love is that while we were yet sinners, Christ died for us."

In one moment of grace, Zacchaeus experienced a transformation. From being a man consumed by self-indulgence, he became a child of God, obedient to the spirit. His encounter with Jesus was profound and his conversion was immediate, radical, and permanent. He experienced a radical change of heart, change of purpose, and change of values. His life took on a whole new meaning. He had found a new love, a new set of priorities, and a new reason to live. This is what real encounter with Jesus does: it enables us to take our attention away from ourselves, and to focus on God and others around us.

Our Encounter and Call to Conversion

We are often like Zacchaeus. Because of our sin, we are often too short and too unworthy of God's holy company. The good news is that, though God hates our sin, he loves us nevertheless. He takes notice of us, calls us by name, and invites us to dine with him in the Eucharist. Each of us stands in need of daily conversion. We need conversion from a closed heart to an open heart, from a heart of stone to a heart of flesh, from a life of self-indulgence to a life of sacrificial love, from a life of hatred and vengeance to a life of love and forgiveness, and from a life of pride and arrogance to a life of humility and self-effacement.

Conclusion

God loves everyone he has created and does not want anyone to perish (John 3:16). Jesus did not come for the righteous, but he came to call sinners to repentance. There is a core of decency, a potential for goodness, even in the worst sinner. We too can become good, but we must be willing to let go of certain things if Jesus is to find a place in our hearts. With Christ, sinners have a future, not just a past.

Questions to Ponder

1. Mention two reasons from the 1st Reading why God shows mercy to sinners.
2. What point does St. Paul make in the 2nd Reading?

3. Compare today's Gospel story with last Sunday's. What are the parallels and how are they related to the Parables of the Lost Sheep, Lost Coin, and Lost Son?
4. What did Zacchaeus have to give up in order to have a meaningful conversion? And what are you prepared today to give up so that you may enjoy true union with God in Christ?

Additional Reading
Psalm 36; Matthew 9:9-13; Luke 7:36-50, 15:1-31

32nd Sunday of the Year

The Truth of Life After Death

Readings: 2 Maccabees 7:1-2, 9–14 | Psalm 17 |
2 Thessalonians 2:16-3:5 | Luke 20:27-38

Summary

Death is inevitable but it does not have the final word. For the children of God, death is not the end of everything. Our God is the God of life: he is the God of Abraham, Isaac and Jacob, the God of the living, not of the dead. The virtuous shall live and reign in everlasting peace with God, while the wicked will go into everlasting damnation.

An Example of Faith, Hope, and Courage

Seven Hebrew boys and their mother were ordered by a pagan king to eat swine's flesh which is against the Law of Moses. They refused to defile themselves and to disobey their God, and they were thus sentenced to a cruel death which they readily embraced rather than commit sin.

As they died one after the other, they each affirmed their faith that death is not the end; that there is life after death; and that there is the resurrection of the just. As their tormentors put pressure on them to renounce their faith and obey the king, they demonstrated that they were willing to undergo any torture and be killed, rather than break the law of their ancestors.

In this refusal to sin against God even at the cost of their lives, they left us some key Christian doctrinal principles, such as faith in a God of love and justice, and faith that death is not the end of everything, but rather a passage to new life. They had the hope that the dead shall rise again, that there will be judgement after death where the just will be vindicated; and that ultimately, good shall be victorious over evil, love shall triumph over hatred, and life shall conquer death. They stood firm with courage when their faith was tested. They never compromised with evil. They embraced suffering and paid the ultimate price for what they believed.

These brothers and their mother aptly demonstrated that whereas physical human life is good and precious, it is not an absolute good; that life in its earthly state is not the highest good; and that obedience to God and the defence of truth must be considered higher goods than physical human life. The brothers and their mother teach us that one must be ready to sacrifice one's life if clinging to it will mean sinning against God or violating truth and justice. They teach us in a most graphic manner that it is better to obey God rather than men (see Acts 4:18-19; 5:29).

God's covenant relationship with his people is one that calls for unwavering commitment and absolute fidelity. God does not play games with us and would not want us to play games with him. He demands and deserves unwavering commitment and absolute fidelity from us. The early apostles were confronted with similar circumstances, and they also told their tormentors, "It is better to obey God rather than men" (Acts 4:18-19; 5:29). The consequence of such a choice in the early Church was often martyrdom. According to Norman Cousins, an American author, death is not the greatest loss (in life); the greatest loss is what dies inside of us while we live. It matters not therefore whether we live or die; what matters most is what we live for and what we are ready to die for.

The Resurrection and the Afterlife
The Sadducees were a very powerful group in Israel with great religious, political, and economic influence, but they did not believe in the immortality of the soul or in the resurrection. They believed that this life is all there is. Life after death was, for them, ridiculous, and the idea of the resurrection was laughable. Jesus' teaching was a threat to their power and influence. So, they set out to make a fool of him with their mischievous question. The ridiculous story of the woman who had married and lost seven husbands in quick succession before her death was their attempt at this, but Jesus ignored their ensnaring question and instead asked them about the fate of some of the greatest men in their history, such as Abraham, Isaac, Jacob, and Moses.

Can you imagine that God created the patriarchs and people like the Blessed Virgin Mary, John the Baptist, Simon Peter, Francis of Assisi, Mother Teresa of Calcutta, Pope John Paul II, etc., only to blot them out of his memory? Do you really think that such righteous and faithful people died and simply perished for ever? Do you really think that God who loved them so much and influenced their lives so intensely, would have forgotten those that even we still remember? For Jesus, to imagine that such beautiful and glorious lives would simply dissolve into nothingness is the height of absurdity!

Today's readings raise some of the fundamental questions that have caught the attention of religious people through the ages. They include the following:

> What is the purpose of human existence?
> Why do we have to die?
> What happens after death?
> Does the suffering of the innocent have any meaning?
> What will be the reward for the just?
> What will be the punishment for the unjust?

The Sadducees had no answers to these questions, but Jesus says: "I am the resurrection…Anyone who believes in me, even though he dies, will live, and whoever lives and believes in me will never die…" (John 11:25-26). And St. Paul adds that if the dead are not raised, then "we are, of all people, most to be pitied" (1 Corinthians 15:19).

An Indian mystic says that death is not the extinguishing of the light; it is simply putting out the lamp because dawn has come. In the Preface for Mass of the Dead, we read: "In Him the hope of blessed resurrection has dawned, that those saddened by the certainty of dying might be consoled by the promise of immortality to come. Indeed, for your faithful, Lord, life is changed not ended, and when this earthly dwelling turns to dust, an eternal dwelling is made ready for them in heaven."

Every Christian should be interested in, and become increasingly familiar with, life on "the other side of Calvary". In the last speech he gave before he was assassinated, Martin Luther King Jr. reflected briefly on this other side beyond the horizon, as follows:

> ...But it really doesn't matter with me now,
> because I've been to the mountaintop.
> And I don't mind.
> Like anybody, I would like to live a long life.
> Longevity has its place. But I'm not concerned about that now.
> I just want to do God's will. And He's allowed me
> to go up to the mountain. And I've looked over.
> And I've seen the Promised Land. I may not get there with you.
> But I want you to know tonight, that we, as a people,
> will get to the promised land!
> And so I'm happy tonight.
> I'm not worried about anything.
> I'm not fearing any man!
> Mine eyes have seen the glory
> of the coming of the Lord!!

This is the typical disposition of the champions of our faith through the course of the centuries. For many of them physical death is not such a tragedy to dread. It is often seen as a release from the bondage of the flesh. They often looked forward with joyful expectation to their death (which many called their "transition") to a new and more glorious life of eternal bliss in the presence of the Lord Jesus, and in the company of the saints.

Belief in the Resurrection and the Afterlife

How does believing in the resurrection and the afterlife challenge our life here and now? How do we live daily as believers in the resurrection? What are the implications of our excessive pursuit of and devotion to sensual pleasure, material wealth, and positions of power and influence? Those looking for the powers of this world by any means may get them, but many would have put their spiritual life at risk, and some in their desire for these earthly goods have inflicted on themselves all kinds of fatal wounds. A critical question to always ask ourselves is, what is our real mission on earth?

Conclusion

The hope of conquering death and living eternally with God should strengthen us as we daily face the challenges of witnessing to Christ. This hope gave strength to the martyrs of the Church and still gives strength to all who live faithful Christian lives today.

Questions to Ponder

1. What is the overriding theme of today's readings?
2. The seven brothers and their mother would rather submit themselves to violent death than commit the slightest sin against God. What motivated them? What gave them strength? What are the lessons for us?
3. Name three key virtues that the seven brothers and their mother in the 1st Reading exhibited.
4. Do you really believe in the resurrection? How does this belief influence your daily life if you do? And what are you prepared to sacrifice for this belief?

Additional Reading

Wisdom 3:1-12; Matthew 10:28, 17:1-8; Luke 16:19-31; Romans 8:38-39

33rd Sunday of the Year

Christian Witnessing Amid Trials and Tribulations

Readings: Malachi 3:19-20 | Psalm 97 | 2 Thessalonians 3:712 Luke 21:5-19

Summary:

In the face of the great difficulties to come between now and the second coming of Jesus Christ, many believers will lose faith in Christ. Others will get discouraged and join the bandwagon in a life of debauchery. But it is our endurance that will win us our lives. Our only path to victory is patience and endurance or perseverance through hardship and tribulations.

Malachi's Consoling Prophecy

We live in a world of multiple contradictions. We come into the world expecting much good from life, but we are often confronted with trials and tribulations, tragedy and disaster, violence and war, disappointments and betrayals, wickedness and folly, as well as sickness and disease. It sometimes appears as if the devil is in total control and there is no basis for our faith and hope in a God of love and justice.

The Israelites too never had it easy. They suffered trials and tribulations, including enslavement and deportation. To lift their drooping spirit, the prophet Malachi came declaring that the day of the Lord will come as surely as the sunrise, and that justice will be done equally to the good and evil people alike. Malachi's words were a re-assurance that God will set things right, the evil one shall not have the last laugh, good shall triumph over evil, light shall conquer darkness, those who follow the path of goodness shall be exalted, evil doers shall face everlasting disgrace, and the faithful ones of Yahweh shall sing the song of victory.

The Day of the Lord

The coming day of the Lord will spell doom for the arrogant and the evil doer. For them it will be a day of judgement and condemnation, but for the righteous, it will be a day of liberation and glorification. For those who fear the Lord, the day of the Lord will mean salvation and vindication. For them, "the Sun of righteousness shall rise with healing in its wings." The same sun that shall scotch the evil doer, shall bring healing in its wings for the righteous. This is a beautiful image representing joy, victory, salvation, and glorification. The Lord who comes to judge the earth, judges with righteousness. Faithful believers, therefore, need not fear the day of the Lord. For those who have been faithful to God, the day of the Lord shall bring vindication and salvation. But for the unfaithful and the wicked, the day will bring judgement and damnation.

From the very beginning of the Christian religion, believers looked forward with excitement to this day, the day when Jesus Christ will come back in glory to judge the living and the dead. A classic prayer of the ancient Church was Maranatha: Come Lord Jesus! We constantly pray: "Christ come quickly," as we earnestly desire and await that glorious day with joyful expectation. St. Peter says of this day:

> "Since all things are to vanish, your way of life must be holy and religious as you wait for the day of the Lord and long for its coming, when the heavens will dissolve in fire and the elements melt away in the heat. We wait for a new heaven and a new earth in which justice reigns according to God's promise" (2 Peter 3:11-13).

In today's gospel, Jesus overhears some people discussing the beauty of the Jerusalem Temple - its fine architecture, elaborate stonework, and visual splendour and decorations. But Jesus tells them that very soon the temple shall be laid waste. It will be so completely destroyed that not a stone shall be left on another. This prediction came to pass seventy years after Christ.

Jesus wants us to recognise that we have no lasting city, treasure or house in this world. When we make ourselves too comfortable here below, we often forget the afterlife. If we are surrounded with too much wealth or too many possessions here, there is the tendency to forget the afterlife. Jesus warns that all the things we often count as important here will pass away. So, we must guard against investing too much of our life and passion into anything that death can destroy, and instead pursue the only thing that cannot be taken away by death, which is the love of God and neighbour.

When his followers heard the prediction of the imminent destruction of the Temple of Jerusalem, they thought it heralded the end of the world. So, they asked him, "When will this happen?" (Luke 21:7). But Jesus demonstrated to them that they were asking the wrong question. He told them that no one knows, and that there is no need speculating, because that will be a complete waste of time. He said there will be signs and wonders and great trials and tribulations, but that the end will not come so quickly.

Christ, the expected Messiah, has already come and, though he has inaugurated the glorious kingdom of God by his suffering and death, this kingdom shall not be consummated until the end of time. He said there will certainly be an end to time, but we are not to allow ourselves to be deceived by rumour mongers or false prophets who will arise and claim to have the answers and, thereby, deceive many. These false prophets, he said, will pose as saviours; they will claim to know when the world will end, cashing in on the people's fears and anxieties, and leading many astray. He warned that we should not follow such false prophets, because only God knows when the world will end.

Meanwhile, in the period between the first coming and the second coming, the Christian Church and individual believers have to pass through a period of trials and tribulations, rejection and persecution, suffering and pain, betrayals and divisions, as well as violence and death, on account of their faith in Jesus Christ.

Witnessing to Christ in Times of Trial
The early Christians looked forward to the end time with such excitement that some of them resigned from their work and were simply waiting for death, because they were about to meet the Lord whom they have come to love so much. But Jesus made a realistic

prediction of what the situation will be like in the period between his first coming and his second coming. He said his faithful followers will find themselves in precarious circumstances, but that their persecution will present an opportunity to bear witness to the gospel. This is one of the major paradoxes on which the Christian religion is built, namely, that God can turn around even the worst tragedies, and bring utmost good out of them, to his own glory, and for the ultimate good of his beloved ones.

Faith that Thrives in Adversity

The message of Jesus was not sugar-coated. He did not preach the prosperity message. He told believers what the stark reality will be: persecution, imprisonment, betrayal, hatred and death. Although crises often bring out the worst in human beings, they are also capable of bringing out the best in human beings. For Christians, trials and tribulations present an opportunity for them to give credible witness to the gospel, to demonstrate audacious faith, sacrificial love, ardent hope, rare courage, endurance and perseverance, as well as fortitude and long-suffering. Faced with trials and tribulations we are called to endure and persevere, to "hang in there" as it were.

What inspires such endurance are: the rightness of our cause, the meaning we see in our suffering, the example and support of other believers, the firm belief that good will triumph over evil, and the belief that God will have the last say. Indeed, the quality of our faith is shown or demonstrated through periods of pain and distress, not amid abundance and prosperity. Christ did not promise to protect those who preach his name against every hardship or painful situations. All that the Christian knows for sure is that God will eventually bring good out of evil, and that love and justice will prevail at the end.

Conclusion

Faith often thrives in adversity, and sometimes faith is even born out of adversity. Amid the crises and challenges of life, we can experience profound joy, because we are comforted by the assurance that God is with us. Such assurance gives us the strength to live through tragedy with our spirit unbroken. Jesus Christ says that when these things begin to happen, we should stand erect and hold our heads high, because our Lord is present with us, and our liberation is near.

Questions to Ponder

1. In our 1st Reading (Malachi 2:19-20) the "Day of the Lord" means two different things. What are these two different meanings?
2. Why do you think some early Christians in Thessalonica stayed idle, and refused to do any work? What example did Paul leave behind for them?
3. With the widespread unemployment in our land today can we rightly say as Christians that the one who does not work should not eat?
4. In three short sentences, summarise the message of Jesus in today's Gospel reading (Luke 21:5-19).

Additional Reading

2 Maccabees 7:1-14; John 16:33; Romans 8:31-39; 2 Corinthians 11:23-27

Solemnity of Christ the King

The Crucified One is the King of Kings

Readings: 2 Samuel 5:1-3 | Psalm 122 | Colossians 1:11-20 | Luke 23:35-43

Summary:

David had already been anointed King over his own tribe of Judah. In our first reading, the northern tribes now came to him in Hebron to invite him to be king over the whole of Israel. David then became king over a united country. This kingship of David prefigures the universal kingship of Christ. The second reading is a hymn of thanksgiving to Christ, "the image of the invisible God, and the firstborn of all creation." It is through his death on the cross that God has reconciled all things to himself. The Gospel shows how all those around Jesus while he was in agony on the cross, except the one called "the good thief," jeered at, sneered at, mocked, and derided him. Through it all, the goodness of Jesus continued to shine to the very end.

The Kingship of Jesus

Today we celebrate the feast of Christ the Universal King, declaring to the world that the innocent One who stood condemned before Pilate, the One who suffered the greatest humiliation of death on the cross of Calvary, the One who at the last supper gave up his body as food and his blood as drink, is the same One who was raised from the dead and given a name that is higher than every other name. The crucified Jesus, the Jesus in the Blessed Sacrament, is the same Jesus whom we proclaim today as the universal king, with sovereignty and power and glory. As St. Paul says in our second reading, "thrones, dominions, sovereignties, powers - all things, were created through him and for him" (Colossians 1:16). And as John says in the book of Revelation 1:5-8, He is the universal king before whom everyone will prostrate, even the ones who persecuted, betrayed and killed him. They will eventually acknowledge him as the Alpha and the Omega, the King of kings, the Lord of lords, the Almighty.

In today's Gospel of Luke (23:35-43) we see Jesus the King of the world hanging on the cross, having been crucified by the corrupt and sinful powers of this world. But he is victorious. His kingship is of a different kind. His glory is beyond the reach of earthly trials and failures. His divine kingship may not save him from physical pain and death, but he is nevertheless victorious. It is through the suffering of pain and physical death that he triumphs.

In John 1:29 Jesus is introduced to us as "the Lamb of God who takes away the sin of the world." He did this consistently, and even while dying on the cross he forgave the sin of the repentant thief and promised him an instant share in his paradise. We are reminded today of the kingship of David, and the promise God made to raise up from the stock of David the Messiah who will free the people from oppression, who will rule in love, justice, and righteousness, and the one who will direct the kingdom in the fear of the Lord. The Messiah is the Prince of Peace, whose dominion shall be established in justice and integrity, and in the kind of peace that has no end (Isaiah 9:6-7).

When Jesus Christ appeared, he proclaimed that he is the anointed one; that he has been sent to bring the good news to the poor, to proclaim liberty to captives and new sight to the blind, to set the downtrodden free, and to proclaim the Lord's year of favour (Luke 4:18). He announced that unlike the thief who comes to steal, to cheat and to destroy, he has come so that his people may have life and have it abundantly (John 10:10). He announced that his Kingdom is about peace; that he gives us peace, the kind of peace which the world cannot give (John 14:27).

The kingship of Christ however is one that is attained through suffering. The glory of Christ is one that comes after enormous sacrifice. The dominion of Christ came after he denied himself of his rightful place as Son of God. His Royal Crown came after he went through humiliation and the agony of the cross. Thus, as we read in Philippians 2:6-11,

> His state was divine, yet he did not cling to his equality with
> God but emptied himself to assume the condition of a slave

and became as men are; and being as all men are, he was humbler yet, even to accepting death, death on a cross. But God raised him high and gave him the name which is above all other names so that all beings in heaven, on earth and in the underworld, should bend the knee at the name of Jesus and that every tongue should proclaim Jesus Christ as Lord to the glory of the Father.

Again, John the Seer says that "The Lamb that was sacrificed is worthy to be given power, riches, wisdom, strength, honour, glory and blessing" (Revelation 5:12).

Jesus presents for us a different model of leadership and kingship than we are used to in many parts of the world. Jesus is the leader who is meek and humble of heart, whose yoke is easy, and whose burden is light (Matthew 11:29-30). Jesus is the leader who takes pity on his suffering people, a leader whose compassion for the poor, the weak and the distressed, moved him to perform miracles of healing and multiplication of loaves (Mark1:40-45, 6:30-44). Jesus is the king whose leadership means service. He did not come to be served, but to serve. He told his disciples that among the pagans the rulers lord it over them, and their great men make their authority felt. He warned that this should not happen among them. Instead, he said:

> ...anyone who wants to be great among you must be your servant, and anyone who wants to be first among you must be your slave, just as the Son of Man came not to be served but to serve and to give his life as a ransom for many (Matthew 20:24-27).

Before he went ahead to offer his body and his blood on the cross of Calvary, Jesus did something unique. He taught his disciples a lesson in leadership by service that will continue to challenge all leaders in the world. He stooped down to wash the feet of his disciples and told them to follow his example. He said "If I then the Lord and Master, have washed your feet, you should wash each other's feet. I have given you an example so that you may copy what I have done to you" (John 13:1-15).

Christ's model of leadership is one of compassion and solidarity with the poor, not one that alienates and further impoverishes the poor. His kingship is one that frees the oppressed, not one that oppresses, intimidates and terrorizes the weak and the lowly. Christ's model of leadership is one that is assumed through suffering, not one that is usurped through the naked use of raw power. The throne of Christ is not erected with the crushed bones of the poor, but rather the wooden cross of Calvary. The palace of Christ is painted not with the blood of the poor, but with his own blood, the blood which he offered in sacrifice for the salvation of mankind. Christ is the leader, the king, whose body was broken, and whose blood was shed for the salvation of his people (Matthew 26:26-28; Mark 14:22-24; Luke 22:19-20).

Christ Jesus, even though he was God, remained humble and unassuming. He was born in a manger. He lived a humble life in Galilee. He gathered around himself lowly fishermen as his companions. He reached out to the poor and the despised, including tax-collectors and prostitutes. He took note of the poor widow in the temple who offered two pieces of coins. He was rejected by the powerful in society. He was insulted, he was mocked and jeered at, but his goodness continued to shine.

The kingship of Christ is one of purposeful leadership, a leadership with vision, with the fear of the Lord, and with commitment to the well-being of all the people. Our celebration today therefore challenges the apathy and acquiescence of many Christians in the face of widespread injustice and misrule in many societies. As we celebrate the feast of Christ the King, and reflect on Christ's model of leadership, this is the most opportune time for Christians to look critically at the quality of leadership in their societies, and denounce all authority structures that exploit, oppress, intimidate, alienate and impoverish the people of God. The feast of Christ the King challenges Christians to commit their resources into programmes and projects aimed at the promotion of human dignity and respect for human rights and freedoms wherever they are. Our celebration challenges us to stand up and be counted on the side of the poor, the oppressed and the downtrodden, whom Jesus identifies as the least of his brethren (See Matthew 25:31-46).

Conclusion

As we pray today in the Lord's Prayer that "May Your Kingdom Come", let us understand that the kingdom of Christ is the kingdom of righteousness, truth and justice, and that there can be no partnership between righteousness and iniquity, and no fellowship of light and darkness. Let us recognise that sin cannot co-exist with the reign of God which Christ has come to inaugurate, and therefore let the holy word of God be the lamp for our feet and the light for our way.

Questions to Ponder

1. On what grounds does St. Paul establish the kingship of Jesus in today's second reading (Colossians 1:12-20)?
2. What kind of king was the earthly Jesus? What kind of battles did he engage in? And what kind of weapons did he deploy to fight these battles?
3. When you say in the Lord's prayer, "May your Kingdom Come," what exactly are you asking for? And what part will you play towards the realisation of such a kingdom?

Additional Reading

Isaiah 61:1-2; John 13:1-15; Philippians 2:6-11; Revelation 5:12

Feasts & Solemnities

Solemnity of Mary Mother of God

New Year, New Beginning

Readings: Numbers 6:22-27 | Psalm 67 | Galatians 4:4-7 | Luke 2:16-21

Summary:

When the appointed time came, God sent his Son, born of a woman. God's entry into human history was aided by the "Yes" of a young Jewish woman. This entry heralds a new beginning of endless possibilities in God through Christ Jesus, our saviour.

Mary Mother of God

The incarnation is the work of the Holy Spirit, but it is also a result of the faith of Mary. The "Yes" of Mary facilitated the momentous event of the incarnation. We know for sure that Mary is the mother of Jesus. We believe that Jesus is God. It follows therefore that Mary is the mother of God. Mary is the new Eve. By the singular act of her obedience, she reverses the curse incurred by humanity on account of the first Eve's disobedience. She is the mother of the new dispensation, the mother of the true Israel, the mother of the Christian Church, and as the paradigm of faith, and the mother of all believers (see John 19:26-27).

Mary Champion of New Possibilities

Mary is the human vessel of ultimate possibility. God used her to demonstrate the mystery of the incarnation, by which God took flesh and dwelt among us. In Mary the world was given a new start, a new beginning. In Mary humanity was offered a new slate. In Mary's purity and holiness, we see new possibilities of purity and holiness for all of us believers. God used Mary to fulfil the great promise (of new things) which he made through the prophets of old. A great new beginning for humanity was launched when the angel said to Mary, "Hail Mary full of grace, the Lord is with you!" (Luke 1:28).

This new beginning is what St. Paul talks about when he says, "When the fullness of time had come, God sent his Son, born of a woman, born under the law, in order to redeem those who were under the law, so that we might receive adoption as children" (Galatians 4:4-5). This new beginning is always available to be embraced at the wake of each new day and each new year!

New Year New Possibilities
New Year Day is dedicated to Mary because it is a day to dream about, to reflect upon, to pray for, and to wish one another new beginnings and new possibilities. Each New Year Day, we celebrate Mary's faith and obedience, and we declare that Paradise lost can be regained even for us in our own time. With every child that comes into this world come new possibilities. Each new birth announces that God has not despaired of the world.

In a world of rampant immorality and human degradation, corruption and injustice as well as widespread criminality and political instability, when soon after celebrating Christmas, we Christians say "Happy New Year" to our friends, family members and colleagues, it means that we desire for one another, new life - life in abundance; new joy - the joy of an exuberant life; new love - love in its purest form; new hope - hope that does not disappoint; new freedom - freedom from all forces that enslave; and new peace - peace that surpasses understanding. For Christians, a New Year following the celebration of the incarnation is about a new creation. The old creation was destroyed with the sin of Adam and Eve (Genesis 3:1-19).

When Adam and Eve disobeyed God, human beings were expelled from paradise, the garden of happiness. We became proud and arrogant, selfish and greedy, lustful and blind, wicked and brutal, insensitive and oppressive, hateful and violent. There is no evil of which we were not capable. Sin brought about separation and alienation from God, from neighbour, and even from self. Sin brought about pain and sorrow from trials and tribulation. Sin also brought about death and damnation. There is perhaps no better time than a new year for us to remind ourselves that with Christ a new world of peace and prosperity for everyone is possible; a new form of humanity, solidarity and collaboration can emerge; and a new life of humility, service, and sacrificial love is possible.

As a new year dawns, and we mark the first day of the year with the Solemnity of Mary, Mother of God, we proclaim to the world our belief that in Christ the son of Mary, God's image in each human being, which was defaced with the disobedience of Adam and Eve, has been restored in all its beauty. We proclaim today as we begin a new calendar year that true, authentic happiness is now possible in this world, and that love can now reign in the hearts of men and women, because of Jesus Christ the son of Mary.

A new year is an opportune time to heed the call of Christ to be born again from above, and to begin to live our lives according to the purpose for which we were created. Each new year we are given one more opportunity to embrace fully the call to be born anew of the Spirit, for as Jesus says to Nicodemus, "…what is born of flesh is flesh, and what is born of Spirit is spirit (John 3:6); and begin to live our lives from inside out rather than from outside in.

Living in Christ: The Imperative of a New Creation

St. Paul teaches that anyone in Christ is a new creation. Everything old has passed away, everything has become new (2 Corinthians 5:17). One who lives in Christ dies to the old life of Adam and is reborn "in Christ." This new life will be marked by dying and rising with Christ; dying to our ego or false selves, and rising to our true identity, obtained in Christ, inspired by the Spirit, and directed toward God. The new life is characterised by love, joy, peace, patience, kindness, goodness, faithfulness, gentleness, and self-control (Galatians 5:22-23); as well as wisdom and understanding, knowledge and good counsel, fortitude and piety, and the fear of the Lord (Isaiah 11:2).

Conclusion

All believers in Christ are challenged to learn something from Mary, the one who obeyed God, the one who pondered everything in her heart, and embrace all that she represents: humility, submission, obedience, sacrifice, love, fear of the Lord. We ought to see each new year as a providential opportunity for a new beginning and seek to dwell always in the God of all possibilities.

We are reminded every New Year Day to trust that God will see us through all the challenges on the way of our Christian commitment; to ponder daily in our hearts God's word that we read or those that come through others; to count every day and make every day count in our lives, and to see each new day as the first day of the rest of our life.

Questions to Ponder
1. The Church dedicates January 1 to Mary the Mother of Jesus (Mother of God). In what ways can we say she represents New Beginnings?
   What Marian virtues are you determined to emulate this new year?
2. Christians observe January 1 as a Day of Prayer for Peace. But by what kind of individual and group behaviour do we sometimes make peace difficult to attain even as we pray daily for it?
3. Jesus the Prince of Peace says "Blessed are the Peacemakers…"
   What kind of conduct must we exhibit this year for the Lord to identify us as Peacemakers?
4. What are the Christian virtues we require the most in order to survive as good Christians this year in the ever-challenging circumstances of our society?

Additional Reading
Isaiah 7:14-16 | Luke 1:46-55 | John 1:1-18, 2:1-11 |
2 Corinthians 5:17

Solemnity of the Birth of John the Baptist

A New Era Has Come

Readings: Isaiah 49:1-6 | Psalm 139 | Acts 13:22-26 | Luke 1:57-66, 80

Summary:

Our first reading tells us about the prophecy of Isaiah regarding the faithful servant of God who will be light to all nations. Then, Paul explains the role of John the Baptist in heralding the coming of Jesus. He prepared the people through his preaching and the baptism of repentance. The Gospel story is about the birth of John the Baptist and the miraculous events of his naming.

Why a Solemnity for John's Birth?

In the Church's Liturgical Calendar, birthdays of saints are not celebrated; only their "death-days," the days of their translation to heaven, are celebrated. But in the case of John the Baptist the Church celebrates both his birth and his death. His birthday is celebrated so solemnly that it even takes precedence over Sunday celebrations. John is the only one after Jesus Christ whose birthday is celebrated with a solemnity. Why is it so?

John was not a very attractive person. He dressed rather badly, wearing camel's hair. He lived an austere life and ate weird food. He harassed people to repent in the most crazy and un-diplomatic manner. Yet in the Gospels and in the Acts of Apostles, John is treated like a celebrity. Today's feast is the Church's way of declaring with Jesus that, "*of all who are born of women no one is greater than John*". In the birth of John the Baptist, God showed mercy and blessed not only Zachariah and Elizabeth, but the whole of humanity, because in him God opened a new era for Israel and for humanity. In John the Baptist, the prophetic voice which had been silent for 400 years emerged again in Israel.

The annunciation of John's birth happened in almost the same way as the annunciation of the birth of Jesus. The angel Gabriel announced to the old priest Zachariah that "God has heard your prayer. You and your barren wife will have a son. You will name the child John." The child will be filled with the Holy Spirit from the womb. His life will be entirely dedicated to the service of God in the spirit of Elijah, and he will herald the coming of the Messiah.

The Church celebrates the birthday of John as solemnly as she celebrates Christmas because she understands that with the birth of John the Baptist a new era has come - a new era of grace, and of God's favour. John has come to prepare the people to receive the graciousness of God. The Church also recognises that John is like a boundary between two testaments, the bridge that connects the Old and the New. He represents the Old (made up of the Law and the Prophets) and heralds the New, which is established in Jesus Christ. After John, the fruitful womb of Mary brought forth the Incarnate Son who would conquer both sin and death and show the way to God's kingdom. John's birth is a decisive turning point in the history of humanity. The fortunes of the world changed decisively and permanently when John introduced Jesus to the world as "the Lamb of God who takes away the sin of the world" (John 1:29).

John, A Special Name

Today's Gospel is about the naming of the child of Zachariah and Elizabeth. Zachariah had been struck dumb and when Elizabeth told the elders that the child is to be named John they protested: *It is not a common name for the clan, none of the relations bears that name (Luke 1:61).* When they signalled to Zachariah, he asked for a writing pad and wrote: HIS NAME IS JOHN! John is the name given to the child by the angel Gabriel before he was conceived (Luke 1:13).

But what is in a name? In biblical times and in traditional African societies the names of persons had deep, profound meanings. Names reflected a person's family or birth circumstances, identity, purpose and mission in life. Parents gave names to point the child in a particular direction. And that is how the child found its fulfilment. God revealed to the parents the purpose of the child, and then they point the child in that direction. Names showed what a person stood for or will live for. So, names could be an expression of the child's entire personality and identity.

John means "God is gracious". His birth launched for Israel and for humanity a new era characterised by Grace, not Law. The name, given before he was conceived shows that God had a specific plan for the child. The words of Prophet Isaiah apply to John: "The Lord called me before I was born… he formed me in the womb to be his servant" (Isaiah 49:1, 5).

Living a Purpose-Driven Life

In John we see that everyone comes into the world with a specific God-given purpose. Our task as we journey through life is to discover this unique purpose and to ensure that it is realised. For John the purpose required that he lived in the desert and be uncontaminated by the prevailing fads and fashions. He dressed in an unusual way (rough animal skin). He ate strictly vegetarian food (locusts and wild honey). He lived in the desert where he learnt to hear God's voice. There he cultivated courage and discipline, virtues that helped him to walk faithfully the path that God set for him. He came out now and again, yelling and screaming, calling people to repent from sin and be baptised.

Conclusion

What name do you bear? How is it related to your purpose in life? If you were to receive a new name today - a name that reflects your true identity and purpose, a name that reflects all that God sent you into the world to be and to become, what will that name be? We often will need some desert experience to discover our true purpose in life. We now and again need an environment where we can hear God's voice like Samuel (See 1 Samuel 3:1-10). Now and again we need to retreat from our regular activities to evaluate ourselves. Failure to discover our purpose or refusal to take the path that leads to its realisation is perhaps the greatest source of sadness in the world.

Many people are sad, depressed distressed or traumatized, because they are bent on pursuing a particular course in life which may not be God's plan for them. We must therefore be constantly seeking to do the will of God rather than our own. John found his purpose and he lived it to the full. This is the reason for his greatness, and the reason why we mark his birth as a solemnity. Like John the Baptist, we too can discover the purpose for which God created us, and in Christ live that purpose to the full. This is the way in which we too will achieve our own greatness.

Questions to Ponder
1. Take a close look at the first reading, was Isaiah's prophecy about Isaiah himself or someone else? Discuss briefly.
2. Explain how the birth of John the Baptist marks a turning point in the history of Israel and in the history of humanity.
3. In what way is the birth and ministry of John the Baptist a source of encouragement for Christians who are daily threatened by terrorist insurgency and violence?

Additional Reading
Matthew 3 | Mark 6:17-29 | Luke 1:67-70, 7:24-28 | John 1:29

Solemnity of Saints Peter and Paul

Heroes of Our Faith

Readings: Acts 12:1-11 | Psalm 34 | 2 Timothy 4:6-8, 17-18 | Matthew 16:13-19

Summary:

Today's first reading is the account of how, after Peter was thrown into prison by Herod for proclaiming Jesus as Lord, the Church went into fervent prayers. The Lord then sent an angel to release him miraculously from his prison. The second reading is an excerpt of Paul's 2nd Letter to Timothy, where he expresses his acknowledgement that the end of his earthly life is very near. He is convinced that he has spent his life in the mission of the gospel, and he declares his belief that the Lord will continue to strengthen him, rescuing him from all evil threats, and bringing him safe into the heavenly Kingdom. The Gospel reading is the account of the spectacular event at Caesarea Philippi, where Simon Peter first declares that Jesus is "the Christ, the Son of the living God." Upon this declaration of faith in Jesus, Simon's named was changed to Peter, the rock upon which Jesus will build his Church!

Peter, Leader of the Early Church

Peter was the brother of Andrew. Along with James and John the sons of Zebedee, he was one of the first four disciples of Jesus (See Mark 1:16-20). Jesus frequented Peter's family house at Capernaum, where on one occasion he healed Peter's mother-in-law who was down with fever (Matthew 8:14). The Lord made him one of his closest companions. Peter had been inspired by the Spirit of God to recognize and confess that Jesus is the Messiah – the Son of God (Matthew 16:16). When, following Jesus' uncompromising teaching on the Bread of Life, many people stopped following him, and Jesus asked the disciples if they too will leave, it was Peter who answered: "Lord to whom shall we go? You have the words of eternal life. We have come to believe and know that you are the Holy One of God." Peter demonstrated that he loved Jesus immensely.

Peter was however a human being with many weaknesses. He was impulsive, impetuous, fearful and even cowardly. Not long after promising Jesus that even if everyone else should abandon the Master, he, Peter, will never abandon him, at a crucial moment of need, when he was identified as one of Jesus' disciples from Galilee, Peter denied vehemently that he ever knew Jesus (See Matthew 26:33 and John 18:13-27). Despite these glaring human weaknesses, Jesus appointed him to lead the Church, to be Shepherd over the flock of Christ, and to hold the Church together in the integrity of the faith. When after the resurrection Peter re-affirmed his love for Jesus, the Lord commanded him to "look after my sheep." Thus, it is understood that Jesus handed over his Church to Peter to oversee. Peter was given the keys of the Kingdom: to lock and to unlock, to bind and to loose, to maintain discipline and the right tradition, etc (Matthew 16:19). As leader, he was to be the rallying point of all Christians, the source of unity for what would be a diverse company of followers.

After receiving the Holy Spirit at Pentecost, it was Peter who stood up in Jerusalem and proclaimed with great power and unusual courage that Jesus Christ the crucified one has risen from the dead; that he is the stone that was rejected by the builders that has now become the cornerstone; and that it is in his name, and in no other name that men and women could be saved. This is the first recorded Christian sermon, and it was delivered by Peter (See Acts 2:14-36). The first miracle in the Christian Church was performed by Peter in the company of John, when they were approached by a lame beggar who sat at the temple gate. He told the beggar, "I have neither silver nor gold, but what I have I give you. In the name of Jesus Christ of Nazareth, stand up and walk" (Acts 3:6).

Paul, once persecutor, now Apostle of Christ
Paul who used to be called Saul from Tarsus, was an ardent and fanatical Pharisee. He was a major persecutor of the early Christian faith and all who followed the Way. He was on his way to Damascus, Syria, with a license from the authorities to destroy adherents of the

new Christian religion, when he was miraculously "arrested" by the Lord and commissioned to go and champion the Church's missionary endeavours, especially towards the Gentiles (See the story of Paul's spectacular conversion in Acts 9:1-29). After his conversion, Paul applied the same energy, zeal and fervour which he had used in persecuting the Church, for the furtherance of the mission of Christ. He promoted the Gospel of Christ with great power and charisma, like no one else ever did.

Paul used his immense intelligence and his vast knowledge of the Jewish religion and history, and the works of the secular philosophers of the time, combined with his oratorical skills, to proclaim the Christian message of salvation. He engaged in many missionary journeys and planted many young Churches, which he nurtured with his well-crafted regular "epistles." Paul traversed land and sea to plant and visit the newly established churches, especially in pagan territories, and endured untold hardship, eventually suffering martyrdom (like Peter) in Rome. Towards the end of his life, as he looked forward to crowning his Christian witnessing with martyrdom, he was able to say to his followers: "I have fought the good fight. I have run the race to the finish. I have kept the faith…" (2 Timothy 4:6-8).

Though Paul never met Jesus in the flesh, he demonstrated in his ministry that indeed he had a profound encounter with the Lord, during which time he was commissioned as an apostle to the Gentiles. Paul is an example of Christian missionary zeal. He is recognized as the Christian missionary par excellence. He had an all-consuming passion for spreading the Christian message of salvation across the world. He was convinced that getting to know Jesus (in spite of his sinful past) was an act of God's mercy and graciousness, and that to be sent on mission to proclaim Christ to others was a rare privilege (See Galatians 1:15-16). He looked upon his entire life and mission as the grace of God at work. He therefore worked for God with a spirit of gratitude and lived his entire life in thanksgiving and praise.

Peter and Paul, the Pillars of the Christian Church

We call Peter and Paul the pillars of the Church because they represent the fundamental columns on which the Christian faith thrives, namely Faith and Mission. In their different personalities and in the conduct of their ministries, Peter and Paul represent the complementary elements of "institution" and "spirit," "law" and "liberty," and "authority" and "charism," which checkmate each other and are often responsible for some creative tension within the Church. Peter and Paul kept each other in balance. They had major differences on how the mission of Christ should be accomplished, but they both received the same vision from Christ. Peter showed an immense love for the Lord, and Paul on his part was on fire with zeal and enthusiasm to see the mission of Christ accomplished. They both worked hard to transform the world for Christ and their lives were crowned with martyrdom!

As we celebrate the feast of Peter and Paul today, we are challenged to seek daily the personal encounter with Jesus that made them such powerful witnesses of Christ and his message of salvation. We are challenged today to cultivate the spirit of repentance and perfect contrition for our sins that Peter and Paul exhibited so clearly. We are challenged today to see our Christian calling and our membership of the Body of Christ as a rare privilege – an act of grace, on account of which we should live the rest of our lives in thanksgiving and praise. As we honour these two heroes of our faith today, we are challenged to commit ourselves passionately to the task of Christian evangelization, using our various talents and privileged exposures.

Conclusion

Saints Peter and Paul are celebrated on the same day because Jesus founded his church on Saint Peter and Saint Paul was the greatest evangelist in the history of the church. These two saints were very different from each other. Each of the two Apostles had a different mission, but together they built up the church that Jesus Christ founded. We owe our Christian faith in a large part due to them. We have personally benefited from their efforts, so it is very fitting that we honour them today.

Questions to Ponder
1. Saints Peter and Paul are celebrated as heroes of the faith. However, they did not earn this honour without suffering. To what extent are you prepared to suffer for the sake of the faith?
2. Each of the Apostles was different in character and gift, yet they were able to work together for the church. How might this unity of purpose guide Christian churches today?
3. Peter declared Jesus as the "Son of the living God." What would your answer be if you hear Jesus say to you: 'Who do you say that I am?'

Additional Reading
John 1:42 | Acts 9:1-19, 22:6-21 | 1 Corinthians 15:9 | Galatians 2 | 2 Peter 3:14-16

The Transfiguration of the Lord

Jesus' True Identity Revealed

Readings: Daniel 7:9-14 | Psalm 97 | 1 Peter 1:16-19 | Matthew 17:1-9

Summary:

The Transfiguration is a rare event at which the veil which separates the visible from the invisible, and the present from the future, was removed. At that (brief) moment on Mount Tabor, the visible and the invisible became one and there was no distinction between the present and the future. The event of that day was an epiphany, whereby Peter, James, and John were, in a moment, shown the future glory of Jesus and themselves.

Jesus' True Identity Revealed

The event of the Transfiguration is recorded almost word for word by all the three synoptic gospels (Matthew 17:1-9; Mark 9:2-10; and Luke 9:28-36). It is one of the few stories that are reported by the three gospels and recorded the same way.

In each Gospel account, the event is set on Jesus' Road to Jerusalem where he was bound to face a violent death like other prophets before him. He was on his way to the city where he would be rejected and condemned, and then tortured and crucified. One would naturally recoil at such a fate, yet Jesus was committed to his Father's will, so he was determined to go on.

On their way he went up a high mountain, Mount Tabor, taking with him Peter, James, and John to reflect and pray over the adversity that was soon to follow. He went up there to seek the face of the loving Father, to find encouragement, and to obtain strength (for the journey). As he prayed, he had a marvelous experience. He was transfigured: his face shone like the light, his clothes became dazzlingly white; and then something significant happened: there appeared with him Moses and Elijah (Moses had passed on for more than two thousand years, and Elijah for about seven hundred years before this incident).

Then the voice of the Father was heard from heaven, saying, "This is my Son, the beloved, listen to Him" (Matthew 17:5; Mark 9:7; and Luke 9:35). It was a most glorious moment for the disciples who had never seen or heard anything like this before. Perhaps the nearest they had heard from their ancestors is that Elijah rode a chariot to heaven. They were mesmerized as the glory they witnessed was beyond description. It is in this state that Peter then requested that they remain there! It was too good an experience to abandon and start coming down.

Something similar happened at the baptism of Jesus in the Jordan when the Spirit of the Lord descended upon Him, and a voice was heard from heaven which said: "This is my Son, the beloved, my favour rests on him" (Matthew 3:17).

Between the Cross and Crown
For Jesus, the Transfiguration was a moment of profound encounter with God. He needed that encounter just as we also need to encounter God from time to time for our confirmation, encouragement, and as a source of strength. During this extraordinary encounter the spirit exploded with brilliance on Jesus; he had a rare glimpse of God's face; heaven broke through to earth; a chord of indescribable joy was struck within him at this experience even though he was going to Jerusalem to suffer and die; and he experienced in a profound way and felt very clearly, the love of God.

That Jesus was going to his definite end through suffering and a painful, violent death, and he still felt clearly and in a profound way the love of God, is the part of the Christian gospel that has not often been well preached in our society, or perhaps it is being preached and we have refused to accept it. For many, the love of God can only be felt by him taking us away from the situation of suffering.

The assurance that Jesus got from the transfiguration experience gave him strength to face the grim future. Memories of the event, we believe, sustained him through the passion. Perhaps we all need that kind of encounter with the Lord, which will be our source of strength when we go through the tunnel of night, because believers in our religious history who had such privileged encounters including St. Paul on the way to Damascus, and Moses at the Burning Bush, were never the same again after the profound encounters.

Such persons never lose faith, and they always keep going, even in the face of great adversities, when they remember the phenomenal experience of their encounter. The Transfiguration experience came at a very difficult time for Jesus: a time of uncertainty, loneliness, and fear. On that mountain, he was affirmed by Moses and Elijah, and comforted by the voice of the Father. He knew that the Father was with him and that he enjoyed the Father's favour. With such knowledge he could face any adversity, for nothing could separate him from the love of God (Romans 8:31-39).

The presence of Moses and Elijah is very significant. Moses represents the Law (by which God established a covenant with his people), and Elijah represents the Prophets (by which God guided them). It then means that everything in the Old Testament came out to confirm that this is the One the world has been waiting for. Moses the ancient law giver, and Elijah, the ancient quintessential prophet, the prophet of all prophets, the one that the Jews speak about with a lot of nostalgia because never was there a prophet like him - both of whom were reputed not to have been buried anywhere under the sky - were around to bear witness, to testify, and confirm that God has indeed finally intervened in history by sending his Son.

Their presence there was an attestation from heaven that God has intervened in history by sending this Person they were standing with. It was a confirmation that indeed this Person is the Messiah. For the disciples, the Transfiguration was meant to reveal the true glory of Jesus to them, to confirm the course Jesus had taken, and to strengthen them for the scandal of the cross.

The cross has always been a scandal because human beings naturally run away from suffering and pain. The disciples' fragile faith in Jesus would soon be shaken, tried, and tested. It is in a bid to prepare them for the ordeal ahead that the Transfiguration event happened. It was demonstrated to them that Jesus is both the glorious Son of God and the Suffering Servant of Isaiah. He is the same person that Daniel 7:13-14 and Isaiah 53 describe. He is the

One presented before the Ancient of Days, and before whom peoples of all nation bow in worship, as well as the Suffering Servant.

Jesus was transformed in order that the disciples who were watching might see the future that awaited them, and we who are celebrating it today may also see the future that awaits us. In this way, when we are enjoying good times in life, we may not settle so fully and so completely for those good times that we forget where we are supposed to be going. Likewise, when we are facing bad times and experiencing adversities, we may not get so distracted by the pain and sadness, that we forget the glory that awaits us.

From experiencing the Transfiguration, the disciples knew that they had a lot of potential. They realised that they could become much more than they were, and that they could do much more than anyone in the world expected of them. Yet they did not understand the implications of all these, until after Jesus had risen from the dead.

A Ray of Light and Hope

The Transfiguration event is filled with light and hope, foreshadowing the light and hope of the resurrection which is for us cause for profound joy and stimulating hope. With the Transfiguration the disciples saw themselves in a new light – as they will be when glorified. As we celebrate the event, we too can see ourselves in this new light.

The Transfiguration reveals the destiny of every human being in God, namely, that in the fullness of time everyone will recognise the Lord in his full splendour and glory and majesty. For us believers the Transfiguration is not meant to be only a future event. We already have some experience of the Transfiguration as we read the gospel and reflect upon it. We also have some more of the Transfiguration experience every time we celebrate the Eucharist, as transubstantiation takes place, and as at communion we become one with the Lord.

Connecting with God at Times of Adversity

As with Jesus on his way to Jerusalem, life for many of us could be very hard sometimes. We could be faced with poverty and unemployment, sickness and pain, failure in career or family life, loneliness and rejection, persecution and unfair judgement, humiliation and condemnation, etc. At such times of adversity, do we, like Jesus, know how to ascend to the "mountaintop," to connect with the Lord who has a purpose for our lives, who gives meaning to every event of our lives? At times of adversity, do we remember to ascend to the mountaintop, so as to hear those consoling words of the Father, "You are my beloved son/daughter," "My grace is sufficient for you," etc.?

Conclusion

The critical question in life is not whether there will be suffering or not, but what kind of attitude we will adopt in the face of life's inevitable problems and difficulties. At such times, do we know how to go up to "the mountaintop" to pray and to reflect, in order to receive the light of hope, to see the larger picture, to seek the face of God, and to be re-assured by God's consoling words?

Questions to Ponder

1. Is there a relationship between the 1st Reading (Daniel 7:9-14) and the Gospel passage? What is it?
2. What is St. Peter saying to us in the 2nd Reading of today (2 Peter 1:16-19)?
3. "The event of the Transfiguration reveals the true identity of Jesus Christ to his disciples and to us." Discuss.
4. Reflect for a moment on the story of the Transfiguration of Christ. What is the Lord saying to you in your life circumstances as you reflect on this story now?

Additional Reading
Exodus 33:22-23; Luke 9:28-36; Mark 9:2-7

Solemnity of the Assumption

Celebrating Mary's Assumption
of the Blessed Virgin Mary

Readings for Vigil Mass: 1 Chronicles 15:3-4, 15-16, 16:1-2| Psalm 132 | 1 Corinthians 15:54-57 | Luke 11:27-28

Readings for Day Mass: Revelation 11:19, 12:1-6,10 | Psalm 45 | 1 Corinthians 15:20-27 | Luke 1:39-56

Summary:

The reading from the first book of Chronicles shows the central place that the Ark of the Old Covenant occupied in Judaism, and the great reverence the people had for it. In the New Testament times the Church sees Mary as the ark of the New Covenant. The second reading for the vigil mass from 1 Corinthians 15 celebrates the victory of Christ over death. Mary the mother of Jesus shares fully and pre-eminently in this victory. In the Gospel for the vigil mass Mary is presented as blessed, not only because she is the mother of Jesus, but also because she heard the word of God and obeyed it.

For the day mass the first reading from Revelation is an account of the battle between the agents of God and Satan. Mary and her child were at the heart of the battle. The agents of God ultimately triumph. In the second reading for the mass during the day, St. Paul demonstrates that by his death on the Cross, Christ (the new Adam) has overturned the damage done by the old Adam and Eve. The Church sees Mary as the new Eve who by her obedience to God undoes the harm done by the old Eve. The Gospel of this day mass narrates Mary's visit to her cousin Elizabeth after the gracious and spectacular event of the annunciation. A significant part of this Gospel is the *Magnificat* – Mary's hymn of praise to God for his goodness to her and to his chosen people.

Celebrating Mary's Assumption

In our first reading for the Assumption Day Mass, John the Seer tells us that,

> "A great sign appeared in heaven: a woman clothed with the sun, with the moon under her feet, and on her head a crown of twelve stars. She was pregnant and was crying out in birth pangs, in the agony of giving birth. Then another sign appeared in heaven: a great red dragon, with seven heads and ten horns, and seven diadems on his heads... Then the dragon stood before the woman who was about to bear a child, so that he might devour her child as soon as it was born. And she gave birth to a son, a male child, who is to rule all nations with a rod of iron. But her child was snatched away and taken to God and to his throne... Then I heard a loud voice in heaven proclaiming, 'Now have salvation and power come, and the kingdom of our God and the authority of his Christ, for the accuser of our brethren who accuses them day and night before our God has been thrown down" (Revelation 12:1-10).

The Dogma of the Assumption

On the Feast of All Saints, November 1, 1950, Pope Pius XII pronounced the dogma of the Assumption of the Blessed Virgin Mary, with the apostolic constitution, *Minificentissimus Deus,* declaring that "Mary, perpetually immaculate, the Virgin Mother of God, after the completion of her earthly life, was assumed body and soul into the glory of heaven."

The Gospels present no details about the death of Mary the mother of Jesus. However, the dogma of the Assumption has its origin in the popular faith of the Christian community all through its two-thousand-year history. It is on record that in the early Centuries of Christianity, Mary was already taken as a symbol of faith and hope for the Christian faithful, who believed that her death had to be an extraordinary event such as befits the extraordinary person that she was. Just as the Jews saw the death of Moses as a graceful event in which angels carried his body to God, Christians began describing the death of Mary as her return (in wholeness) to God. They were so persuaded of her unique holiness and special place in God's plan for the salvation of humanity, that their imaginative faith supplied details regarding her death and glorification which the New Testament could not supply.

Visual artists and poets competed with one another in celebrating their love for Mary the mother of Jesus, and their faith in her glorious assumption. Numerous images abounded of Mary being carried by angels on celestial flights, of saintly choirs celebrating her arrival in heaven, and of the grand events of her coronation or crowning as "Queen of Heaven," such that by the 6th Century A.D. the Christian community already began to celebrate many Marian Feasts, which have survived till today in the official calendar of the Church.

In the Apostolic Constitution defining the Assumption, Pope Pius XII situates the dogma in the context of a humanity in a major crisis of moral, spiritual and human values. The declaration was coming when the world had just witnessed two World Wars with attendant atrocities that were hitherto unimaginable. The Pope notes in the Apostolic Constitution that "while the illusory teachings of materialism and the corruption of morals that follows from these teachings threaten to extinguish the light of virtue and to ruin the lives of men by exciting discord among them, in this magnificent way all may see clearly to what a lofty goal our bodies and souls are destined" (See paragraph 42).

Also in a 1974 Apostolic Exhortation, *For the Right Ordering and Development of Devotion to the Blessed Virgin Mary*, Pope Paul VI states that,

> "The solemnity of August 15 celebrates the glorious Assumption of Mary into heaven. It is a feast of her destiny of fullness and blessedness, of the glorification of her immaculate soul and of her virginal body, of her perfect configuration to the Risen Christ, a feast that sets before the eyes of the Church and all mankind the image and the consoling proof of the fulfilment of their final

hope, namely, that this full glorification is the destiny of all those whom Christ made His brothers..."

Pope John Paul II suggests that in our love for Mary the mother of Jesus, we are sensing the "feminine face of God." At a time when many are shamelessly displaying the ugly face of humanity through the celebration of hatred and violence, unmitigated consumerism, as well as reckless promiscuity, symbolised perhaps most graphically in modern-day pornography, those of us believers who today are celebrating the beauty of Mary - Our Lady of the Assumption, are taking on the responsibility of counteracting the ugliness of evil that abounds everywhere in the world, by showing humanity the beautiful, feminine face of God that is loving, graceful, tender, elegant and dignified.

Yes, it is this beautiful face of God that will save our world which today is ravaged by multiple manifestations of evil. As we celebrate the Assumption, we are announcing to the modern world the same message that John the Seer proclaimed two thousand years ago: that the agents of God have been victorious over Satan; that goodness and beauty have triumphed; and that love and mercy have overcome hate and vengeance.

The Example of Mary
As we celebrate the Assumption, we reflect on the life of Mary, the very first Christian believer, who heard the word of God and kept it, who recognised in all humility that she was only a handmaid and asked that God's will be done in her life. We celebrate the life of the one whose soul "magnified" and proclaimed the greatness of the Lord. Mary allowed God to be God in her life. Unlike the first Eve, Mary recognised that obedience to God does not diminish human freedom, but instead expands it. She knew that if God is great, and if His will is done, then we too could be great.

In the account of Genesis, Adam and Eve thought that if God wins, they will lose. But Mary was very clear in her understanding that human life is not oppressed or diminished by obedience to God, but that by obedience to God the Creator, human life expands and flourishes in splendour, and reaches its ultimate fulfilment. Her "Yes" to God therefore overturned the disobedience of the first Eve.

Mary was simple and uncompromising in her submission to God. She was imbued with the Word of God. She was at home with the word of God. She meditated on the word of God, treasuring it in her heart (see Luke 2:19). She spoke the word of God. She was totally immersed in and penetrated by the word of God. This love of and familiarity with the word of God endowed her with inner enlightenment, wisdom and prudence, and the strength and courage that comes from God to resist evil and to foster goodness. Mary demonstrated absolute commitment and fidelity to God's purpose, which she embraced wholeheartedly. She said, "I am the handmaid of the Lord, let it be done to me according to your word" (Luke 1:38).

As we celebrate the Assumption of Mary the mother of Jesus, the Church calls upon us to embrace her as our mother and model of spirituality and Christian conduct. She emptied herself completely to be full of grace. She believed God simply because he is God. She trusted that God knows best and placed herself completely at God's disposal. Mary's Assumption should be a source of encouragement for all believers who look forward to their own ultimate glorification.

Conclusion

The Solemnity of the Assumption of the Blessed Virgin Mary commemorates the death of Mary and her bodily assumption into Heaven before her body could begin to decay. But to share in Mary's glory, we must obey God at every turn in our lives. Such obedience is risk-taking because you never know all the implications. However, the history of our religion sufficiently demonstrates that those who take risks in doing God's will are never disappointed. To share in Mary's glory, we must appreciate that true happiness is to be found in the loving acceptance of duty and fidelity to one's commitment.

Questions to Ponder
1. Which of the qualities of the Blessed Virgin Mary do you admire the most?
2. How does the Assumption of Mary inspire in you the hope of resurrection?

3. How would you explain today's celebration to a non-believer?

Additional Reading
1 Samuel 15:22 | Isaiah 7:14 | Hebrews 10:7 | Revelation 12

Solemnity of All Saints

Called to Be Saints

Readings: Revelation 7:2-4, 9-14 | Psalm 24 | 1 John 3:1-3 | Matthew 5:1-12

Summary:

The Solemnity of All Saints commemorates all those holy men, women, children, martyrs, confessors, and unknown others who lived lives of such holiness that upon death they either entered directly into God's presence in heaven or they had their souls purified of every imperfection in purgatory, before advancing into His presence. Sainthood is not meant only for some special people. All Christians are called to be saints, to be holy (see Matthew 5:48; Ephesians 1:1; 1 Corinthians 1:1-2).

Who are the Saints?

The Church Triumphant is made up of the saints who have been through suffering and pain, persecution, and martyrdom and have come off victorious. They are the sanctified brethren who have overcome sin and death. They are people who were discriminated against because of their faith in Jesus, who lived during the time of great persecutions, who endured indescribable suffering, and who died for the sake of the Gospel.

These are the ones who persevered to the end and whose names are written in the book of life (Revelation 20:12). They are the great multitude from every tribe and language and people and nation who have come out of the great ordeal and washed their robes sparkly white in the Blood of the Lamb (Revelation 7:9, 14). They were convinced of who they were deep within them and so they dared to live the Christian life in an uncompromising manner.

Saints are those who loved God and their neighbours passionately, whose lives were a witness to the love of Christ. They are those who accomplished deeds of heroism, who achieved greatness of heart, who had nobility of spirit, who lived by the norms of the beatitudes, and who attained the best they could be. The aspiration of every Christian should be to become saint because that is what God desires for us. When we live like saints then we are living our highest potential.

The saints are models of radical Christian discipleship. They were ordinary people who lived extraordinary lives by doing ordinary things in an extraordinary manner. They are the best and brightest stars of humanity whose integrity, kindness, and generosity make up for the greed and selfishness of others. They are the ones whose lives were dedicated to the establishment of God's kingdom. They knew that the only real cause of sadness is to live far away from God.

What are the Beatitudes?
The beatitudes are the Magna Carta of the Christian life. They are Jesus' charter for his followers, the roadmap to the kingdom of heaven, and the compass that ought to guide our navigation through this world. They are virtues like humility, mercy, patience, purity, hunger and thirst for righteousness, and fortitude, etc., which characterise the sanctified life. The beatitudes are elements of the virtuous life, and the foundation upon which to build the Christian life of faith. They are the summary of the gospel and the boundaries within which the Christian life is lived.

Jesus did not teach these words while walking from one town to the other, but he climbed the top of a mountain, sat down, and taught his disciples and the people. This is where the Catholic Church took the idea of the "cathedral" (the seat of the teacher) from. When the Pope speaks *ex-cathedra* he speaks officially from his seat. So, Jesus the teacher of all teachers sat down to proclaim the Beatitudes.

The mere fact that he taught sitting down signifies that this teaching is a very significant part of his entire message. What he taught was a complete reversal of conventional values and standards. He practically turned everything they knew upside down. In a world where people are competing for power to control others, who wants to be meek? Yet here was Jesus saying that blessed are the meek for they shall inherit the earth. Where people do not want to be associated with mourning, he is saying that those who mourn are blessed. Jesus does not function in accordance with our mortal ways. He tells the truth of things as they are and as they will be.

He said that we are blessed when men revile, persecute, abuse us, and when they utter all kinds of calumny against us on his account. He even enjoins us to rejoice and be glad in such circumstances. We need to give this a thought and prayerfully reflect on it. If we do, it will affect our daily conduct, our daily choices, and the kind of relationship we keep.

What Does Holiness Mean?

Holiness means goodness in all its dimensions. It is a wholesome life of love and compassion, truth and justice, as well as purity and integrity. It is being close to others while being close to God, forgiving others and not holding grudges against them, getting rid of one's prejudices, and eschewing resentment. Holiness is being pure in heart, revealing the truth of who one is, and not being dubious. It means living holistically with God and being filled with his Holy Spirit. Holiness can be measured perhaps by the level of our compliance with the beatitudes. The prayers, vigils, novenas, and other religious activities we embark on are meant to help attune us to the beatitudes, and if they do not, then they are not of much use. The beatitudes are indeed the eight keys that unlock the treasures of happiness.

Conclusion

As we reflect on the lives of the saints today we are called upon to share in their heavenly jubilation, to reflect on the glory that is theirs in the divine firmament, to see the ones who shine like stars in the presence of God, to taste the joy of the heavenly host, and be filled with the desire to be like them. We are called to "walk the walk" of the saints not just "talk the talk" (John 12:24-26). The saints are our models, our examples, our teachers, our guides, and our friends. They inspire, encourage, and comfort us. They intercede for us as our advocates; and their lives challenge and motivate us to live better and strive harder towards holiness. Their example gives strength to those who are struggling, courage to the fearful, and comfort to the suffering.

Questions to Ponder
1. What kind of human beings were the saints whom we venerate today?
2. Explain how the Beatitudes are an excellent guide or roadmap to the kingdom of heaven.
3. How can we who live in the modern world (and in our different societies today) become saints? What virtues must we cultivate? What challenges must we overcome?
4. Who is your Patron Saint? What were his/her principal virtues? How are you struggling to emulate him/her?

Additional Reading
Leviticus 19:2 | Matthew 5-7, 25:14-46 | John 12:24-26

Feast of All Souls

The Resurrection is Our Consolation

Readings: Wisdom 3:1-9 | Psalm 23 | Romans 5:5-11 | John 6:37-40

Summary:

The bitter experience of death is an ever-present reality. We all know about it. Death is a reality every single living creature will experience. No one's health, wealth, status, or riches ever saved them from dying and being committed to mother earth. Unfortunately, human beings tend to be very short-sighted. As we plan for our education, career, family, children, and retirement, we often lose sight of the ever-present reality of death, which can strike at any time. Today, as we remember and pray for the departed, we are reminded of the need to reflect now and again on our own inevitable death.

The sense of loss

Life is intertwined with losses. We lose many things as we journey through life, but the most painful loss of all is death. The death of friends and relations, and finally our own death. Nothing throws us off balance as much as the death of a loved one. We can be insured against many ills in our society, but when it comes to death, no insurance is possible. We shall all suffer the loss occasioned by death.

The Reality of Death

The book of Genesis 3 tells us that death is not what God intended for humanity. Death is the consequence of human misadventure, by way of disobedience. The death that Genesis speaks about is not just physical death, it is also spiritual death, the ultimate separation of human creatures from their God. It is this death that Saint Paul refers to in Romans 6:23 when he speaks of the wages of sin as death.

Physical death would have been the most terrible and most unfortunate event for us, but the resurrection of Jesus and his assurance of our own resurrection have changed everything. This is the good news of Christianity.

In Jesus the prophecy of Isaiah 25:6-9 has been fulfilled, that the Lord will destroy death forever; that he will remove the mourning veil covering all peoples; that he will wipe away the tears from every cheek; that he will take away his people's shame. In the face of the brutal reality of death, our consolation as Christians is that the Lord who has conquered death, now assures us that we who believe in him will also conquer death and rise to a new and fuller life in God's presence where death shall be no more. The central teaching of the Gospel is that by rising from the dead, Jesus has taken on our death and is the guarantee of eternal life for all of us who believe.

The Resurrection: Our Consolation

Our greatest consolation comes from the words of Christ to Martha in John's Gospel (11:25). He says, "I am the resurrection and the life, if anyone believes in me even though he dies, he will live, and if anyone lives and believes in me, he will never die." The resurrection was the centre of the Apostles' message. When Paul went to see the Areopagites in Athens and spoke to them, he was applauded until he spoke about the resurrection, and they told him, "We shall hear you again" (Acts 17:32). Yet the resurrection is so central to Christianity that those who, like the Areopagites reject the message of the resurrection, also reject Christianity.

Christianity would, indeed, be a monumental fraud if there was no resurrection, and if Jesus has not risen from the dead. Saint Paul captures this in 1 Corinthians 15:19, when he says that if there is no resurrection of the dead, if Christ had not risen from the dead, and if all our hope in Christ was for this world alone, then of all people we are to be most pitied. All our beliefs and emphasis on living the moral life are anchored on the fact that we shall die, but thereafter we shall rise. With the death and resurrection of Christ and the eternal life he has won for us, there is now hope of eternal life for us and for our beloved departed ones in God's presence

We believe that the human spirit never dies. Everything that can be destroyed by death has limited, short-term value. The more important element of the human reality, the soul, does not die. That's why Jesus Christ tells us not to be afraid of the one who can destroy the body but can do nothing about the soul. Rather he says, "fear the one who can destroy the body and cast the soul into hell." At death, our vain body will end up six feet below and be food for termites.

The death of our loved ones brings a lot of grief. Our faith in the death and resurrection of Christ does not take away such grief. The fact that we believe that Christ died and has risen from the dead, and that we too shall rise again, does not take away the pain and sorrow we suffer over the loss of our loved ones. However, our faith should moderate and transform our grief when we lose our loved ones. St. Paul admonishes us not to grieve like people who do not believe (see 1 Thessalonians 4:13-18). So, even though our firm belief in the resurrection does not remove the pain of loss, there should be a difference in the way a Christian believer mourns.

Though faith does not remove the pain of separation, faith enables us to accept the loss and continue with our lives, confident that the separation is only temporary, that our departed ones have gone to be with God, and that we shall meet again, never to part. Such belief makes our losses easier to bear. Our faith affirms the truth that all life is a gift of God and will return to the source of life. Indeed, who we are is what we have been given. None of us owns his or her life. In this way, death is not the doorway to darkness, it is the doorway to eternal life, to eternal light.

A Day to Reflect and Pray
So, the Feast of All Souls, is an occasion for us who are alive to remember all our departed friends and relations, and to pray for them, that God may have mercy on them, cleanse them of their impurities, and receive them into his kingdom of everlasting peace. As we celebrate the memory of our departed friends and relations, we demonstrate that love is stronger than death. As we pray for them, we demonstrate that not even death can destroy the bond of love between us and our loved ones who have died.

On this day, we also pray for ourselves, that Christ may strengthen our faith in his victory over death so that in our daily struggles we may constantly look forward to our own resurrection. Today's celebration should remind us of the shortness of life and the certitude of death. It is therefore an occasion for us to reflect on the quality of our Christian vocation today in this world, in view of our eternal destiny.

Conclusion

Death is a certainty. But it is not our finality. The resurrection of Jesus Christ is our sure pledge of eternal life with God. However, while awaiting this glory, divine justice requires that we run away from sin and iniquity and pursue a life of virtue and holiness. While Jesus has opened the doorway to eternal life for every believer, we must remember that we are still responsible for the choices we make, which will determine whether we shall go in (to heaven) or stay out (in hell). Because Jesus has risen from the dead, death is no longer a major threat for believers. As we live the Christian life, we are assured that when we depart this world, we too shall be welcomed into the glorious company of the saints.

*May the souls of all the faithful departed,
through the Mercy of God, rest in peace. Amen.*

Questions to Ponder

1. Death is a reality. How does today's celebration challenge you about the certainty of your own death?
2. Jesus says, "I am the Resurrection and the Life." How should this assurance moderate our sense of loss and our grieving over the death of a loved one?
3. What would you love to be remembered for? What must you do now to realise this desire?

Additional Reading

Psalm 146:4 | Ezekiel 18:32 | John 11:25-26, 14:1-4 | Romans 6:23, 8:38-39

www.ingramcontent.com/pod-product-compliance
Lightning Source LLC
Chambersburg PA
CBHW021755230426
43669CB00006B/78